The Heart Healthy Cookbook for Beginners 2020

600 Low Sodium, Low Fat Recipes to Drop Pounds, Improve Health and Lower Blood Pressure (21 Day Meal Plan Included)

By Adele Wilson

Table of Content

Introduction

The health of the heart is very important in the life of a human being. It is imperative that you take your time to understand the foods that you want to consume before ingestion because they will determine the longevity of your heart's functionality. Heart diseases have become rampant in the modern era because of the lifestyle and foods that we consume. Coronary heart disease is the most common form of heart disease and it is the leading cause of death for men and women in the united states with stroke or heart attacks being ranked third. Luckily, the health of your heart is in your hands and you can do something about to ensure that you live a long and healthy life. With every action that you take towards protecting your heart, you will be in a better place because your heart will function optimally and you will not risk developing any complication.

Over the years with experience and knowledge in heart health I have come across so many patients with cardiac or heart problems and these problems usually stem from diet and lifestyle. With adequate knowledge I believe that walking the talk will not only help people get the type of life they want but also eating healthy is a priority in my life right now. Many people across the world are struggling with similar challenges and we can help them by generating a book that will encompass all healthy meals prepared from scratch and what you can avoid to have a healthy heart. Temptations usually surround us and we are bound to make poor choices, however with this guide you will be able to look into a new direction and make the right choices. This book will act as a critical nutritional driver of your heart with simple and satisfying recipes that are designed to help you follow three major healthy eating patterns mainly DASH, vegetarian/vegan and Mediterranean.

The recipes in this book are designed for efficiency and speed so that you can make the meals even when you have a short time to prepare the meals or you are low on energy. In this book, you will get to know some of the best meals that you can prepare in the comfort of your kitchen without requiring too much effort. You will find hearty meals that cover breakfasts, lunch, dinner, snacks, and beverages that are designed to cater to any craving that you might have without causing any problem to your heart. The current recipes are updated which means that you can get them at your local grocery. There are many strategies that you can use to protect your heart and you should commit to sticking to the ideas daily. A healthy diet is the best weapon against any heart disease. You will get to understand the different aspects of nutrition as well as a healthy lifestyle that will help you avoid any challenges that are often characterized by an unhealthy lifestyle and eating habits.

Chapter 1 The Heart Healthy Diet Basics

What Does A Heart-Healthy Recipe Mean?

With the current changes in the world of health and fitness, people are looking for ways that will help them maintain optimum heart functions as well as body function. The guideline released is meant to help people to shift towards a dietary change that contains more fruits, vegetables and eat more lean proteins and whole grains as opposed to fine processed foods. Based on recent evidence there is a direct correlation between the cholesterol in the blood and the type of food that is consumed. Foods that are rich in low-density lipoproteins will increase the level of cholesterol in the system. However, dieticians and doctors have had to urge people to consume high-density lipoproteins which are good fats for the body. It is important to note that the body still needs fats therefore you need to consume the right type of fats which will boost the functionality of the body system without increasing cholesterol levels.

So, what do experts recommend when it comes to heart-healthy eating? for cardiovascular disease prevention, it is recommended that you should consult a dietary pattern that emphasizes the consumption of low-fat dairy products, whole grains, and legumes, poultry, fish and nuts. You should limit sugar-sweetened beverages, sweets, red meats and your healthy diet must:

- Limit intake of saturated fat intake to 5% to 6% of total calorie intake
- Reduce calorie intake of trans fats and saturated fats
- Maintain your sodium intake to less than 2300 mg to 1500 mg per day for people prone to cardiovascular diseases.
- Limit the intake of added sugars to at least 10% of the total calories consumed per day.

When you implement this type of eating pattern you are likely to reduce your chances of having any cardiovascular disease. It is important to note that the dietary patterns written in this book are not fads or diets, but it is a healthy diet plan that is based on scientific evidence on ways of decreasing the risk of chronic diseases. It is all about the interaction of many antioxidants, minerals, vitamins and phytochemicals that are critical in boosting the functionality of the body cells.

How To Conform To Heart-Healthy Eating Patterns

The recipes that are written in this book conform to international standards that will maintain a heart-healthy dietary pattern by focusing on the use of whole and unprocessed ingredients. Tropical oils like coconut oil cannot be used in such a case because of the high low-density lipoproteins. The sodium levels are kept in check and these recipes do not contain any trans fats. one integral fact that you must know is that the recipes are not nonfat. However, they include sources of healthy fat which are rich in high-density lipoproteins that helps in maintaining body processes. Oils from plant sources are the best because they give the body the much-needed fats and also contain antioxidants and phytonutrients which are all important because they act as cardioprotective agents. These fats replace polyunsaturated and monounsaturated fats.

Why Change To A Heart-Healthy Eating Pattern?

Heart-healthy eating pattern is essential because there are other benefits of taking this diet apart from a healthy lifestyle. The people following this heart-healthy eating pattern are those who:

- Have metabolic syndrome
- Are on their menopause or post menopause
- Have high levels of triglycerides
- Have excess weight in the middle or belly fat
- Are known to have a polycystic syndrome
- Are prone to diabetes or hypertension

It is imperative to note that when you are taking whole foods, a plant-based diet that includes daily change of habits, as well as exercises, will go a long way in boosting your overall body health.

Focusing On Heart Healthy Pattern

Focusing on a quality diet is integral in achieving your objectives. It is vital to note that it all comes to what the mind perceives and how you plan to implement it. When you have your full attention on what you can do to make the diet more nutrient-filled rather than thinking of what you can reduce then you are heading in the right direction. However, there are nutrients that you should always take time to check to ensure that your body does not run out of the essential factors.

Sodium

Sodium is essential for the functioning of the nervous system because it aids in the transformation of signals from one neuron to another. It is recommended that you should not consume more than 1500mg of sodium per day. This is the amount that is categorized as safe for the body and does not increase the chances of developing heart disease. It is imperative to note that most of the sodium that many people consume is from processed and packaged foods. Therefore, dieticians recommend that if you prepare your meals you will be able to regulate the level of sodium intake.

Dietary fats

Dietary fats are some of the essential fats that the body requires for optimal functioning. They are critical because they provide the energy required to support cell growth and development. Besides, they are essential in keeping the body warm, protecting vital organs, and helping the body absorb vital vitamins. The American heart association usually recommends that you should limit your intake of saturated trans fats with heart-healthy polyunsaturated and monounsaturated fats. If you are prone to high cholesterol or you already record-high levels of cholesterol you should limit your fat intake to a maximum of 6% of your daily intake. There are two kinds of fats that are harmful to your body.

- Saturated fats- this is a class of fats that are obtained from animal sources and it is solid at room temperature and it raises the levels of low-density lipoproteins which in turn increases the levels of cholesterol in the system.
- Trans fats- this is naturally occurring fats and most are manufactured through partial hydrogenation. These fats are known to also increase the level of low-density lipoproteins which increases cholesterol levels in the system.

However, there are three categories of fats that are highly beneficial to the body and these include:
- Monounsaturated fats- this is a class of fats that are found in vegetable oils and foods such as nuts and avocados. Foods that have high levels of monounsaturated fats are known to improve cholesterol levels by reducing their conversion. This is critical because it will lower the total cholesterol level in the system hence low risk of heart conditions. This is also beneficial for people with insulin resistance or type 2 diabetes. Monounsaturated fats can be found in sesame, olives, and canola.
- Polyunsaturated fats- this is a category of fats that is usually plant-based and eating foods that are rich in polyunsaturated fats is vital because they help in reducing the levels of cholesterol in the body thereby giving you the best heart health. Polyunsaturated fats can be obtained from sunflower, corn, and soybeans.
- Omega-3 fats- this is a class of polyunsaturated fatty acids that are beneficial to the heart because they capture vital vitamins and boost heart muscle functioning. They are usually in fish and they lower the risks of heart diseases.

Eating foods with fat is a part of the heart-healthy diet and you should not work towards eliminating them in your diet because they are critical for bodily functions. You should focus more on replacing saturated fats with unsaturated fats and balance the number of calories that you are consuming. Aiming for a dietary pattern that emphasizes the intake of fruits, vegetables, and whole grains and that which limits the intake of sweets, sugars, red meat, and sugar-sweetened beverages means that your diet will be both low on trans and saturated fats.

Ways Of Handling Fiber

Vegetables, fruits, and whole grains contain a huge chunk of fiber and this can influence so many areas of your health. The fiber is essential in boosting weight loss and the bacterial nutrient on the gut. Fibers are a fundamental part of a healthy diet. There are two categories of fibers and these are soluble and non-soluble fibers. Soluble fibers can bind with water effectively and the insoluble partners do not blend with water and they pass through the digestive tract more or less intact. You must have both classes of fibers in your diet because they will help you achieve balanced digestion.

Oats, fruits and beans are the common sources of soluble fibers and this is a class of fiber that can help in lowering the levels of cholesterol in the body. They increase the feeling of fullness, controls blood sugar through slowing down nutrient absorption. On the other hand, nuts, seeds, whole grains are vital because they are a good source of insoluble fiber which is critical in increasing fecal bulk and it helps in preventing cases of constipation. Experts recommend that you should aim for at least 30 grams to 40 grams of fiber per day.

Revamp Your Kitchen Staples

Eating saturated fat, less sodium, sugar, and trans fat and eating more vegetables, fruits, and whole grains is essential in boosting your energy and will improve your overall health. However, for you to regain this kind of eating pattern, there are things that you must change for the eating pattern to work. This can be quite challenging especially if you do not know where to start from or what kitchen items to get fresh items. However, here are some of the techniques that will help you overcome the early challenges that people face when they are getting on a new diet.

- Understand that it is a process- making changes in your life especially those that involve foods and habits that you are used to for a very long time can be very challenging. It is vital to note that this cannot happen overnight, however, with constant change in habits and learning of the new technique you will accomplish what you want.
- Review your pantry - one of the ways that you can change into a hearty heating pattern is by changing your pantry. You should review what you currently have in your refrigerator, pantry, and freezer. You should list the processed foods that you currently consume. Read the ingredients and understand their sodium, calorie and sugar levels. If any of the ingredients in the foods that you are consuming have partially hydrogenated oils or additional sugars you should avoid.
- Think about addition, not subtraction – once you have decided which foods that you need to go you can make a list of the whole foods, grains among others that you will have to replace. It is really easy and super simple if you follow classic techniques that help in changing habits. You change processed foods for those that include fruits and vegetables. A cup of vegetables like cauliflower, broccoli, carrots, and celery is a better option.
- Get whole grains – you should strive to stock up healthier alternatives to the foods that you know you love. You should swap your white rice for brown rice, whole-wheat couscous, millet, quinoa, amaranth, rolled oats among others.
- Get cooking at home more often – one of the main reasons why people fail to achieve a better heart-healthy eating pattern is because they still eat meals outside. Eating meals outside is not a problem but you will not be in control of the ingredients and the cooking process. However, if you cook your meals at home you will control all the ingredients effectively.
- Use healthier condiments - mustard and kinds of ketchup are known to contain high amounts of sugar and sodium and you can make your condiments or use nontraditional condiments such as curry powders, hummus, and sriracha. You can use fresh dried salt instead of the salt shaker.
- Choose your canned foods carefully - many canned foods are known to have preservatives and salt during their processing. You should choose alternatives that do not have added salt and always drain and rinse beans and vegetables before using them.
- Seek a support system – making changes is not always easier and you must have a support system in place. When you have a support group you will be able to get better each day because they will encourage you to make healthy choices.

Embrace Healthy Cooking Techniques

There are many ways of cooking up flavorful and juicy foods without adding unnecessary salt or frying. You can use healthy cooking techniques which eliminates excessive amounts of fat and salt and this can help you cut calories while retaining the flavor and nutrient in the food. You should try to prepare your food using the following techniques:
- Steaming - for you to steam food effectively use a perforated basket and suspend above the simmering liquid. Your food will have more flavor and you will not need any salt. Foods that can be made this way include vegetables like broccoli, green beans, chicken and fish.
- Poaching – for you to gain the best, you can gently simmer your food in a flavorful liquid such as vinegar, wine, low sodium broth or plain water with added spices and herbs. Choose a covered pan if you plan to poach food with a minimal amount of liquid.
- Grilling or broiling – these two techniques are known to expose food to direct heat. You can grill food outdoors or place a grill rack above a bed of charcoal and cook the food until tender. If you want

to broil, place the food in a broiler rack below your heat source. Both techniques are known to allow fat to drip away from the food and it is a great method for vegetables, fish, chicken or fruits.

- Baking – Baking is a technique that is known not to use any additional fats and you can bake seafood, fruits, vegetables, poultry, and meats. Besides, baking will allow you to cover your food with a foil and the food will cook with the moisture that is within.
- Stir-frying – this is a traditional Asian technique that allows you to quickly stir fry small amounts of foods and set them aside. This method usually uses low amounts of oil therefore highly effective for cooking chicken, pork, meat, vegetables among others.
- Roasting- Roasting is a technique that uses dry heat to cook food. The technique is similar to baking but the food is usually cooked at higher temperatures and you can roast your food in a baking sheet or pan.

What You Need To Know Before Incorporating Heart Healthy Eating Patterns In Your Schedule

For you to reduce the risk of future heart problems you need to fuel yourself with minimally processed foods which include whole grains, nuts, legumes, lean meat, dairy, and fish. You should always feel the essence of adding foods with cardioprotective properties. These foods will go a long way in helping you prevent any occurrence of heart problems. Moderation of alcohol is important if you want to achieve this objective.

The most important aspect of changing your eating habits is to know why, when, how and where you eat will matter a lot because you will be able to regulate yourself in different ways. Habits like sharing meals, honoring cultural traditions can contribute to heart health than your regular kales and lentils. You will need to practice eating away from the television or any other distraction so that you can enjoy your meal and you truly experience the satisfaction when you start feeling full. I hope this book will enlighten you and help you achieve your heart-healthy eating plan.

Chapter 2 Breakfast Recipes

Cucumber 'n Tomato Breakfast Wrap

Serves: 1 , Cooking time: 0 minutes

Ingredients:
- 2 tbsp hummus
- 1 whole-wheat tortillas (8-inch)
- 1 Plum Tomato
- 1/4 whole Long English Cucumber
- 1/4 medium red onion
- 1 cup Baby Lettuce Mix
- 8 leaf fresh mint leaves
- 1 tsp 100% Lemon Juice
- 1/2 tsp lemon zest
- 1/2 tsp ground black pepper

Directions for Cooking:
1. Spread tortilla on a plate.
2. Add hummus and spread all over tortilla.
3. Pile remaining ingredients on top of tortilla. Roll like a burrito.
4. Serve and enjoy.

Nutrition Information:
Calories per Serving: 320.9; Protein: 10.8g; Carbs: 52.1g; Fat: 7.7g; Saturated Fat: 2.5g; Sodium: 300mg

Spinach 'n Tomato Egg Scramble

Serves: 1 , Cooking time: 10 minutes

Ingredients:
- 2 eggs
- 1 teaspoon of fresh basil, chopped
- ½ teaspoon cayenne pepper
- ¼ cup Swiss cheese
- ½ cup packed Spinach, chopped
- 1 medium chopped tomato
- 1 tsp olive oil

Directions for Cooking:
1. In a small bowl, whisk well eggs, basil, pepper, and swiss cheese.
2. Place a medium fry pan on medium fire and heat oil.
3. Stir in tomato and sauté for 3 minutes. Stir in spinach and cook for 2 minutes or until starting to wilt.
4. Pour in beaten eggs and scramble for 2 to 3 minutes or to desired doneness.
5. Enjoy.

Nutrition Information:
Calories per Serving: 323.7; Protein: 21.7g; Carbs: 8.6g; Fat: 22.5g; Saturated Fat: 9.3g; Sodium: 167mg

Avocado Cup with Egg

Serves: 4 , Cooking time: 25 minutes

Ingredients:
- 2 ripe avocados
- 4 dashes of pepper
- 4 medium eggs
- 1 stalk scallion, chopped
- 4 dashes paprika
- 4 tsp Parmesan cheese

Directions for Cooking:
1. Preheat oven to 375ºF.
2. Slice avocadoes in half and discard seed.
3. Slice the rounded portions of the avocado, to make it level and sit well on a baking sheet.
4. Place avocadoes on baking sheet and crack one egg in each hole of the avocado.
5. Season each egg evenly with pepper, and paprika.
6. Pop in the oven and bake for 25 minutes or until eggs are cooked to your liking.
7. Serve with a sprinkle of Parmesan.

Nutrition Information:
Calories per Serving: 277.6; Protein: 9.4g; Carbs: 15g; Fat: 20g; Saturated Fat: 3.9g; Sodium: 112mg

Serves: 6 , Cooking time: 45 minutes

Ingredients:

- 6 medium zucchinis
- ¾ lb. turkey breast, sliced into 4 strips
- 2 medium tomatoes, seeded and chopped
- 1/2 cup panko (Japanese) breadcrumbs
- 1/3 cup grated Parmesan cheese
- 1/3 cup minced fresh parsley
- 2 tablespoons minced fresh oregano
- 2 tablespoons minced fresh basil
- 1/4 teaspoon pepper
- 3/4 cup shredded part-skim mozzarella cheese

Directions for Cooking:

1. Preheat oven to 350ºF and lightly grease a glass baking dish with cooking spray.
2. Slice zucchinis lengthwise and scoop out the pulp creating a hollow in the middle. Reserve pulp in a bowl.
3. Place zucchinis in glass dish and microwave for 3 minutes. Rearrange zucchinis and microwave for another 2 minutes or until crisp tender.
4. Meanwhile, chop up the zucchini pulp.
5. Place a large fry pan on medium high fire and pan fry turkey meat for 4 minutes per side. Remove turkey and chop roughly.
6. Return to pan and cook until no longer pink, around 5 minutes. Turn off fire and mix in breadcrumbs, parmesan, parsley, oregano, basil, and pepper Mix well.
7. Evenly spoon sausage mixture into middle of zucchinis. Cover dish with foil and bae in the oven for 20 minutes.
8. Remove foil, sprinkle mozzarella evenly on top of zucchini. Bake for another 5 minutes.
9. Serve and enjoy.

Nutrition Information:

Calories per Serving: 180.8; Protein: 23.5g; Carbs: 10g; Fat: 5.2g; Saturated Fat: 2.5g; Sodium: 298 mg

Serves: 1 , Cooking time: 0 minutes

Ingredients:

- 1/4 cup dried cranberries
- 1/3 cup oat bran
- ½ cup orange juice
- ½ cup water

Directions for Cooking:

1. In a bowl, combine all ingredients.
2. For about 2 minutes, microwave the bowl then serve with sugar and milk. You may also add honey.
3. Enjoy!

Nutrition Information:

Calories per Serving: 288.7; Protein: 6.2g; Carbs: 59.9g; Fat: 2.7g; Saturated Fat: 0.4g; Sodium: 7mg

Serves: 1 , Cooking time: 0 minutes

Ingredients:

- 2 tbsp oats
- 1 tsp sunflower seeds
- 5 whole almond pieces
- 1 tsp chia seeds
- 1 tbsp craisins
- 1 ½ cup low fat milk

Directions for Cooking:

1. In a jar or mason bottle with cap, mix all ingredients.
2. Refrigerate overnight.
3. Enjoy for breakfast. Will keep in the fridge for up to 3 days.

Nutrition Information:

Calories per Serving: 294.2; Protein: 17.6g; Carbs: 37.5g; Fat: 8.2g; Saturated Fat: 1g; Sodium: 157mg

Cheddar & Kale Frittata

Serves: 6 , Cooking time: 50 minutes

Ingredients:
- 1 tsp olive oil
- 5 oz baby kale and spinach
- 1 red pepper, diced
- 1/3 cup sliced scallions
- 12 eggs
- 3/4 cup non-fat milk
- 1 cup sharp low-fat cheddar cheese, shredded
- 1/4 tsp pepper

Directions for Cooking:
1. Preheat oven to 375°F.
2. With olive oil, grease a glass casserole dish.
3. In a bowl, whisk well all ingredients except for cheese.
4. Pour egg mixture in prepared dish and bake for 35 minutes.
5. Remove from oven and sprinkle cheese on top and broil for 5 minutes.
6. Remove from oven and let it sit for 10 minutes.
7. Cut up and enjoy.

Nutrition Information:
Calories per Serving: 210.7; Protein: 18.7g; Carbs: 8.1g; Fat: 11.5g; Saturated Fat: 4g; Sodium: 343mg

Bagels Made Healthy

Serves: 8 , Cooking time: 30 minutes

Ingredients:
- 2 tsp yeast
- 1 ½ tbsp olive oil
- 1 ¼ cups bread flour
- 2 cups whole wheat flour
- 1 tbsp vinegar
- 2 tbsp honey
- 1 ½ cups warm water

Directions for Cooking:
1. In a bread machine, mix all ingredients, and then process on dough cycle.
2. Once done or end of cycle, create 8 pieces shaped like a flattened ball.
3. Make a hole in the center of each ball using your thumb then create a donut shape.
4. In a greased baking sheet, place donut-shaped dough then cover and let it rise about ½ hour.
5. Prepare about 2 inches of water to boil in a large pan.
6. In a boiling water, drop one at a time the bagels and boil for 1 minute, then turn them once.
7. Remove them and return to baking sheet and bake at 350oF for about 20 to 25 minutes until golden brown.

Nutrition Information:
Calories per Serving: 228.1; Protein: 6.9g; Carbs: 41.8g; Fat: 3.7g; Saturated Fat: .5g; Sodium: 47mg

Breakfast Oatmeal in Slow Cooker

Serves: 8 , Cooking time: 8 hours

Ingredients:
- 1 tsp cinnamon
- 2 packets stevia or to taste
- 1/3 cup dried apricots, chopped
- 1/3 cup dried cherries
- 1/3 cup raisins
- 2 cups steel-cut oats
- 4 cups water
- 4 cups almond milk

Directions for Cooking:
1. In slow cooker, mix well all ingredients.
2. Cover and set to low.
3. Cook for 8 hours.
4. You can set this the night before so that by morning you have breakfast ready.

Nutrition Information:
Calories per Serving: 175.6; Protein: 5.1g; Carbs: 31.6g; Fat: 3.2g; Saturated Fat: .3g; Sodium: 90mg

Scrambled Eggs with Mushrooms and Spinach

Serves: 1 , Cooking time: 7 minutes

Ingredients:

- 1 tsp olive oil
- 1 cup fresh spinach, chopped
- ½ cup fresh mushrooms, sliced
- 1 whole egg
- 2 egg whites
- 2 tbsp fat free American cheese, shredded
- Pepper to taste
- 1 slice whole wheat toast

Directions for Cooking:

1. On medium high fire, place a nonstick fry pan and add oil. Swirl oil to cover pan and heat for a minute.
2. Add spinach and mushrooms. Sauté until spinach is wilted, around 2-3 minutes.
3. Meanwhile, in a bowl whisk well egg, egg whites, and cheese. Season with pepper.
4. Pour egg mixture into pan and scramble until eggs are cooked through, around 3-4 minutes.
5. Serve and enjoy with a piece of whole wheat toast.

Nutrition Information:

Calories per Serving: 298.6; Protein: 25.3g; Carbs: 22.8g; Fat: 11.8g; Saturated Fat: 2.7g; Sodium: 325mg

Oats 'n Blueberry Pancakes

Serves: 10 , Cooking time: 50 minutes

Ingredients:

- 1 ½ cups water
- ½ cup steel cut oats
- 1 egg
- ½ cup plain Greek yogurt
- 1 1/2 cups almond milk
- ½ tsp baking soda
- ½ tsp baking powder
- 1 cup whole wheat flour
- 2 packets stevia
- 1 cup frozen blueberries

Directions for Cooking:

1. On high fire, place a medium pot, add water and bring to a boil.
2. Once boiling add oats. Lower fire to a simmer and cook for ten minutes or until oats are tender. Turn off fire and set aside.
3. Whisk egg in a medium bowl. Add yogurt and milk. Whisk well.
4. Sift in baking soda, baking powder, whole wheat flour, and stevia. Whisk well to combine.
5. Fold in cooked oats and blueberries.
6. On medium fire, place a nonstick fry pan and grease with cooking spray.
7. Pour ¼ cup of the batter. Cover and cook on medium low for 2-3 minutes or until pancake is bubbly. Turnover pancake and cook for a minute. Remove pancake and place in a serving plate.
8. Repeat process for remaining batter until done.
9. Serve and enjoy. Or store extra pancakes in a lidded container and store in fridge for 5 days. You can also store batter for up to 5 days in the fridge.

Nutrition Information:

Calories per Serving: 116.6; Protein: 5.9; Carbs: 18.3g; Fat: 2.2g; Saturated Fat: .4g; Sodium: 102mg

French Toast with Applesauce

Serves: 6 , Cooking time: 18 minutes

Ingredients:

- 6 slices whole wheat bread
- ¼ cup unsweetened applesauce
- 2 packets Stevia
- 1 tsp ground cinnamon
- ½ cup skim milk
- 2 eggs

Directions for Cooking:

1. Mix well applesauce, sugar, cinnamon, milk and eggs in a mixing bowl.
2. One slice at a time, soak the bread into applesauce mixture until wet.

3. On medium fire, heat a large nonstick skillet.
4. Add soaked bread on one side and another on the other side. Cook in a single layer in batches for 2-3 minutes per side on medium low fire or until lightly browned.

5. Serve and enjoy.

Nutrition Information:
Calories per Serving: 121; Protein: 6.5g; Carbs: 17.9g; Fat: 2.6g; Saturated Fat: .7g; Sodium: 175mg

Breakfast Grains and Fruits

Serves: 6 , Cooking time: 20 minutes

Ingredients:
- 3 cups water
- ¾ cup bulgur
- ¾ cup quick cooking brown rice
- 1 orange
- 1 Red delicious apple
- 1 Granny Smith apple
- 1 8-oz low fat vanilla yogurt
- 1 cup raisins

Directions for Cooking:
1. On high fire, place a large pot and bring water to a boil.
2. Add bulgur and rice. Lower fire to a simmer and cook for ten minutes while covered.
3. Turn off fire, set aside for 2 minutes while covered.
4. In baking sheet, transfer and evenly spread grains to cool.
5. Meanwhile, peel oranges and cut into sections. Chop and core apples.
6. Once grains are cool, transfer to a large serving bowl along with fruits.
7. Add yogurt and mix well to coat.
8. Serve and enjoy.

Nutrition Information:
Calories per Serving: 121; Protein: 3.8g; Carbs: 24.2g; Fat: 1g; Saturated Fat: .5g; Sodium: 32mg

Zaalouk a Moroccan Tomato-Eggplant Recipe

Serves: 4 , Cooking time: 45 minutes

Ingredients:
- 1 large eggplant, equally cut into bite-sized pieces
- 3 tsp olive oil, divided
- ½ tsp salt
- 3 cloves garlic, minced
- 1 large onion, thinly sliced
- 1 tbsp ground cumin
- 1 tbsp smoked paprika
- 1 tsp coconut aminos
- 6 large tomatoes
- 1 cup water, divided
- 1 cup cooked chickpeas, rinsed and drained well
- 1 packet stevia or to taste
- 2 tbsp harissa paste

Directions for Cooking:
1. Preheat oven to 425ºF.
2. On baking sheet add eggplant. Drizzle with 2 tbsp olive oil and season with salt. Toss well to coat and spread evenly in pan. Pop in the oven and roast for 35 minutes. Toss and mix once 20-minutes of cooking time has elapsed.
3. Meanwhile, place a large nonstick pot on medium fire. Heat remaining oil for a minute.
4. Add garlic and sauté for a minute. Stir in onion and cook for 3 minutes.
5. Stir in cumin, paprika, and tomatoes. Sauté for 7 minutes until tomatoes are wilted and turned into a mush.
6. Add ½ cup water and deglaze pot. Continue cooking tomatoes until water has fully evaporated, around 10 minutes.
7. Stir in coconut aminos, chickpeas, and harissa paste. Mix well. Turn off fire.
8. Once eggplants are done cooking, transfer to pot and turn fire on to medium.
9. Add remaining water and simmer for 5 minutes.
10. Season with stevia to taste. Mix well and let sit for another 5 minutes.
11. Serve and enjoy.

Nutrition Information:
Calories per Serving: 222.2; Protein: 8.4g; Carbs: 34.1g; Fat: 5.8g; Saturated Fat: .8g; Sodium: 321mg

Serves: 4 , Cooking time: 55 minutes

Ingredients:

- 3 tsp olive oil, divided
- 4 cloves garlic, minced
- 2 1/2 tbsp cornstarch
- 1 1/2 cups unsweetened almond milk
- 1/2 cup vegetable broth, low sodium
- 1/8 tsp ground nutmeg
- 1/4 tsp black pepper
- 1 tbsp coconut aminos
- 4 tbsp nutritional yeast
- 3 medium Yukon gold potatoes, very thinly sliced
- 1/4 cup fat free parmesan cheese, divided
- 1/4 tsp paprika

Directions for Cooking:

1. Place a large nonstick saucepan on medium fire and heat 1 ½ tsp olive oil for a minute.
2. Stir in garlic and cook for a minute.
3. Whisk in the cornstarch and mix well while cooking for a minute.
4. Slowly whisk in the almond milk until fully incorporated and no clumps are seen.
5. Add the broth and mix well.
6. Stir in pepper, coconut aminos, and nutmeg. Cook until sauce has thickened.
7. Turn off fire and stir in nutritional yeast. With an immersion blender, puree sauce until creamy.
8. In a cast iron pan, place on medium low fire just to heat up pan. Oil pan with remaining olive oil.
9. Place half of potatoes in cast iron pan and evenly spread. Sprinkle with half of parmesan cheese. Layer the remaining half of potatoes on top of cheese and then sprinkle remaining parmesan on top.
10. Pour white sauce on top of cheese and push down potatoes to submerge in sauce.
11. Cover pan with foil and pop in the oven for 20 minutes.
12. Remove foil and continue baking for another 40 minutes until bubbly and golden brown.
13. Sprinkle paprika on top before serving.

Nutrition Information:

Calories per Serving: 281.5; Protein: 11.2g; Carbs: 47.7g; Fat: 5.1g; Saturated Fat: 0.7g; Sodium: 180mg

Serves: 4 , Cooking time: 30 minutes

Ingredients:

- 2 Portobello mushroom caps, stemmed and sliced into 1/8-inch thick
- 2 tbsp avocado oil
- 1 ¼ tbsp maple syrup
- 1 ¼ tbsp apple cider vinegar
- 1 tbsp coconut aminos
- 1 heaping tsp smoked paprika
- 1 dash liquid smoke
- 1 rounded tsp miso paste
- 3/4 tsp ground black pepper, plus more to taste

Directions for Cooking:

1. Set a stainless-steel rack on top of a baking sheet and lightly grease with cooking spray.
2. Preheat oven to 400°F.
3. In a large shallow dish, mix well avocado oil, maple syrup, vinegar, coconut aminos, paprika, liquid smoke, miso paste, and pepper.
4. Add sliced Portobello and toss well to coat.
5. Place mushrooms on a single layer on the rack.
6. Pop in the oven and bake for 25 minutes or to desired crispness. Mushrooms are done cooking by the 15-minute mark and just continue to bake to make it crisp.
7. Serve and enjoy.

Nutrition Information:

Calories per Serving: 189.6; Protein: 3.6g; Carbs: 7.8g; Fat: 8g; Saturated Fat: 1.1g; Sodium: 86mg

Black Bean 'n Sweet Potato on Pita Bread

Serves: 8 , Cooking time: 20 minutes

Ingredients:

- 2 medium sweet potatoes, cut into ¼-inch cubes
- 2 tbsp olive oil
- ½ + ¾ tsp ground cumin, divided
- 1 tsp chili powder, divided
- 1 ripe avocado
- 3 tbsp lime juice
- 1/4 tsp sea salt
- 1 to 2 tbsp minced jalapeño, to taste
- 1 15-ounce can black beans, rinsed well and drained
- 1/4 cup finely chopped cilantro
- 1/4 cup red onion, finely diced
- 1 cup whole corn kernels
- 4 large pita bread

Directions for Cooking:

1. On a baking sheet toss well to coat cubed sweet potatoes, ½ tsp cumin, and ½ tsp chili powder. Pop in a preheated 375°F oven and bake until lightly browned, around 20 minutes. Halfway through baking time, toss around sweet potatoes to ensure even cooking.
2. Meanwhile, in a large bowl mash and mix well remaining cumin and chili powder, avocado, lime juice, salt, and minced jalapeno.
3. In same large bowl, mix in remaining ingredients and toss well to coat.
4. Add sweet potatoes once done cooking and toss well to coat.
5. Serve and enjoy with toasted pita bread halves.

Nutrition Information:

Calories per Serving: 330.8; Protein: 14.4g; Carbs: 56.9g; Fat: 8.4g; Saturated Fat: 1.3g; Sodium: 211mg

Mushroom 'n Egg Bake

Serves: 4 , Cooking time: 35 minutes

Ingredients:

- pepper to taste
- 4 eggs, beaten
- ½ small onion sliced
- ½ cup mushrooms, chopped
- 1 stalk green onions, chopped

Directions for Cooking:

1. Whisk well all ingredients except for green onions.
2. Preheat oven to 400°F.
3. Lightly grease an oven safe dish with olive oil.
4. Pour egg mixture and cover top with foil.
5. Bake in oven for 20 minutes.
6. Remove foil and sprinkle green onions.
7. Broil top for 3 minutes.
8. Let it rest for 10 minutes, serve and enjoy.

Nutrition Information:

Calories per Serving: 76.6; Carbs: 2.6g; Protein: 6.2g; Fats: 4.6g; Saturated Fat: 1.4g; Sodium: 64mg

Garlic Beef & Egg Brekky Frittata

Serves: 4 , Cooking time: 30 minutes

Ingredients:

- A dash of salt
- ¼ tsp pepper
- 3 eggs, beaten
- 3 cloves of garlic, minced
- 1 onion, chopped
- ½ pound lean ground beef

Directions for Cooking:

1. Place a small cast iron pan on medium fire and heat for 2 minutes.
2. Add beef and crumble. Cook for 5 minutes.
3. Add onion and garlic, continue cooking beef until browned, around 5 minutes more. Discard any fat.
4. Season with pepper and salt.
5. Spread beef in pan and lower fire to low.
6. Meanwhile whisk eggs in a bowl. Pour over meat, cover and cook for 10 minutes on low.

7. Place pan in oven and broil on low for 3 minutes. Let it set for 5 minutes.
8. Serve and enjoy.

Nutrition Information:

Calories per Serving: 179.5; Carbs: 3.8g; Protein: 19.7g; Fats: 9.5g; Saturated Fat: 3.5g; Sodium: 122mg

Marinara Sauce Over Eggplant Bake

Serves: 4 , Cooking time: 45 minutes

Ingredients:
- 1 large eggplant
- 1 clove garlic, sliced
- 1 tablespoon olive oil
- A dash of salt
- 1/4 teaspoon red pepper flakes
- 1-1/2 cups prepared marinara sauce, low sodium
- ¼ tsp freshly ground black pepper
- 2 tablespoons shredded pepper jack cheese
- 1/4 cup water, plus more as needed
- 1/4 cup grated Parmesan cheese
- 1/4 cup and 2 tablespoons ricotta cheese
- 1/4 cup and 2 tablespoons dry breadcrumbs

Directions for Cooking:
1. Cut eggplant crosswise in 5 pieces. Peel and chop two pieces into ½-inch cubes.
2. Lightly grease a large nonstick pan with 1 tbsp olive oil. For 5 minutes, heat oil at medium high fire. Add half eggplant strips and cook for 2 minutes per side. Transfer to a plate.
3. In same pan, add garlic and cook for a minute. Add chopped eggplants. Season with pepper flakes and a dash of salt. Cook for 4 minutes. Lower heat to low and continue cooking eggplants until soft, around 8 minutes more.
4. Stir in water and marinara sauce. Cook for 8 minutes until heated through. Stirring every now and then. Transfer to a bowl.
5. In a bowl, whisk well pepper, pepper jack cheese, Parmesan cheese, and ricotta. Evenly spread cheeses over eggplant strips and then fold in half.
6. Lay folded eggplant in an oven safe dish. Pour marinara sauce on top.
7. In a small bowl whisk well olive oil, and breadcrumbs. Sprinkle all over sauce.
8. Cook for 15 minutes at 400ºF preheated oven until tops are lightly browned.
9. Serve and enjoy.

Nutrition Information:
Calories per Serving: 234.9; Carbs: 18.3g; Protein: 11.4g; Fats: 12.9g; Saturated Fat: 3.1g; Sodium: 81mg

Bell Pepper, Beef & Egg Scramble

Serves: 4 , Cooking time: 45 minutes

Ingredients:
- A dash of salt
- ¼ tsp pepper
- 4 large eggs, beaten
- 3 cloves of garlic, minced
- 8-oz ground beef, 85% lean
- 1 onion, chopped
- 1 green bell pepper, seeded and chopped

Directions for Cooking:
1. Preheat oven to 400ºF.
2. On medium high fire, heat oil in a nonstick pan for a minute.
3. Sauté beef and crumble, for 5 minutes. Stir in garlic and onion. Cook for another 3 minutes.
   Add bell pepper and continue sautéing for 3 minutes.
4. Season with a dash of salt and pepper.
5. Transfer to an oven safe dish and discard any fat.
6. Pour beaten eggs over meat and pop in the oven.
7. Cook for 25 minutes. Turn off oven and let it sit for another 10 minutes.
8. Serve and enjoy.

Nutrition Information:
Calories per Serving: 217; Carbs: 3.9g; Protein: 22.9g; Fats: 11.6g; Saturated Fat: 4.2g; Sodium: 161mg

Fluffy Egg 'n Spinach Casserole

Serves: 2 , Cooking time: 35 minutes

Ingredients:

- A dash of salt
- ¼ tsp pepper
- 4 large eggs, beaten
- 1 teaspoon garlic powder
- 1 tablespoon olive oil
- 1 small onion, chopped
- 1 ½ cups spinach, chopped and excess water squeezed out
- ¼ cup low fat mayonnaise

Directions for Cooking:

1. Preheat oven to 400°F.
2. In a mixing bowl, combine all ingredients except for the spinach and oil. Whisk until well-incorporated.
3. Rub oil all over a baking dish, spread spinach on bottom, and pour the egg mixture over.
4. Place in the oven and cook for 15 minutes.
5. Turn off oven and let it sit for another 10 minutes or until eggs are set.
6. Serve and enjoy.

Nutrition Information:

Calories per Serving: 249.5; Carbs: 7.1g; Protein: 11.4g; Fats: 19.5g; Saturated Fat: 6.5g; Sodium: 243mg

Egg on Avocado Cup Bake

Serves: 4 , Cooking time: 20 minutes

Ingredients:

- 2 medium avocados
- 4 small eggs
- 1 tsp garlic powder
- 4 dash of salt
- 1 tsp pepper
- 1/4 cup Parmesan cheese, low fat, shredded
- 1/4 tsp black pepper

Directions for Cooking:

1. Preheat oven to 400°F.
2. Slice avocados in half lengthwise and discard seed. Thinly slice the other side of avocado so it sits stable on a flat surface. Place on a baking sheet.
3. Break an egg on each avocado hole. Season each egg with ¼ tsp garlic powder, a dash of salt, and ¼ tsp pepper.
4. Pop in the oven and bake for 15 minutes. Turn off oven.
5. Sprinkle evenly with cheese and leave in oven for 5 minutes.
6. Serve and enjoy.

Nutrition Information:

Calories per Serving: 262.9; Carbs: 11.5g; Protein: 9g; Fats: 20.1g; Saturated Fat: 4.2g; Sodium: 330mg

Healthy Avocado Toast

Serves: 4 , Cooking time: 10 minutes

Ingredients:

- One 8-ounce ripe avocado, halved, pitted and peeled
- ¼ tsp freshly ground black pepper
- 4 slices whole grain or whole wheat bread
- 1 clove garlic, peeled and halved
- ¼ tsp crushed red pepper flakes

Directions for Cooking:

1. In a shallow bowl, mash the avocado with a fork until chunky. Season with black pepper.
2. Toast the bread until browned and crisp. Lightly rub 1 side of each slice with the cut side of the garlic until fragrant; discard the garlic.
3. Divide the mashed avocado evenly among the toasts, and top with red pepper flakes.
4. Serve and enjoy

Nutrition Information:

Calories per Serving: 181.4; Carbs: 19g; Protein: 5.2g; Fats: 9.4g; Saturated Fat: 1.4g; Sodium: 150mg

Serves: 4 , Cooking time: 1 hour and 30 minutes

Ingredients:

- 1 1/2 tsp freshly ground black pepper
- 8 ounces lasagna noodles (about 12)
- 6-oz ground beef, lean
- 1 bunch scallions, whites cut into 1/2-inch pieces and greens thinly sliced
- 1/4 cup all-purpose flour
- 2 cups skim milk
- 1/2 teaspoon freshly grated nutmeg
- 1 cup shredded low-fat mozzarella cheese
- 1/2 cup grated Parmesan, low fat
- Two 10-ounce packages frozen chopped spinach, thawed and excess liquid squeezed out
- 1/4 cup fresh parsley leaves, chopped

Directions for Cooking:

1. Bring a large pot of water to a boil. Add the noodles and cook according to the package directions, minus the oil and salt.
2. Strain into a colander and cool with running tap water. Drape the noodles over and around the side of the colander.
3. Meanwhile, heat a large nonstick skillet over medium-high heat. Add the ground beef. Cook and crumble for 5 minutes.
4. Add scallion whites. Continue cooking and stirring for another 5 minutes.
5. Sprinkle the flour over the cooked beef and stir until it is completely absorbed.
6. Add 1 cup milk. Stir until it starts to thicken. Add remaining milk, bring to a simmer and stir until the sauce is thick enough to coat the back of a spoon, about 2 minutes.
7. Stir in 1 1/2 teaspoons pepper and the nutmeg. Remove the sauce from the heat and set aside.
8. Mix together the mozzarella and Parmesan in a medium bowl.
9. Lightly grease with cooking spray a 9- by 13-inch baking dish.
10. Spread about 4 tablespoons of the sauce (without pieces of meat) over the bottom. Arrange 4 slightly overlapping noodles to fully cover the bottom of the dish. Spread 1/3 of the remaining sauce over the noodles. Spread 1/2 the spinach in an even layer. Sprinkle with about 1/3 of the scallion greens, a few grinds of pepper and 1/3 of the cheese mixture.
11. Repeat layering process until all ingredients ae used.
12. Cover the top with plastic wrap and refrigerate overnight. Do the same with the remaining scallion greens.
13. Preheat the oven to 350°F. Remove the plastic wrap from the baking dish, and cover with foil. Bake until the cheese is melted and bubbly, about 45 minutes.
14. Remove foil and continue to bake until tops are slightly browned, 10 to 15 minutes.
15. Top with the remaining scallions, parsley and a sprinkle of black pepper. Let sit for at least 15 minutes, then slice and serve.

Nutrition Information:

Calories per Serving: 389; Carbs: 25.8g; Protein: 35.3g; Fats: 16.2g; Saturated Fat: 8.8g; Sodium: 374mg

Serves: 2 , Cooking time: 10 minutes

Ingredients:

- 2 eggs, beaten
- 2 egg whites
- ½ cup white onion, chopped
- Juice of ½ lime, freshly squeezed
- 1 tsp olive oil
- 1 tablespoon jalapeno, chopped
- 1 handful cilantro, chopped

Directions for Cooking:

1. Whisk eggs, egg whites, and jalapeno. Set aside.
2. Place a medium nonstick pan on medium fire and heat oil for a minute.
3. Sauté onions for 3 minutes.
4. Stir in cilantro and cook for 2 minutes or until wilted.
5. Add eggs and scramble to desired doneness.
6. Serve and enjoy with lime juice.

Nutrition Information:

Calories per Serving: 155.4; Carbs: 9.6g; Protein: 9.9g; Fats: 8.6g; Saturated Fat: 2g; Sodium: 207mg

Savory 'n Herby Scrambled Eggs

Serves: 4 , Cooking time: 10 minutes

Ingredients:

- 6 large eggs
- 1/4 cup skim milk
- 1 tablespoon thinly sliced fresh chives
- 2 tablespoons minced fresh flat-leaf parsley leaves
- 1 1/2 teaspoons finely chopped fresh tarragon leaves
- ¼ tsp freshly ground black pepper
- 1 tsp olive oil

Directions for Cooking:

1. In a medium bowl, whisk together the eggs, milk, chives, parsley, and tarragon. Season with pepper.
2. On medium low fire, heat oil in a medium non-stick skillet for a minute.
3. Add the egg mixture and cook, stirring almost constantly, for 4 to 7 minutes depending on the desired firmness of the eggs.
4. Serve immediately.

Nutrition Information:
Calories per Serving: 102.3; Carbs: 3.2g; Protein: 4.6g; Fats: 7.9g; Saturated Fat: 2.6g; Sodium: 20mg

Easy Breakfast Potatoes 'n Veggies

Serves: 8 , Cooking time: 20 minutes

Ingredients:

- 5 pounds red potatoes, roughly chopped/diced
- 4 cloves garlic, minced
- 1 onion, chopped
- 1 green bell pepper, seeded and roughly chopped
- 1 red bell pepper, seeded and roughly chopped
- 1 tbsp olive oil
- 1 tsp coconut aminos
- 1/2 teaspoon cayenne pepper
- ½ tsp freshly ground pepper
- ½ tsp dried rosemary
- ½ tsp dried basil

Directions for Cooking:

1. In a large nonstick pan, heat oil over medium fire.
2. Stir in potatoes, garlic, onion, and coconut aminos. Sauté for 5 minutes.
3. Cover and let cook for 8 minutes, stirring occasionally.
4. Remove cover, add remaining ingredients, increase fire to high and stir fry for 7 minutes.
5. Serve and enjoy.

Nutrition Information:
Calories per Serving: 231.3; Carbs: 47.4g; Protein: 5.7g; Fats: 2.1g; Saturated Fat: .3g; Sodium: 160mg

Easy Brekky Bread Pudding

Serves: 8 , Cooking time: 60 minutes

Ingredients:

- 5 extra-large whole eggs
- 2 extra-large egg yolks
- 1/2 cup half-and-half
- 2 cups skim milk
- 1/3 cup honey
- 1 1/2 teaspoons pure vanilla extract
- 2 teaspoons orange zest (2 oranges)
- Brioche loaf
- 1/2 cup golden raisins
- Maple syrup, to serve

Directions for Cooking:

1. Preheat the oven to 350ºF.
2. In a medium bowl, whisk together the whole eggs, egg yolks, half-and-half, milk, honey, vanilla, and orange zest. Set aside.
3. Slice the brioche loaf into 6 (1-inch) thick pieces. Lay half brioche slices flat in a 9 by 13 baking dish. Spread the raisins on top of the brioche slices and place the remaining slices on top. Make sure that the raisins are between the layers of brioche or they will burn while baking. Pour the egg mixture over the bread and allow to soak for 15 minutes, pressing down gently.

4. Bake for 55 to 60 minutes or until the pudding puffs up and the custard is set.
5. Remove from the oven and cool for 10 minutes before serving.

Nutrition Information:
Calories per Serving: 258.8; Carbs: 44.9g; Protein: 9g; Fats: 4.8g; Saturated Fat: 1.6g; Sodium: 187mg

Delicious Breakfast Burritos

Serves: 4 , Cooking time: 15 minutes
Ingredients:
- 2 medium tomatillos (about 4 ounces), husked and rinsed
- 1 jalapeno pepper (remove seeds for less heat)
- 1 small red onion, quartered
- 2 cups roughly chopped fresh cilantro (leaves and tender stems)
- Juice of 1 lime
- freshly ground pepper
- 3 1/2 cups frozen shredded or diced hash brown potatoes (about 1 pound)
- 4 large eggs, lightly beaten
- 1 16-ounce can low-sodium refried beans
- 4 10-inch flour tortillas, warmed
- 1 cup shredded mozzarella cheese (about 4 ounces)

Directions for Cooking:
1. Preheat the broiler. Put the tomatillos, jalapeno and red onion on a baking sheet and broil, turning once, until tender and charred in spots, about 5 minutes per side.
2. Transfer the vegetables to a blender and add the cilantro, lime juice, 1/4 cup water and a few grinds of pepper. Process until smooth.
3. Meanwhile, cook the potatoes in a skillet. Cover and cook, stirring halfway through, until golden brown around, 8 to 10 minutes. Put in a bowl.
4. Add eggs to the skillet and cook over medium heat, stirring, until scrambled, about 1 minute. Transfer to a bowl and cover.
5. Wipe skillet with paper towel and add the beans. Cook until warmed, around 3 minutes.
6. Season with pepper and turn off the fire.
7. Spread the beans in the center of each tortilla and top with the potatoes, eggs and cheese. Fold the bottom edge of the tortilla over the filling, then fold in the sides and roll up. Serve with the tomatillo salsa.

Nutrition Information:
Calories per Serving: 437.6; Carbs: 64g; Protein: 23.8g; Fats: 9.6g; Saturated Fat: 2.8g; Sodium: 981mg

Smoked Salmon Scrambled Eggs

Serves: 6 , Cooking time: 10 minutes
Ingredients:
- 1/4-pound sliced smoked salmon
- 6 eggs
- 1/2 cup skim milk
- ¼ tsp freshly ground black pepper
- 1 tablespoon olive oil
- 8 blades of fresh chives, finely chopped
- 3 cups packed spinach

Directions for Cooking:
1. Reserve 2 slices of salmon for garnish. Chop the remaining salmon into very small pieces.
2. Whisk eggs and milk together. Add 1/2 of your chopped chives and season eggs with pepper.
3. Preheat a large nonstick skillet over medium heat. Add oil and heat for a minute.
4. Add spinach and cook for 3 minutes until wilted.
5. Pour in eggs and scramble for 4 minutes. Once it has come together, but still wet, stir in chopped salmon. Scramble some more and continue to cook to desired doneness.
6. Garnish with chopped chives and reserved salmon.
7. Serve and enjoy.

Nutrition Information:
Calories per Serving: 127.5; Carbs: 3.6g; Protein: 10.5g; Fats: 7.9g; Saturated Fat: 2g; Sodium: 165mg

Serves: 8 , Cooking time: 20 minutes

Ingredients:

- 8 ounces low-fat cream cheese, at room temperature
- 1/3 cup sugar
- 2 extra-large egg yolks, at room temperature
- 2 tablespoons ricotta cheese
- 1 teaspoon pure vanilla extract
- 1 tablespoon grated lemon zest (2 lemons)
- 2 sheets (1 box) frozen puff pastry, defrosted
- 1 egg beaten with 1 tablespoon water, for egg wash

Directions for Cooking:

1. Lightly grease with cooking spray a baking sheet.
2. With a mixer, cream the cream cheese and sugar until smooth. Stir in egg yolks, ricotta, vanilla and lemon zest. Mix until just combined on low.
3. Unfold 1 sheet of puff pastry onto a lightly floured board and roll it slightly with a floured rolling pin until it's a 10 by 10-inch square.
4. Cut the sheet into quarters with a sharp knife.
5. Place a heaping tablespoon of cheese filling into the middle of each of the 4 squares. Brush the border of each pastry with the egg wash and fold 2 opposite corners to the center, brushing and overlapping the corners of each pastry so they firmly stick together.
6. Brush the top of the pastries with egg wash. Place the pastries on the prepared sheet pan. Repeat with the second sheet of puff pastry.
7. Refrigerate Danish puff pastry for 15 minutes. Preheat oven to 400ºF.
8. Bake the pastries for about 20 minutes, until puffed and brown. Serve warm.

Nutrition Information:

Calories per Serving: 94.8; Carbs: 6.9g; Protein: 3.3g; Fats: 6g; Saturated Fat: 3.3g; Sodium: 107mg

Serves: 4 , Cooking time: 35 minutes

Ingredients:

- 8 ounces cooked corned beef, diced
- 1 white onion, finely chopped
- 1 bell pepper, finely chopped
- 2 medium baking potatoes, peeled and shredded (about 2 cups)
- 4 large eggs
- 1 tbsp olive oil
- ¼ tsp freshly ground pepper
- 4 slices cheddar cheese (about 2 ounces), low fat

Directions for Cooking:

1. Heat a medium nonstick pan over high heat.
2. Add the corned beef and cook, stirring with a wooden spoon, until it releases some fat and browns slightly, about 3 minutes.
3. Stir in the onion, bell pepper and potatoes and cook, undisturbed, until browned and crisped on the bottom, about 7 minutes. Continue cooking, turn the hash and let bottom brown evenly for 15 more minutes.
4. Meanwhile, heat the oil in a small nonstick skillet over medium-high heat. Fry the eggs sunny side up to desired doneness. Season with pepper.
5. Place the cheese slices on top of the hash, reduce the heat and let sit until the cheese melts, about 1 minute.
6. To serve, top each portion of hash with a fried egg.

Nutrition Information:

Calories per Serving: 441.2; Carbs: 31.6g; Protein: 28.3g; Fats: 22.4g; Saturated Fat: 9.5g; Sodium: 253mg

Cauliflower and Egg Casserole

Serves: 8 , Cooking time: 45 minutes

Ingredients:
- 10 eggs, beaten
- 1 cup skim milk
- ½ tsp pepper
- ½ tsp dill
- ½ tsp smoked paprika
- 1 tsp olive oil
- 1 cup cauliflower florets, chopped
- 1 onion, diced
- 1 red bell pepper, seeded and diced
- 1 stalk green onions, chopped

Directions for Cooking:
1. Lightly grease a casserole dish with olive oil.
2. In a bowl, whisk eggs and milk well. Season with pepper, paprika, and dill.
3. In prepared dish, evenly spread and layer onion, cauliflower, and bell pepper.
4. Pour in eggs. Cover dish with foil and bake for 30 minutes.
5. Remove foil and broil on low until tops are lightly browned, around 5 minutes.
6. Remove from oven and let it sit for 10 minutes to set.
7. Sprinkle with chopped green onions.
8. Serve and enjoy.

Nutrition Information:
Calories per Serving: 116.8; Carbs: 7.2g; Protein: 8.5g; Fats: 6g; Saturated Fat: 1.8g; Sodium: 203mg

Kale and Mushroom Frittata

Serves: 4 , Cooking time: 25 minutes

Ingredients:
- 1 tsp olive oil
- 2 teaspoons minced garlic
- 1 cup mushrooms, sliced
- 1 cup chopped kale
- 4 large eggs, beaten

Directions for Cooking:
1. On medium fire, place a medium nonstick pan and heat oil. Swirl to coat pan.
2. Sauté mushrooms and garlic for 5 minutes.
3. Add kale and sauté until wilted, around 4 minutes.
4. Add eggs and lower fire to low. Cook for 10 minutes while covered. If needed, insert a spatula underneath frittata to move uncooked egg from the top to the bottom of the pan.
5. Let frittata sit for 5 more minutes before slicing.

Nutrition Information:
Calories per Serving: 69.3; Carbs: 1.5g; Protein: 3g; Fats: 5.7g; Saturated Fat: 1.8g; Sodium: 10mg

Scrambled Eggs with Spinach

Serves: 4 , Cooking time: 10 minutes

Ingredients:
- 4 large eggs, beaten
- 4 large egg whites, beaten
- 1/2 cup almond milk, unsweetened
- 2 cups spinach
- ¼ onion, diced
- ¼ tsp pepper
- ½ tsp garlic
- 1 tsp olive oil

Directions for Cooking:
1. In a bowl, whisk well all ingredients except for oil, spinach and onions.
2. Place a large nonstick frying pan on medium high fire and heat oil.
3. Sauté onions for 3 minutes. Stir in spinach and cook for another 3 minutes until wilted.
4. Add whisked eggs and scramble for 4 minutes or to desired doneness.
5. Serve and enjoy.

Nutrition Information:
Calories per Serving: 104.1; Carbs: 5.2g; Protein: 7.1g; Fats: 6.1g; Saturated Fat: 1.8g; Sodium: 97mg

Savory Basil 'n Tomato Omelet

Serves: 6 , Cooking time: 10 minutes

Ingredients:

- 1 tsp olive oil
- 6 eggs, beaten
- ¼ cup skim milk
- ¼ tsp pepper
- 1 tsp coconut aminos
- 1 cup fresh basil leaves, chopped
- 2 roma tomatoes, sliced

Directions for Cooking:

1. In a bowl, whisk well all ingredients except for oil, basil leaves and tomatoes.
2. Place a large nonstick frying pan on medium high fire and heat oil.
3. Sauté tomatoes for 3 minutes. Stir in basil leaves and cook for another 2 minutes until wilted.
4. Add whisked eggs and scramble for 5 minutes or to desired doneness.
5. Serve and enjoy.

Nutrition Information:

Calories per Serving: 83.5; Carbs: 3.1g; Protein: 6.3g; Fats: 5.1g; Saturated Fat: 1.5g; Sodium: 83mg

Cauliflower and Eggs Skillet

Serves: 4 , Cooking time: 15 minutes

Ingredients:

- 1 tsp olive oil
- 3 cloves of garlic
- 1 head cauliflower, grated and squeezed dry
- 4 large eggs
- 1 small onion, sliced
- ¼ tsp pepper

Directions for Cooking:

1. In a blender, pulse cauliflower and garlic until it looks like rice. Transfer to a bowl and squeeze excess water.
2. In a bowl, whisk well eggs and pepper.
3. Place a large nonstick frying pan on medium high fire and heat oil.
4. Sauté onions for 5 minutes, until soft. Stir in riced cauliflower and cook for another 4 minutes soft but not mushy.
5. Add whisked eggs and scramble for 5 minutes or to desired doneness.
6. Serve and enjoy.

Nutrition Information:

Calories per Serving: 97.1; Carbs: 6.6g; Protein: 4.4g; Fats: 5.9g; Saturated Fat: 1.9g; Sodium: 29mg

Artichoke, Red Pepper and Feta Frittata

Serves: 8 , Cooking time: 35 minutes

Ingredients:

- 1 can artichoke hearts, drained and cut into small pieces
- 2 big red peppers
- ¼ cup sliced green onions
- 8 eggs, beaten
- ¼ tsp pepper
- 4 ounces feta cheese
- 2 tablespoons parsley, chopped

Directions for Cooking:

1. Slice bell peppers in half and discard seeds. Place red bell peppers on a baking sheet and broil for 4 minutes on top rack. Remove from oven and once cool enough to handle chop.
2. In a bowl, whisk eggs and season with pepper.
3. Lightly grease a baking dish with cooking spray.
4. Evenly spread artichoke hearts on bottom followed by chopped bell peppers and parsley.
5. Cover with foil and bake in preheated 400°F oven for 15 minutes.
6. Remove from oven and discard foil.
7. Sprinkle cheese and parsley on top and bake for another 10 minutes.
8. Remove from oven, sprinkle cheese, and let it sit for another 10 minutes.
9. Serve and enjoy

Nutrition Information:

Calories per Serving: 180.8; Carbs: 4.7g; Protein: 11.7g; Fats: 12.8g; Saturated Fat: 4.7g; Sodium: 243mg

Chapter 3 Appetizer Recipes

Sour Cream and Onion Dip Carrot Sticks

Serves: 8 , Cooking time: 0 minutes

Ingredients:
- 1 sweet onion, peeled and minced
- ½ cup sour cream
- 2 tbsp low fat mayonnaise
- 4 stalks celery, cut into 3-inch lengths
- 2 cups carrot sticks

Directions for Cooking:

1. In a bowl, whisk well sour cream and mayonnaise until thoroughly combined.
2. Stir in onion and mix well.
3. Let it sit for an hour in the fridge and serve with carrot and celery sticks on the side.

Nutrition Information:
Calories per Serving: 60; Protein: 1.8g; Carbs: 7.8g; Fat: 1.8g; Saturated Fat: 1g; Sodium: 43mg

Crab Stuffed Mushrooms

Serves: 6 , Cooking time: 25 minutes

Ingredients:
- 2 tbsp minced green onion
- 1 cup cooked crabmeat, chopped finely
- ¼ cup Monterey Jack cheese, shredded, low fat
- 1 tsp lemon juice
- ½ tsp dill
- 1 lb. fresh button mushrooms

Directions for Cooking:
1. Destem mushrooms, wash and drain well.
2. Chop mushroom stems.
3. Preheat oven to 400oF and lightly grease a baking pan with cooking spray.

4. In a small bowl, whisk well green onion, crabmeat, lemon juice, dill, and chopped mushroom stems.
5. Evenly spread mushrooms on prepared pan with cap sides up. Evenly spoon crabmeat mixture on top of mushroom caps.
6. Pop in the oven and bake for 20 minutes.
7. Remove from oven and sprinkle cheese on top.
8. Return to oven and broil for 3 minutes.
9. Serve and enjoy.

Nutrition Information:
Calories per Serving: 58; Protein: 12.1g; Carbs: 58.1g; Fat: 2.5g; Saturated Fat: 1.1g; Sodium: 135mg

Ricotta and Pomegranate Bruschetta

Serves: 12 , Cooking time: 12 minutes

Ingredients:
- 6 slice Whole Grain Nut Bread
- 1 cup Low Fat Ricotta Cheese
- 1/2 tsp Grated lemon zest
- 1/2 cup Pomegranate Arils
- 2 tsp Thyme, Fresh

Directions for Cooking:
1. Toast bread until lightly browned.
2. Meanwhile, in a small bowl whisk well cheese and lemon zest.

3. Slice the toasted bread in half. Slather top with cottage cheese.
4. Top with thyme and pomegranate.
5. Serve and enjoy.

Nutrition Information:
Calories per Serving: 69; Protein: 4.1g; Carbs: 11.1g; Fat: 1.0g; Saturated Fat: 0.2g; Sodium: 123mg

Buffalo Chicken Dip

Serves: 8 , Cooking time: 10 minutes

Ingredients:

- 1-piece chicken breast half, sliced into strips
- ½ cup cottage cheese, fat free
- 1 tbsp ranch dressing
- 2 tbsp hot sauce
- ¼ cup low fat cheddar cheese
- 6 stalks celery, cut into 4-inch lengths

Directions for Cooking:

1. Place a fry pan on medium fire and pan fry chicken pieces until cooked, around 8 minutes.
2. Stir in ranch dressing, hot sauce, and cheddar cheese until melted.
3. Turn off fire and transfer to a bowl. Mix in cottage cheese and stir well.
4. Serve with celery sticks on the side.

Nutrition Information:

Calories per Serving: 71; Protein: 8.7g; Carbs: 1.3g; Fat: 3.3g; Saturated Fat: 1.3g; Sodium: 290 mg

Deviled Eggs Guac Style

Serves: 12 , Cooking time: 0 minutes

Ingredients:

- 1 ripe avocado
- 1 tbsp green onion, chopped
- 1 tbsp Cilantro
- 1 tbsp Lime
- 1/2 jalapeno chili pepper
- 1 tbsp light sour cream
- 6 medium eggs, hard boiled and peeled

Directions for Cooking:

1. In a medium bowl, mash avocado. Mix in green onion, cilantro, lime, pepper, and sour cream. Mix well.
2. Slice hard boiled eggs in half lengthwise.
3. Scoop out yolk and place in bowl of avocadoes. Mix well.
4. Scoop out avocado yolk mixture and spoon into egg white holes.
5. Serve and enjoy or refrigerate for future use.

Nutrition Information:

Calories per Serving: 60; Protein: 3.1g; Carbs: 1.8g; Fat: 4.7g; Saturated Fat: 1.1g; Sodium: 34mg

Homemade Spinach Artichoke Dip with Pita Chips

Serves: 16 , Cooking time: 10 minutes

Ingredients:

- 1 1/4 cups raw cashews
- 1 tsp olive oil
- 5 cloves garlic, peeled
- 3/4 cup chopped shallot
- 1 1/2 cups unsweetened almond milk
- 5 tbsp nutritional yeast, for cheesy flavor
- 1/2 tsp black pepper
- 1 tsp coconut aminos
- 2 tbsp water
- 4 cups loosely packed chopped fresh spinach
- 1 14-ounce can artichoke hearts, rinsed, drained well, and roughly chopped
- 2 tbsp fat free parmesan cheese
- 4 large whole wheat pita bread, quartered

Directions for Cooking:

1. Place cashews in a bowl, cover with boiling water and let it soak for an hour. Then drain well.
2. Place a cast iron pan on medium fire and heat oil. Add garlic and cook for a minute. Stir in shallots and cook for 4 minutes or until soft.
3. In a blender, add half of garlic and shallot mixture. Add drained cashews, almond milk, nutritional yeast, pepper, and coconut aminos. Puree until smooth and creamy. Scrape sides of blender and blend once more.
4. Preheat oven to 350oF.
5. Return same cast iron pan to medium fire and add water, spinach, and artichoke hearts. Cook until spinach is wilted, around 4 minutes.
6. Pour pureed mixture into pan and mix well. Turn off fire. Sprinkle cheese on top.

7. Pop in the oven and bake for 8 minutes.
8. Serve with your favorite bread or cracker.

Nutrition Information:
Calories per Serving: 108; Protein: 5.2g; Carbs: 15.6g; Fat: 3.5g; Saturated Fat: 0.6g; Sodium: 209 mg

Cornbread with Southern Twist

Serves: 8 , Cooking time: 20 minutes

Ingredients:
- 1 tbsp olive oil
- 1 ¼ cups skim milk
- ¼ cup egg substitute
- 4 tbsp sodium free baking powder
- ½ cup flour
- 1 ½ cups cornmeal

Directions for Cooking:
1. Prepare 8 x 8-inch baking dish or a black iron skillet then add shortening.
2. Put the baking dish or skillet inside the oven on 425oF and leave there for 10 minutes.
3. In a bowl, add milk and egg then mix well.
4. Take out the skillet and add the heated oil into the batter and stir well.
5. Once all ingredients are mixed, pour mixture into skillet.
6. Then cook for 15 to 20 minutes in the oven until golden brown.

Nutrition Information:
Calories per Serving: 206.7; Protein: 4.9g; Carbs: 38g; Fat: 3.9g; Saturated Fat: .9g; Sodium: 40mg

Easy Potato Casserole

Serves: 10 , Cooking time: 20 minutes

Ingredients:
- 1 tsp dried dill weed
- ¼ tsp black pepper
- ¼ cup green onions, chopped
- 2 tbsp olive oil
- 16 small new potatoes, around 5 cups

Directions for Cooking:
1. Using water and vegetable brush clean all potatoes.
2. For about 20 minutes, boil potatoes then drain and cool them for 20 minutes.
3. Mix spices, onions, and olive oil. Then cut potatoes into quarters and combine with the mixture.
4. Refrigerate and enjoy!

Nutrition Information:
Calories per Serving: 237; Protein: 5.6g; Carbs: 46.9g; Fat: 3.0g; Saturated Fat: .4g; Sodium: 22.5mg

Carrot Sticks with Dill 'n Garlic Dip

Serves: 10 , Cooking time: 0 minutes

Ingredients:
- 1 ½ cups raw sunflower seeds
- 6 cloves garlic, peeled
- 1 tsp coconut aminos
- 1/2 cup lemon juice
- 1/3 cup tahini
- 1 tbsp olive oil
- 1/2 cup water
- 1/2 cup fresh dill
- 4 carrots, peeled and sliced into sticks

Directions for Cooking:
1. Soak sunflower seeds in water overnight or at least 2 hours.
2. In a blender, add soaked sunflower seeds and peeled garlic. Puree.
3. Add remaining ingredients except for water and ¼ cup dill. Puree until smooth and creamy.
4. Add water slowly until desired consistency is reached.
5. Chop the remaining dill and stir in to mix well.
6. Serve with sliced fresh veggies.
7. Can be stored in a lidded container in the fridge for up to a week.

Nutrition Information:
Calories per Serving: 188; Protein: 5.9g; Carbs: 7.5g; Fat: 16.5g; Saturated Fat: 1.7g; Sodium: 13 mg

Celery Sticks with Chipotle Aioli Dip

Serves: 8 , Cooking time: 5 minutes

Ingredients:
- 3/4 cup raw cashews
- 1/2 cup almond milk
- 2 tbsp lemon juice
- 1/2 tsp coconut aminos
- 1 packet stevia
- 2 whole chipotle peppers in adobo sauce, reserving 1 tbsp adobo sauce
- 1 pinch smoked paprika
- 6 stalks celery, cut into 3-inch lengths

Directions for Cooking:

1. In a mixing bowl, place cashews and cover with boiling hot water. Leave for an hour and then drain thoroughly.
2. Place drained cashews in a blender and add remaining ingredients.
3. Puree until smooth and creamy.
4. Serve with celery sticks on the side.

Nutrition Information:
Calories per Serving: 52; Protein: 1.7g; Carbs: 5.0g; Fat: 3.3g; Saturated Fat: 0.5g; Sodium: 22 mg

Appetizing Cucumber Salad

Serves: 8 , Cooking time: 0 minutes

Ingredients:
- 2 cucumber, peeled
- ½ cup sour cream
- 2 tbsp low fat, low sodium mayonnaise
- 1 tsp mustard
- 1 tbsp fresh lemon juice
- 1 garlic clove, peeled and minced
- 1/3 cup fresh dill leaves, chopped roughly
- ½ tsp pepper

Directions for Cooking:
1. Slice cucumber into 3 equal lengths. Then slice lengthwise into quarters or smaller to create cucumber sticks. Drain in a colander and set aside.
2. In a medium bowl whisk well the remaining ingredients.
3. Add the drained cucumber into bowl of dressing and toss well to coat.
4. Serve and enjoy.

Nutrition Information:
Calories per Serving: 37.9; Protein: 1g; Carbs: 3.3g; Fat: 2.3g; Saturated Fat: 1g; Sodium: 24mg

Pesto Stuffed Mushrooms

Serves: 6 , Cooking time: 25 minutes

Ingredients:
- 6 large cremini mushrooms
- 6 bacon slices
- 2 tablespoons basil pesto
- 5 tablespoons low-fat cream cheese softened

Directions for Cooking:
1. Line a cookie sheet with foil and preheat oven to 375oF.
2. In a small bowl mix well, pesto and cream cheese.
3. Remove stems of mushrooms and discard. Evenly fill mushroom caps with pesto-cream cheese filling.
4. Get one stuffed mushroom and a slice of bacon. Wrap the bacon all over the mushrooms. Repeat process on remaining mushrooms and bacon.
5. Place bacon wrapped mushrooms on prepared pan and bake for 25 minutes or until bacon is crispy.
6. Let it cool, evenly divide into suggested servings, and enjoy.

Nutrition Information:
Calories per Serving: 137.8; Carbs: 2g; Protein: 5g; Fats: 12.2g; Saturated Fat: 1g; Sodium: 168mg

Tuna Topped Pickles

Serves: 5 , Cooking time: 0 minutes

Ingredients:

- ¼ tsp pepper
- 1 tbsp fresh dill, and more for garnish
- ¼ cup light mayo
- 1 can light flaked tuna, drained
- 5 dill pickles

Directions for Cooking:

1. Slice pickles in half, lengthwise. With a spoon, deseed the pickles and discard seeds.
2. In a small bowl, mix well the mayo, dill, and tuna using a fork.
3. Evenly divide the mixture into 10 and spread over deseeded pickles.
4. Garnish with more dill on top and sprinkle black pepper.
5. Evenly divide into suggested servings and enjoy.

Nutrition Information:

Calories per Serving: 57; Carbs: 4.6g; Protein: 7.4g; Fats: 1g; Saturated Fat: .2g; Sodium: 313mg

Old Bay 'n Dijon Crab Cakes

Serves: 8 , Cooking time: 20 minutes

Ingredients:

- ½ tsp pepper
- 2 large eggs
- 1-pound lump crab meat
- 1 teaspoon Worcestershire sauce
- 1 teaspoon Dijon mustard
- 1 ½ teaspoon old bay seasoning
- ½ cup panko
- ¼ cup chopped green onion

Directions for Cooking:

1. Preheat oven to 400⁰F.
2. In a mixing bowl, combine all ingredients until everything is well-incorporated.
3. Use your hands to form small patties of crab cakes.
4. Place an oven safe wire rack on a baking pan and lightly grease rack. Place crab cakes on wire rack.
5. Bake in the oven for 15 minutes or until golden brown.
6. Serve an enjoy.

Nutrition Information:

Calories per Serving: 69.9; Carbs: 2.2g; Protein: 11.3g; Fats: 1.9g; Saturated Fat: .6g; Sodium: 196mg

Cajun-Paprika Onion Rings

Serves: 6 , Cooking time: 20 minutes

Ingredients:

- ¼ cup almond milk
- ½ teaspoon Cajun seasoning
- ¾ cup almond flour
- 1 ½ teaspoon paprika
- 1 large white onion
- 1 teaspoon garlic powder
- 2 large eggs, beaten
- 1 tsp pepper

Directions for Cooking:

1. Preheat oven to 400°F.
2. Peel the onion, cut off the top and slice into circles.
3. In a mixing bowl, combine the almond milk and the eggs.
4. Soak the onion in the egg mixture.
5. In another bowl, combine the almond flour, paprika garlic powder, Cajun seasoning, and pepper.
6. Dredge the onion in the almond flour mixture.
7. Place an oven safe wire rack on a baking pan and lightly grease with cooking spray.
8. Place dredged onions on wire rack. Pop in the oven and bake for 15 minutes or until golden brown.
9. Serve and enjoy.

Nutrition Information:

Calories per Serving: 42.6; Carbs: 5g; Protein: 1.6g; Fats: 1.8g; Saturated Fat: .6g; Sodium: 29mg

Garlicky Zucchini Fries

Serves: 6 , Cooking time: 20 minutes

Ingredients:

- ¼ teaspoon garlic powder
- ½ cup almond flour
- 2 large egg whites, beaten
- 3 medium zucchinis, sliced into French fry sticks
- ½ tsp pepper

Directions for Cooking:

1. Mix all ingredients in a bowl until the zucchini fries are well coated.
2. Lightly grease a baking sheet with cooking spray.
3. Evenly spread zucchini fries on baking pan and place on top rack of oven.
4. Broil on low for 5 minutes. Remove from oven and turn over sticks. Return to oven and continue cooking for another 3 to 5 minutes until lightly browned and crisped.
5. Serve and enjoy

Nutrition Information:

Calories per Serving: 11; Carbs: .7g; Protein: 1.5g; Fats: 0.1g; Saturated Fat: 0g; Sodium: 0.5mg

Kale Taters Garlic Flavored

Serves: 4 , Cooking time: 20 minutes

Ingredients:

- cooking spray
- 4 cups kale, rinsed and chopped
- 2 cups boiled potatoes, finely chopped
- 1/8 teaspoon black pepper
- 2 tbsp almond milk
- 1 teaspoon extra-virgin olive oil
- 1 clove of garlic, minced

Directions for Cooking:

1. Heat oil in a large skillet and sauté the garlic for 2 minutes. Add the kale until it wilts. Transfer to a large bowl.
2. Add the potatoes and almond milk. Season with pepper to taste.
3. Evenly divide into 4 and form patties.
4. Lightly grease a baking pan with cooking spray. Place patties on pan. Place pan on top rack of oven and broil on low for 6 minutes. Turnover patties and cook for another 4 minutes.
5. Serve and enjoy.

Nutrition Information:

Calories per Serving: 89.4; Carbs: 18g; Protein: 2.1g; Fats: 1g; Saturated Fat: .1g; Sodium: 25mg

French Fried Butternut Squash

Serves: 6 , Cooking time: 20 minutes

Ingredients:

- 1 medium butternut squash
- 1 tablespoon olive oil
- 1 tablespoon chopped fresh thyme
- 1 tablespoon chopped fresh rosemary
- 1/2 teaspoon salt

Directions for Cooking:

1. Heat oven to 425°F. Lightly coat a baking sheet with cooking spray.
2. Peel skin from butternut squash and cut into even sticks, about 1/2-inch-wide and 3 inches long.
3. In a medium bowl, combine the squash, oil, thyme, rosemary, and salt; mix until the squash is evenly coated.
4. Spread onto the baking sheet and roast for 10 minutes.
5. Remove baking sheet from the oven and shake to loosen the squash.
6. Return to oven and continue to roast for 10 minutes or until golden brown.
7. Serve and enjoy.

Nutrition Information:

Calories per Serving: 62; Carbs: 11.0g; Protein: 1.0g; Fats: 2.0g; Saturated Fat: 0g; Sodium: 168mg

Sweet 'n Spicy Trail Mix

Serves: 12 , Cooking time: 45 minutes

Ingredients:

- 2 cans (15 ounces each) garbanzos, rinsed, drained and patted dry
- 2 cups wheat squares cereal
- 1 cup dried pineapple chunks
- 1 cup raisins
- 2 tablespoons honey
- 2 tablespoons Worcestershire sauce
- 1 teaspoon garlic powder
- 1/2 teaspoon chili powder
- 1 tsp olive oil

Directions for Cooking:

1. Heat the oven to 350°F. Lightly grease a large baking pan with cooking spray.
2. Place a large nonstick pan on medium fire and heat oil. Add garbanzos and cook until lightly browned, around 10 minutes while stirring frequently.
3. Transfer to prepared pan, bake for 20 minutes or until crisped. Shake pan halfway through cooking time. Remove from oven.
4. Measure the cereal, pineapple and raisins and add to pan of garbanzos. Stir to mix evenly.
5. In a large glass measuring cup combine honey, Worcestershire sauce and spices. Stir to mix evenly. Pour the mixture over the snack mix and toss gently.
6. Bake for about 10 to 15 minutes, stirring occasionally to keep the mixture from burning.
7. Remove from oven and let cool completely.
8. Evenly divide into suggested servings and enjoy.

Nutrition Information:

Calories per Serving: 170.4; Carbs: 32.3g; Protein: 5.8g; Fats: 2g; Saturated Fat: .2g; Sodium: 122mg

Tender-Crisp Cauliflower Bites

Serves: 3 , Cooking time: 10 minutes

Ingredients:

- 2 cups cauliflower florets
- 1 tablespoon olive oil
- ¼ tsp salt
- ½ tsp pepper
- 2 clove garlic minced

Directions for Cooking:

1. In a small bowl, mix well olive oil salt, pepper, and garlic.
2. Place cauliflower florets on a baking pan. Drizzle with seasoned oil and toss well to coat.
3. Evenly spread in a single layer and place pan on top rack of oven.
4. Broil on low for 5 minutes. Turnover florets and return to oven.
5. Continue cooking for another 5 minutes.
6. Serve and enjoy.

Nutrition Information:

Calories per Serving: 68.7; Carbs: 4.9g; Protein: 1.7g; Fats: 4.7g; Saturated Fat: .7g; Sodium: 216mg

Chapter 4 Soup Recipes

Delicious Carrot Soup

Serves: 6 , Cooking time: 40 minutes
Ingredients:
- 10 carrots, scraped and sliced
- 1 1/2 tablespoons sugar
- 2 cups water
- 3 tablespoons all-purpose (plain) flour
- 1/4 teaspoon ground black pepper
- 1/4 teaspoon ground nutmeg
- 4 cups fat-free milk
- 2 tablespoons fresh parsley, chopped

Cooking Directions:
1. Heat the water, carrots, and sugar in a saucepan. Simmer while covered for 20 minutes. Then drain, reserve some of the liquid.
2. Whisk in medium-high heat the flour, nutmeg, milk, and pepper. Stir constantly until it thickens.
3. Blend the white sauce and carrots in a food processor. Puree until smooth. Add reserved liquid until desired consistency is achieved.
4. Garnish with parsley and serve.

Nutrition Information:
Calories per serving: 137; Carbs: 27g; Fats: 9g; Protein: 7g; Saturated fat: 1g; Sodium: 164mg

Fresh Vegetable Soup

Serves: 6 , Cooking time: 40 minutes
Ingredients:
- 2 tablespoons extra-virgin olive oil
- 1 medium onion, chopped
- 2 medium carrots, chopped
- 2 stalks celery, chopped
- 12 ounces fresh green beans, cut into ½-inch pieces
- 2 cloves garlic, minced
- 8 cups no-salt-added chicken broth or low-sodium vegetable broth
- 2 (15 ounce) cans low-sodium cannellini or other white beans, rinsed
- 4 cups chopped kale
- 2 medium zucchinis, chopped
- 4 Roma tomatoes, seeded and chopped
- 2 teaspoons red-wine vinegar
- ¾ teaspoon salt
- ½ teaspoon ground pepper
- 8 teaspoons prepared pesto

Cooking Directions:
1. Sauté garlic, green beans, celery, carrot, and onion in medium-high heat. Cook for 10 minutes or until vegetables soften.
2. Add broth and bring to a boil then reduce to a simmer. Stir often until veggies are soft. Star for another 10 minutes.
3. Add Vinegar, tomatoes, beans, kale, zucchini, pepper, and salt. Cook until zucchini and kale are soft. Top each serving with pesto.

Nutrition Information:
Calories per serving: 300; Carbs: 52g; Fats: 4g; Protein: 14g; Saturated fat: 1g; Sodium: 306mg

Wild Rice Soup

Serves: 4 , Cooking time: 50 minutes
Ingredients:
- 1/2 tablespoon canola oil
- 1 1/2 cups diced yellow onion
- 1 cup diced carrot
- 1 cup diced celery
- 2 cloves garlic, minced
- 1 1/2 cups chopped kale
- 1 tablespoon minced parsley
- 2 cups low-sodium vegetable stock
- 1 teaspoon fennel seeds, crushed
- 1 teaspoon ground black pepper
- 1 cup unsalted prepared white beans (or about 1/2 of a 15.5 ounce can of white beans, rinsed and drained)
- 2 cups 1 percent milk

- 1/2 cup wild rice, cooked

Cooking Directions:
1. With canola oil, sauté garlic, onion, celery, and carrots in medium-high heat. Stir in parsley, stock, spices, and kale. Bring to a Boil.
2. Puree beans and milk then add mixture to the soup.
3. Add the rice and cook for 30 minutes.
4. Serve

Nutrition Information:
Calories per serving: 264; Carbs: 37g; Fats: 8g; Protein: 11g; Saturated fat: 1g; Sodium: 173mg

Roasted Butternut Squash Soup

Serves: 2 , Cooking time: 60 minutes

Ingredients:
- 1 Butternut Squash, cut into cube pieces (or frozen, cubed butternut Squash)
- 2 tsp. Canola Oil, divided
- 1 cup Celery, diced
- 1 ½ cup Yellow Onion, diced
- 1 ½ cup Fresh Spinach
- 2 cloves Garlic, minced
- 1 cup Carrots, diced
- 3 cup low-sodium Vegetable Broth
- 1 cup Water
- 1 tsp. Sage
- ½ tsp. Nutmeg
- Black Pepper to taste

Cooking Directions:
1. Toss squash with oil.
2. Roast at 400 ° for 40 minutes.
3. Puree the squash then set aside.
4. Add leftover oil to a pot and sauté vegetables until soft.
5. Add the spices, broth, water, and squash. Simmer for 10 min

Nutrition Information:
Calories per serving: 215; Carbs: 38g; Fats: 3g; Protein: 9g; Saturated fat: .5g; Sodium: 97mg

Creamy Asparagus Soup

Serves: 6 , Cooking time: 25 minutes

Ingredients:
- 2 cups peeled and diced potatoes
- 1/2-pound fresh asparagus, cut into 1/4-inch pieces
- 1/2 cup chopped onion
- 2 stalks celery, chopped
- 4 cups water
- 2 tablespoons butter
- 1/2 cup whole-wheat (whole meal) flour
- 1 1/2 cups fat-free milk
- Lemon zest, to taste
- Cracked black pepper, to taste

Cooking Directions:
1. Combine potatoes, onions, celery, water, and asparagus in a large soup pot over high heat. Bring to a boil. Reduce heat until veggies are tender (around 15 minutes).
2. Mix in butter.
3. Whisk together milk and flour then pour mixture into the soup pot whilst stirring. Increase heat and continue stirring until soup reaches desired consistency. (5 minutes).
4. Serve with lemon zest and pepper.

Nutrition Information:
Calories per serving: 144; Carbs: 22g; Fats: 4g; Protein: 5g; Saturated fat: 3g; Sodium: 75mg

Avocado Chicken Soup

Serves: 6 , Cooking time: 6-8 hours

Ingredients:
- 1-pound boneless chicken breast
- 5 cups low-sodium chicken broth
- 1 medium poblano chili chopped
- 1 medium tomato chopped
- 3 baby carrots chopped
- 1 medium onion chopped
- 2 Tablespoons garlic minced
- 1/2 medium avocado, cubed optional

Cooking Directions:

1. Combine all ingredients into the slow cooker (except for avocado)
2. Cook for 6-8 hours.
3. Shred chicken and add the chopped avocado to each serving.

Nutrition Information:
Calories per serving: 98; Carbs: 5g; Fats: 2g; Protein: 15g; Saturated fat: 2g; Sodium: 112mg

Carrot Curry Soup

Serves: 6 , Cooking time: 30 minutes

Ingredients:
- 1 tablespoon olive oil
- 1 teaspoon mustard seed
- 1/2 yellow onion, chopped (about 1/2 cup)
- 1-pound carrots, peeled and cut into 1/2-inch pieces
- 1 tablespoon plus 1 teaspoon peeled and chopped fresh ginger
- 1/2 jalapeno, seeded
- 2 teaspoons curry powder
- 5 cups low-sodium chicken stock, vegetable stock or broth
- 1/4 cup chopped fresh cilantro (fresh coriander), plus leaves for garnish
- 2 tablespoons fresh lime juice
- 1/2 teaspoon salt (optional)
- 3 tablespoons low-fat sour cream or fat-free plain yogurt
- Grated zest of 1 lime

Cooking Directions:
1. Sauté mustard seed until they start to pop. Add the onion and saute until translucent. Mix in jalapeno, ginger, carrots, and curry powder. Cook for a few minutes. Add in 3 cups of the stock and bring to a boil. Cook until carrots are tender.
2. Puree the soup in small batches with a food processor. Stir in remaining stock.
3. Before serving put in lime juice and cilantro. Season with salt if desired.

Nutrition Information:
Calories per serving: 104; Carbs: 12g; Fats: 4g; Protein: 5g; Saturated fat: 1g; Sodium: 116mg

Chicken Noodle Soup

Serves: 4 , Cooking time: 40 minutes

Ingredients:
- 1 teaspoon olive oil
- 1 cup chopped onion
- 3 cloves garlic, minced
- 1 cup chopped celery
- 1 cup sliced, peeled carrots (2 medium)
- 4 cups Maureen's Chicken Broth (separate recipe)
- 4 ounces dried linguini, broken
- 1 cup cooked non-brined chicken breast, cut into desired size (skin and bones removed)
- 2 tablespoons snipped fresh parsley

Cooking Directions:

1. Sauté onion and garlic over medium heat.
2. Then add carrots and celery and cook for 3 minutes. Bring to a boil and reduce heat after adding chicken broth.
3. Keep pot covered for 5 minutes then stir in linguini. Cook linguini.
4. Reduce heat to a simmer while stirring constantly for 10 minutes.
5. Top with chicken and parsley

Nutrition Information:
Calories per serving: 104; Carbs: 12g; Fats: 4g; Protein: 5g; Saturated fat: 1g; Sodium: 116mg

Healthy Vegetarian Chili

Serves: 8 , Cooking time: 2 hours

Ingredients:

- 2 cups diced onion
- 1 cup diced celery
- 1 cup diced bell pepper
- 2 cloves garlic, minced
- 2 tablespoons water
- 2 Fresno peppers, diced
- 2 quarts crushed tomatoes (no salt added)
- 2 cups cooked pinto beans (no salt added; if canned, rinse under water)
- 2 tablespoons ground cumin
- 1 tablespoon chipotle pepper (or smoked paprika)
- 1 tablespoon ground black pepper
- 1 tablespoon balsamic vinegar
- 1 tablespoon dried oregano

Cooking Directions:

1. Cook onion, garlic, and bell pepper in a stockpot for 10 minutes with 2 tablespoons of water.
2. Add remaining ingredients. Cover the pot and simmer for 1-2 hours. Stir often until desired consistency is reached.

Nutrition Information:

Calories per serving: 161; Carbs: 31g; Fats: 1g; Protein: 7g; Saturated fat: 1g; Sodium: 116mg

Garbanzo, Lentil, and Vegetable Stew

Serves: 8 , Cooking time: 2 hours

Ingredients:

- 3 cups butternut squash (approximately 1 1/2 - 2 pounds), peeled, seeded and cut into 1-inch cubes
- 3 large carrots, peeled and cut into 1/2-inch pieces
- 2 large onions, chopped
- 3 garlic cloves, minced
- 4 cups low-sodium vegetable stock
- 1 cup red lentils
- 2 tablespoons no-added-salt tomato paste
- 2 tablespoons peeled and minced fresh ginger
- 2 teaspoons ground cumin
- 1 teaspoon turmeric
- 1/4 teaspoon saffron
- 1 teaspoon freshly ground pepper
- 1/4 cup lemon juice
- 1 can (16 ounces) garbanzo beans, drained and rinsed
- 1/2 cup chopped roasted unsalted peanuts
- 1/2 cup chopped fresh cilantro

Cooking Directions:

1. Slowly sweat vegetables in a Dutch oven over low/medium heat. Mix in stock.
2. Add tomato paste, lentils, and seasonings. Keep pot covered for 1 to 1.5 hours
3. Before serving stir in lemon juice and garbanzo beans. Top with peanuts and cilantro.

Nutrition Information:

Calories per serving: 279; Carbs: 41g; Fats: 7g; Protein: 13g; Saturated fat: 1g; Sodium: 258mg

Tart Tomato Soup

Serves: 2 , Cooking time: 20 minutes

Ingredients:

- 1 can (10.5 ounces) condensed low-sodium, low-fat tomato soup
- 1 can (10.5 ounces) filled with fat-free milk
- 1 medium tomato, chopped
- 1 tablespoon chopped fresh basil or cilantro
- 2 tablespoons croutons
- 1 tablespoon freshly grated Parmesan cheese

Cooking Directions:

1. Add milk and soup in a saucepan. Whisk over medium heat for 10 minutes. Whisk constantly.
2. Add in herbs and tomato and cook for another 5 minutes.
3. Garnish with croutons and parmesan.

Nutrition Information:

Calories per serving: 271; Carbs: 48g; Fats: 3g; Protein: 13g; Saturated fat: 1g; Sodium: 224mg

Chicken and Beans Soup

Serves: 8 , Cooking time: 25 minutes

Ingredients:

- 1 can (10 ounces) white chunk chicken
- 2 cans (15 ounces each) low-sodium white beans, drained
- 1 can (14.5 ounces) low sodium diced tomatoes
- 4 cups low-sodium chicken broth
- 1 medium onion, chopped
- 1/2 medium green pepper, chopped
- 1 medium red pepper, chopped
- 2 garlic cloves, minced
- 2 teaspoons chili powder
- 1 teaspoon ground cumin
- 1 teaspoon dried oregano
- Cayenne pepper, to taste
- 8 tablespoons shredded reduced-fat Monterey Jack cheese
- 3 tablespoons chopped fresh cilantro

Cooking Directions:

1. Simmer chicken, beans, chicken broth, and tomatoes over medium heat for 10 minutes.
2. Add garlic, peppers, and onions.
3. Sauté veggies for 5 minutes.
4. Simmer for another 10 minutes after seasoning with oregano, chili powder, cumin, and cayenne.
5. Garnish with cilantro.

Nutrition Information:

Calories per serving: 212; Carbs: 25g; Fats: 4g; Protein: 19g; Saturated fat: 1.5g; Sodium: 241mg

Turkey and Beans Soup

Serves: 6 , Cooking time: 20 minutes

Ingredients:

- 1-pound ground turkey breast
- 2 medium onions, chopped
- 2 stalks celery, chopped
- 1 clove garlic, minced
- 1/4 cup ketchup
- 1 can (14.5 ounces) unsalted diced tomatoes
- 3 cubes low-sodium chicken bouillon
- 7 cups water
- 1 1/2 teaspoons dried basil
- 1/4 teaspoon ground black pepper
- 2 cups shredded cabbage
- 1 can (15 ounces) unsalted cannellini beans, rinsed and drained

Cooking Directions:

1. Cook celery, garlic, onion, and turkey until veggies are soft and turkey is cooked.
2. Add the rest of the ingredients and cover pot and simmer for 30 minutes.

Nutrition Information:

Calories per serving: 242; Carbs: 30g; Fats: 2g; Protein: 26g; Saturated fat: 1g; Sodium: 204mg

Herbed Veggie Soup

Serves: 4 , Cooking time: 20 minutes

Ingredients:

- 1 tablespoon olive oil
- 1/2 cup chopped onion
- 1/3 cup chopped celery
- 1 carrot, diced
- 1 garlic clove, minced
- 4 cups fat-free, unsalted chicken broth
- 2 large tomatoes, seeded and chopped
- 1/2 cup chopped spinach
- 1 can (16 ounces or about 1 1/2 cups) canned chickpeas or red kidney beans, drained and rinsed
- 1/2 cup uncooked whole-grain small shell pasta
- 1 small zucchini, diced
- 2 tablespoons fresh basil, chopped

Cooking Directions:

1. Sauté onion, garlic, celery, and carrots in the olive oil.
2. Stir in broth, pasta, spinach, tomatoes, and beans. Bring to a boil then reduce to simmer.
3. Add zucchini and basil and cook for 5 more minutes.

Nutrition Information:

Calories per serving: 205; Carbs: 30; Fats: 5g; Protein: 10g; Saturated fat: 1g; Sodium: 300mg

Barley and Mushroom Soup

Serves: 9 , Cooking time: 60 minutes

Ingredients:
- 1 tablespoon canola oil
- 1 1/2 cups chopped onions
- 1 cup sliced mushrooms
- 3/4 cup chopped carrots
- 1 teaspoon dried thyme
- 1/8 teaspoon black pepper
- 1/2 teaspoon chopped garlic
- 8 cups vegetable stock
- 3/4 cup pearl barley
- 3 ounces dry sherry
- 1/2 small potato, chopped
- 1/4 cup thinly sliced green onions

Cooking Directions:
1. Sauté onion, garlic, thyme, pepper, mushrooms, and carrots in the olive oil.
2. Stir in broth and add in barley. Bring to a boil then reduce to simmer for 20 minutes.
3. Add potato and sherry and cook for 15 more minutes.
4. Garnish with green onions.

Nutrition Information:
Calories per serving: 120; Carbs: 19; Fats: 4g; Protein: 2g; Saturated fat: 0g; Sodium: 112mg

Roasted Corn Soup

Serves: 12 , Cooking time: 60 minutes

Ingredients:
- 4 cups corn kernels
- 1 1/2 tablespoons olive oil
- 3 cups chopped onion
- 2 cups chopped carrots
- 2 cups chopped celery
- 2 teaspoons chopped garlic
- 1/4 cup all-purpose flour
- 1 teaspoon cumin
- 6 cups vegetable stock
- 2 jalapeno peppers, minced
- 1 1/2 cups half-and-half
- 1 teaspoon salt
- 1/8 teaspoon white pepper
- 1 tablespoon chopped parsley

Cooking Directions:
1. Heat oven to 500 F. Roast corn in the oven for 8 minutes.
2. Sauté onion, carrots, garlic, and celery in medium-high heat. Reduce heat and stir in cumin, flour, and corn. Mix thoroughly.
3. Add in jalapenos and veggie stock. Let it cook for 30 minutes.
4. Stir in half and half, pepper, parsley, and salt. Serve

Nutrition Information:
Calories per serving: 120; Carbs: 17; Fats: 5g; Protein: 3g; Saturated fat: 2g; Sodium: 184mg

Creamy Pumpkin Soup

Serves: 4 , Cooking time: 60 minutes

Ingredients:
- 3/4 cup water, divided
- 1 small onion, chopped
- 1 can (15 ounces) pumpkin puree
- 2 cups unsalted vegetable broth
- 1/2 teaspoon ground cinnamon
- 1/4 teaspoon ground nutmeg
- 1 cup fat-free milk
- 1/8 teaspoon black pepper
- 1 green onion top, chopped

Cooking Directions:
1. In medium heat, boil ¼ cup of water and then add onions and cook for 3 minutes.
2. Add remaining ingredients and bring to a boil then reduce to a simmer for 5 minutes.
3. Stir in milk and heat until it is hot but do not boil.
4. Garnish with green onions and black pepper.

Nutrition Information:
Calories per serving: 125; Carbs: 17; Fats: 5g; Protein: 3g; Saturated fat: 2g; Sodium: 184mg

Black Bean Soup

Serves: 4 , Cooking time: 25 minutes

Ingredients:

- 1 tsp olive oil
- 3 cloves garlic, minced
- 1 cup diced white or yellow onion
- 2 tsp ground cumin
- 1 ½ tsp chili powder
- 1/4 tsp ground coriander
- 1-2 chipotle peppers in adobo sauce, drained well
- 2 15-ounce cans black beans, rinsed and drained well
- 2 cups low sodium vegetable broth
- 3 tbsp chopped dark chocolate
- 2 tbsp chopped cilantro
- 1 lime cut into wedges

Directions for Cooking:

1. Place large nonstick pot on medium fire and heat oil. Swirl oil to coat pan and add garlic. Cook for a minute.
2. Stir in onion and cook for 3 minutes.
3. Stir in cumin, chili powder, and coriander. Continue sautéing for a minute or two.
4. Add chipotle peppers and black beans. Sauté for 3 minutes or until heated through.
5. Stir in chocolate and cook for 2 minutes until starting to melt.
6. Stir in broth. Mix well and bring to a simmer. Once simmering, lower fire and simmer for 5 minutes.
7. Transfer to bowls, garnish with cilantro and lime wedges.
8. Serve and enjoy.

Nutrition Information:

Calories per Serving: 353.5; Protein: 20.8g; Carbs: 60.6g; Fat: 3.1g; Saturated Fat: .6g; Sodium: 105mg

Easy Tom Yum Soup

Serves: 4 , Cooking time: 30 minutes

Ingredients:

- 1 tsp coconut oil
- 1 stalk lemongrass, cut in half then halved lengthwise
- 4 cloves garlic, minced
- 1½ tbsp fresh minced ginger
- 1/2 medium yellow onion, thinly sliced
- 4 red tomatoes, chopped
- ¼ cup water
- 1 Thai red chili pepper
- 1½ cups thinly sliced shiitake mushrooms
- 3 tbsp green curry paste
- 6 cups vegetable broth, low sodium
- 1/2 cup light coconut milk
- 2 medium limes, juiced
- 1 tbsp coconut aminos
- 1 packet Stevia or to taste

Directions for Cooking:

1. Place a large nonstick pot on medium high fire and heat oil for a minute. Swirl to coat pot.
2. Sauté garlic, ginger, and lemongrass for a minute. Add onion and sauté for 3 minutes. Stir in tomatoes and sauté for 8 minutes.
3. Add water and deglaze pot. Stir in chili pepper, curry paste, and mushrooms. Continue cooking until water has evaporated, around 10 minutes.
4. Stir in broth and coconut milk. Season with coconut aminos and a packet of stevia.
5. Bring to a simmer and turn off fire.
6. Season with lime juice and discard lemon grass.

Nutrition Information:

Calories per Serving: 193.8; Protein: 4g; Carbs: 20.6g; Fat: 10.6g; Saturated Fat: 7.6g; Sodium: 253mg

Slow Cooker Tex-Mex Chicken Soup

Serves: 6 , Cooking time: 8 hours
Ingredients:

- 1-pound chicken breast, chopped into bite-sized pieces
- 4 cups water
- 3 large celery stalks
- 3 carrots, sliced
- 2 poblano peppers, seeded and chopped
- 1 onion, chopped
- 3 cloves of garlic, minced
- 1 tablespoons ground cumin
- 1 tablespoon ground coriander
- 2 cans white cannellini beans, rinsed and drained
- 2 tablespoons lime juice

Directions for Cooking:
1. Place all ingredients in a slow cooker.
2. Give a good stir to combine all ingredients.
3. Close the lid and cook on low for 8 hours.

Nutrition Information:
Calories per Serving: 236.2; Carbs: 19.9g; Protein: 18.9g; Fats: 9g; Saturated Fat: 2.2g; Sodium: 246mg

Chicken Barley Soup

Serves: 8 , Cooking time: 1 hour and 35 minutes
Ingredients:

- 8 cups water
- 2 pounds chicken breasts, boneless
- 1 ½ cups chopped carrots
- 1 onion, chopped
- ¾ cup pearl barley
- 3 bay leaves
- 1 teaspoon sage
- ¼ teaspoon ground black pepper
- 2 tablespoons lemon juice

Directions for Cooking:
1. Put water and chicken thighs in a pot and bring to a boil for 15 minutes to make the chicken stock.
2. Take the chicken out and shred. Set aside.
3. To the pot, Add the carrots, onions, pearl barley, bay leaves, and sage.
4. Season with salt and pepper to taste.
5. Close the lid and allow to boil for another 15 minutes.
6. Turn the heat to low and cook for 60 minutes or until the barley is soft.
7. Add the shredded chicken and cook for 5 more minutes.
8. Stir in lemon juice before serving.

Nutrition Information:
Calories per Serving: 352; Carbs: 25.0g; Protein: 27.5g; Fats: 15.4g; Saturated Fat: 3.7g; Sodium: 204mg

Chicken and Beef Spanish Soup

Serves: 5 , Cooking time: 30 minutes
Ingredients:

- 1 ½ pounds beef stew meat, cubed
- ¼ pound chicken breasts, chopped
- 1 daikon radish, peeled and cubed
- 1 turnip, peeled and cubed
- 2 carrots, peeled and cubed
- 2 stalks of celery, chopped
- A pinch of saffron
- 6 cups water
- 1 bay leaf
- Pepper to taste

Directions for Cooking:
1. Place beef ron bottom of pot then followed by chicken. Season generously with pepper.
2. Add carrots and radish and spread in an even layer. Place celery on top.
3. Add saffron, celery, and water.
4. Turn fire to medium high and bring to a boil. Lower fire to a simmer, cover, and cook for 30 minutes or until beef is tender.
5. Adjust seasoning to taste before serving.

Nutrition Information:
Calories per Serving: 176.3; Carbs: 7g; Protein: 5.8g; Fats: 13.9g; Saturated Fat: 6.2g; Sodium: 317mg

Creamy Squash Bisque

Serves: 8 , Cooking time: 25 minutes

Ingredients:

- 1 tablespoons oil
- ½ tablespoon turmeric powder
- ½ teaspoon cumin
- ½ teaspoon nutmeg
- ½ cup onion, chopped
- 2 medium potatoes, grated
- 2 medium-sized kabocha squash, seeded and chopped
- 2 cups water
- 1 cup coconut milk
- Pepper to taste

Directions for Cooking:

1. Place a heavy bottomed pot on medium high fire and heat for 3 minutes.
2. Add oil to pot and swirl to coat sides and bottom of pot. Heat for 2 minutes.
3. Place squash in a single layer, as much as possible, on bottom of pot. Top with potatoes.
4. Season generously with pepper.
5. Sprinkle turmeric, cumin, nutmeg, and onion. Add water.
6. Cover and bring to a boil. Once boiling lower fire to a simmer and let it cook for 10 minutes.
7. With a handheld blender, puree squash and potatoes. Stir in coconut milk and mix well.
8. Serve and enjoy.

Nutrition Information:

Calories per Serving: 158.9; Carbs: 20.6g; Protein: 3.1g; Fats: 8.1g; Saturated Fat: 2.1g; Sodium: 11.9 mg

Chicken-Coconut Thai Soup

Serves: 4 , Cooking time: 25 minutes

Ingredients:

- 2 cups coconut milk, freshly squeezed or Whole 30 compliant
- 1 cup water
- 1 thumb-size fresh ginger, sliced
- 1 stalk fresh lemongrass, cut into 1-inch thick
- 1-pound chicken breasts, cut into chunks
- 1 cup sliced mushrooms
- 1 tablespoon fresh lime juice
- 2 small Thai chilies, chopped
- ¼ cup basil leaves
- ¼ cup fresh cilantro, minced
- Pepper to taste
- 1 tablespoon oil

Dircetions for Cooking:

1. Place a heavy bottomed pot on medium high fire and heat for 3 minutes.
2. Add oil to pot and swirl to coat sides and bottom of pot. Heat for 2 minutes.
3. Place chicken in a single layer, as much as possible, on bottom of pot. Top with ginger, lemon grass, Thai chilies, and mushrooms.
4. Season generously with pepper. Add water.
5. Cover and bring to a boil. Once boiling lower fire to a simmer and let it cook for 15 minutes.
6. Stir in basil leaves and cilantro.
7. Serve and enjoy.

Nutrition Information:

Calories per Serving: 440; Carbs: 6.6g; Protein: 36.4g; Fats: 31.2g; Saturated Fat: 6.8g; Sodium: 116mg

Sweet Potato Soup Cuban Style

Serves: 6 , Cooking time: 20 minutes

Ingredients:

- 2 tablespoons extra virgin olive oil
- 1 onion, chopped
- 5 cloves of garlic, minced
- 1-pound sweet potatoes, peeled and diced
- 1 red bell pepper, chopped
- 1 cup tomatoes
- 1 bay leaf
- 1 teaspoon ground cumin
- 2 teaspoons dried oregano
- Pepper to taste

- 4 cups water

Directions for Cooking:
1. Place a heavy bottomed pot on medium high fire.
2. Add all ingredients and mix well.
3. Bring to a boil. Once boiling, lower fire to a simmer and cook for 15 minutes while covered.
4. Serve and enjoy.

Nutrition Information:
Calories per Serving: 100; Carbs: 18.8g; Protein: 2.0g; Fats: 2.3g; Saturated Fat: 0.4g; Sodium: 68mg

Easy and Beefy Soup

Serves: 6 , Cooking time: 45 minutes

Ingredients:
- 1 ½ pounds stew meat, cut into chunks
- Salt and pepper to taste
- 2 tablespoons olive oil
- 10 baby Bella mushrooms, chopped
- 8 cloves of garlic, minced
- 1 onion, chopped
- 1 stalk of celery, chopped
- 1 carrot, chopped
- 7 cups water
- 2 bay leaves
- ½ teaspoon thyme
- 1 large potato, grated

Directions for Cooking:

1. Place a heavy bottomed pot on medium high fire.
2. Add all ingredients except for celery carrot, and potato. Mix well.
3. Bring to a boil. Once boiling, lower fire to a simmer and cook for 30 minutes
4. Stir in remaining ingredients and continue simmering for another 10 to 15 minutes or until beef is fork tender.
5. Serve and enjoy.

Nutrition Information:
Calories per Serving: 347; Carbs: 19.4g; Protein: 43.0g; Fats: 10.3g; Saturated Fat: 4.9g; Sodium: 87mg

Little Neck Clam Oriental Soup

Serves: 6 , Cooking time: 15 minutes

Ingredients:
- 1-pound fresh little neck clams
- 1-inch thumb ginger, peeled and sliced thinly
- 6 garlic cloves, smashed and peeled
- 1 onion, sliced thinly
- 1 tomato, sliced in lengths
- 1 teaspoon salt
- 1 tablespoon fish sauce
- Pepper to taste
- 1 stalk lemongrass, cut into 5-inch lengths
- 8 cups water

Directions for Cooking:

1. Place a heavy bottomed pot on medium high fire.
2. Add all ingredients except for clams and half of water. Mix well.
3. Bring to a boil and let it boil for 5 minutes.
4. Add remaining water and bring to a boil.
5. Once boiling, add clams, cover and cook until clams have opened, around 5 minutes.
6. Serve and enjoy.

Nutrition Information:
Calories per Serving: 56.5; Carbs: 11.4g; Protein: 1.6g; Fats: .5g; Saturated Fat: .1g; Sodium: 109mg

Italian Soup (Minestrone)

Serves: 6 , Cooking time: 35 minutes

Ingredients:
- 6 cups water
- 1-pound beef bones
- Pepper to taste
- 1 onion, diced
- 3 cloves of garlic, minced
- 2 stalks of celery, minced
- 1 carrot, diced
- 1 zucchini, diced

- 1 cup roma tomatoes, diced
- 1 cup basil leaves
- 1 teaspoon dried oregano
- 1 teaspoon dried basil
- 1 bay leaf
- ½ cup spinach, shredded

Directions for Cooking:
1. Place a heavy bottomed pot on medium high fire.
2. Add water, garlic, half of onion, tomatoes, and beef bones. Bring to a boil and simmer for 30 minutes and season generously with pepper. Discard the bones.
3. Add remaining ingredients except for spinach and basil leaves. Mix well.
4. Once boiling, lower fire to a simmer, cover and cook for 5 minutes.
5. Stir in spinach and basil.
6. Serve and enjoy.

Nutrition Information:
Calories per Serving: 77; Carbs: 4.7g; Protein: 2.9g; Fats: 5.4g; Saturated Fat: 0.4g; Sodium: 413mg

Vegetarian Approved Mushroom-Broccoli Soup

Serves: 4 , Cooking time: 20 minutes

Ingredients:
- 1 onion, diced
- 3 cloves of garlic, diced
- 2 cups mushrooms, chopped
- 4 cups water
- 2 heads of broccoli, cut into florets
- Pepper to taste

Directions for Cooking:
1. Place a heavy bottomed pot on medium high fire and heat for 3 minutes.
2. Add onion, garlic, water, and broccoli. Season generously with pepper.
3. Cover and bring to a boil. Once boiling lower fire to a simmer and let it cook for 7 minutes.
4. With a handheld blender, puree mixture until there are a little bit of chunks left.
5. Stir in mushrooms, cover and simmer for another 8 minutes.
6. Serve and enjoy.

Nutrition Information:
Calories per Serving: 38.2; Carbs: 6g; Protein: 2.2g; Fats: .6g; Saturated Fat: .1g; Sodium: 9mg

Potato and Spinach Soup the Ethiopian Way

Serves: 4 , Cooking time: 13 minutes

Ingredients:
- 1 onion, chopped
- 1 teaspoon garlic powder
- 2 teaspoon ground coriander
- ½ teaspoon cinnamon powder
- ½ teaspoon turmeric powder
- ¼ teaspoon clove powder
- ¼ teaspoon cayenne pepper
- ¼ teaspoon cardamom powder
- ¼ teaspoon grated nutmeg
- 2 cups potatoes, chopped
- 8 cups water
- Pepper to taste
- 2 cups spinach, chopped

Directions for Cooking:
1. Place a heavy bottomed pot on medium high fire.
2. Add all ingredients except spinach. Mix well.
3. Bring to a boil, lower fire to a simmer, cover and cook for 10 minutes.
4. Stir in spinach and cook until wilted, around 3 minutes.
5. Serve and enjoy.

Nutrition Information:
Calories per Serving: 116; Carbs: 18.7g; Protein: 2.7g; Fats: 3.1g; Saturated Fat: 0.9g; Sodium: 29mg

Quail Eggs and Winter Melon in a Soup

Serves: 6 , Cooking time: 40 minutes

Ingredients:
- 1-pound pork bones
- 6 cups water, divided
- 4 cloves of garlic, minced
- 1 onion, chopped
- 1 winter melon, peeled and sliced
- 10 quail eggs, pre-boiled and peeled
- Pepper to taste
- Chopped cilantro for garnish

Directions for Cooking:
1. Place a heavy bottomed pot on medium high fire.
2. Add 5 cups water and pork bones. Season generously with pepper.
3. Bring to a boil, lower fire to a simmer, cover and cook for 30 minutes. Discard bones.
4. Add remaining ingredients except for cilantro. Cover and simmer for another 10 minutes.
5. Serve and enjoy with cilantro for garnish.

Nutrition Information:
Calories per Serving: 65; Carbs: 5.6g; Protein: 4.0g; Fats: 3.0g; Saturated Fat: 0.6g; Sodium: 358mg

Simplified French Onion Soup

Serves: 5 , Cooking time: 30 minutes

Ingredients:
- 2 tablespoons olive oil
- 4 large onions, sliced
- 2 bay leaves
- 5 cups Beef Bone Broth
- 1 teaspoon dried thyme
- Pepper to taste

Directions for Cooking:
1. Place a heavy bottomed pot on medium-high fire and heat pot for 3 minutes.
2. Add oil and heat for 2 minutes. Stir in onions and sauté for 5 minutes.
3. Lower fire to medium low, continue sautéing onions for 10 minutes until soft and browned, but not burned.
4. Add remaining ingredients and mix well.
5. Bring to a boil, lower fire to a simmer, cover and cook for 5 minutes.
6. Let it sit for 5 minutes.
7. Serve and enjoy.

Nutrition Information:
Calories per Serving: 109; Carbs: 12.9g; Protein: 2.3g; Fats: 5.8g; Saturated Fat: 1.3g; Sodium: 268mg

Creamy Soup with Greens and Chicken

Serves: 6 , Cooking time: 30 minutes

Ingredients:
- ½-pounds collard greens, torn to bite sized pieces
- 1 sausage link, low sodium
- 5 cups chicken broth
- 1/2-pounds parsnips
- ½-pounds cauliflower florets
- 2 cloves garlic
- 1 cup diced onion
- 1 tablespoon oil

Directions for Cooking:
1. Place a heavy bottomed pot on medium-high fire and heat pot for 3 minutes.
2. Add oil and heat for 2 minutes. Swirl to coat bottom and sides of pot with oil.
3. Stir in onions and garlic. Sauté for 5 minutes.
4. Add sausage link, cook and crumble for 5 minutes.
5. Add parsnips and chicken broth. Bring to a boil, lower fire to medium low, cover and cook for 10 minutes.
6. Stir in collard greens and cauliflower. Cook for 3 minutes.
7. Let it sit for 5 minutes.
8. Serve and enjoy.

Nutrition Information:
Calories per Serving: 119.6; Carbs: 13.7g; Protein: 6.3g; Fats: 4.4g; Saturated Fat: 1g; Sodium: 162mg

Sweet Potato Chowder

Serves: 8 , Cooking time: 15 minutes

Ingredients:

- 1 cup water
- 4 cups chicken broth, low sodium
- 2-pounds sweet potatoes, peeled, quartered and sliced thin
- 5 garlic cloves, smashed and peeled
- A dash of cayenne pepper
- ¼ teaspoon black pepper
- 1 onion, diced

Directions for Cooking:

1. Place a heavy bottomed pot on medium high fire.
2. Add all ingredients, ring to a boil, lower fire to a simmer, cover and cook for 15 minutes.
3. With a handheld blender, puree until smooth and creamy.
4. Serve and enjoy.

Nutrition Information:
Calories per Serving: 89.7; Carbs: 13.9g; Protein: 5.6g; Fats: 1.3g; Saturated Fat: .4g; Sodium: 45mg

Vietnamese Pho Noodle Soup

Serves: 6 , Cooking time: 45 minutes

Ingredients:

- 6 cups water
- 1 tsp ground cardamom
- 4 whole star anise
- 1 tsp whole black peppercorns
- 1 tsp ground coriander
- 1 tsp ground cinnamon
- 1 tbsp apple cider vinegar
- 2 knobs of ginger, sliced in half
- 2 cloves garlic, peeled
- 2 medium onions, sliced in half
- 4-lbs beef bones
- 1 bunch cilantro
- 1 bunch basil
- 1 box rice noodles, cooked according to package instructions
- 1 cup bean sprouts
- 1 lime, cut into wedges
- ½-lb sirloin steak, very thinly sliced

Directions for Cooking:

1. On a pressure cooker, add water, cardamom, star anise, peppercorns, coriander, cinnamon, vinegar, garlic, ginger, onions, and beef bones.
2. Cover and pressure cook for 45 minutes.
3. Meanwhile, you can cook your noodles according to package instructions.
4. Set out 6 bowls and evenly divide noodles in them. Top each bowl with 1/6 of cilantro, basil, bean sprouts, and raw thinly sliced steak.
5. Once the broth is done cooking, do a quick release.
6. While broth is still boiling hot, scoop and pour on prepared bowls. This will cook the thinly sliced beef.
7. Serve lime wedges on the side.

Nutrition Information:
Calories per Serving: 435; Carbs: 24.2g; Protein: 48.5g; Fats: 16.0g; Saturated Fat: 4.5g; Sodium: 231mg

Barley and Beef Soup

Serves: 6 , Cooking time: 80 minutes

Ingredients:

- 2/3 cup pearl barley, rinsed
- 1 large potato, shredded
- ½ tsp dried thyme
- 2 bay leaves
- 1 cup water
- 6 cups low-sodium beef broth
- 8 cloves garlic, minced
- 1 onion, chopped
- 3 cups mirepoix
- 10 baby Bella mushrooms, quartered
- 2 tbsp oil
- Pepper and salt to taste
- 1 ½-lbs stew meat, sliced into 1-inch cubes

Directions for Cooking:

1. Place a heavy bottomed pot on medium high fire and heat pot for 3 minutes.

2. Meanwhile, season beef with salt.
3. Once pot is hot, add oil and swirl to cover bottom of pot. In 2 batches, brown beef, around 6 minutes in total per batch. Once done browning, transfer to a large bowl and continue browning the next batch and put in the bowl afterwards.
4. Add garlic in same pot and sauté for a minute. Add onions and continue cooking for 3 minutes.
5. Add mushrooms and sauté for 3 minutes.

6. Add thyme and bay leaves and sauté for a minute.
7. Add mirepoix and sauté for 2 minutes.
8. Pour in water and beef broth. Cover and cook for 40 minutes.
9. Stir in barley and potatoes. Cover and cook for 10 minutes.
10. Let it sit for 5 minutes, serve and enjoy.

Nutrition Information:
Calories per Serving: 547.5; Carbs: 60.4g; Protein: 41.6g; Fats: 15.5g; Saturated Fat: 6g; Sodium: 132mg

Comforting Chicken Noodle Soup

Serves: 4 , Cooking time: 35 minutes

Ingredients:
- Pepper to taste
- 6 cups chicken stock, low sodium
- 1 celery stalk, chopped
- 2 medium carrots, chopped
- 1 bay leaf
- 6 white button mushrooms, chopped
- 4 garlic cloves, minced roughly
- 1 small onion, diced roughly
- 1 boneless, skinless chicken breasts, cut into ½-inch cubes
- 1 tbsp lemon juice
- ¼ cup Italian parsley, finely chopped

Directions for Cooking:
1. Place a heavy bottomed pot on medium high fire and heat pot for 3 minutes.
2. Once hot, add oil and stir around to coat pot with oil.

3. Add garlic and cook for a minute. Add onions and continue cooking for 3 minutes.
4. Add mushrooms and chicken. Season with pepper and sauté for 10 minutes or until the juice given off by the mushrooms have evaporated.
5. Add celery, chopped carrots, and bay leaf. Mix well and cook for 3 minutes.
6. Pour in chicken stock and deglaze pot before closing.
7. Cover, bring to a boil, lower fire to a simmer and simmer for 15 minutes.
8. To serve, garnish each bowl with parsley and lemon juice.

Nutrition Information:
Calories per Serving: 169.7; Carbs: 20.9g; Protein: 10.5g; Fats: 4.9g; Saturated Fat: 1.2g; Sodium: 244mg

Lentil and Veggie Soup

Serves: 4 , Cooking time: 25 minutes

Ingredients:
- 1/8 cup chopped fresh parsley
- ¾ tbsp. red wine vinegar
- 6-oz diced tomatoes, canned
- ¼ tsp dried oregano
- 1/8 tsp black pepper
- ¾ tsp garlic, minced
- 1/3 cup carrots, diced
- ¼ cup celery, diced
- 1/3 cup onion, diced
- 3 ¼ cup water
- ¾ cup lentils, brown

Directions for Cooking:
1. Place a heavy bottomed pot on medium high fire and heat pot for 3 minutes.
2. Add all ingredients to pot, except for parsley and mix well.
3. Cover, bring to a boil, lower fire to a simmer and simmer for 15 minutes.
4. Serve and enjoy with a sprinkle of parsley.

Nutrition Information:
Calories per Serving: 38.2; Carbs: 7g; Protein: 2.1g; Fats: .2g; Saturated Fat: .1g; Sodium: 36mg

Vegan Approved Spinach and Lentil Soup

Serves: 2 , Cooking time: 30 minutes

Ingredients:

- 8-oz baby spinach
- 4 cups low-sodium vegetable broth
- 1 cup dry brown lentils, rinsed
- ¼ tsp ground pepper
- 1 tsp dried thyme
- 1 tsp ground turmeric
- 2 tsp ground cumin
- 4 medium garlic cloves, minced
- 1 medium stalk celery, diced
- 2 medium carrots, peeled and diced
- ½ medium yellow onion, diced
- 1 tsp olive oil

Directions for Cooking:

1. Place a heavy bottomed pot on medium high fire and heat pot for 3 minutes.
2. Once hot, add oil and stir around to coat pot with oil.
3. Stir in celery, carrots, onions, and garlic. Sauté for 5 minutes.
4. Stir in pepper, thyme, and cumin. Sauté for a minute.
5. Add broth and lentils. Mix well.
6. Cover, bring to a boil, lower fire to a simmer and simmer for 15 minutes.
7. Stir in spinach, turn off fie, and let it sit for 3 minutes or until spinach is wilted.
8. Serve and enjoy.

Nutrition Information:

Calories per Serving: 270.9; Carbs: 42.8g; Protein: 13g; Fats: 5.3g; Saturated Fat: 1g; Sodium: 228mg

Spicy Fava Bean Soup with Greek Yogurt

Serves: 5 , Cooking time: 60 minutes

Ingredients:

- 1 tbsp cup olive oil
- 2 onions, quartered
- 4 cloves of garlic, minced
- 1 can crushed tomatoes
- 2 teaspoons ground cumin
- ½ teaspoon ground coriander
- ¼ teaspoon ground allspice
- 8 cups vegetable broth
- 1 ½ cups dried fava beans, soaked overnight
- Pepper to taste
- 1/3 cup plain Greek yogurt

Directions for Cooking:

1. Place a heavy bottomed pot on medium high fire and heat pot for 3 minutes.
2. Meanwhile rinse and drain beans.
3. Once hot, add oil and stir around to coat pot with oil.
4. Add onions, garlic, cumin, coriander, allspice, and beans. Sauté for 5 minutes.
5. Add broth and season with pepper.
6. Cover, bring to a boil, boil for 10 minutes, lower fire to a simmer and simmer for another 10 minutes.
7. Turn off fire and let it sit for 30 minutes to soften beans.
8. Turn on fire and bring pot to a boil and turn off.
9. Stir in yogurt.
10. Serve and enjoy.

Nutrition Information:

Calories per Serving: 490.1; Carbs: 19g; Protein: 4.3g; Fats: 44.1g; Saturated Fat: 6.1g; Sodium: 238mg

Chapter 5 Salad Recipes

Nectarine & Shrimp Salad

Serves: 4 , Cooking time: 10 minutes

Ingredients:

- 1 cup fresh or frozen corn
- 2 teaspoons canola oil, divided
- 1-pound uncooked shrimp, peeled and deveined
- 1/2 teaspoon lemon-pepper seasoning
- 1-1/2 teaspoons honey
- 1-1/2 teaspoons Dijon mustard
- 3 tablespoons cider vinegar
- 1/3 cup orange juice
- 1 tablespoon minced fresh tarragon
- 8 cups torn mixed salad greens
- 2 medium nectarines, cut into 1-inch pieces
- 1 cup grape tomatoes, halved
- 1/2 cup finely chopped red onion

Directions for Cooking:

1. On medium high fire, place a nonstick pan and heat 1 tsp oil. Stir in corn and cook for 2 minutes or until tender and crisp. Transfer to a plate.
2. Add a tsp of oil in same pan. Heat for a minute and add shrimp. Season with lemon-pepper seasoning and stir fry for 4 minutes or until shrimp is pink. Add corn to pan and mix well. Turn off fire.
3. In a small bowl, whisk well honey, mustard, vinegar, and orange juice. Stir in tarragon.
4. In a large salad bowl, toss well to mix salad greens, nectarines, tomatoes, and red onion. Drizzle with 1/3 of the dressing and toss well to coat.
5. Top salad with shrimp mixture and drizzle remaining dressing on top.
6. Serve and enjoy.

Nutrition Information:
Calories per Serving: 282.6; Carbs: 32.2g; Protein: 27.6g; Fats: 5g; Saturated Fat: 1g; Sodium: 333mg

Medley of Lentil Salad

Serves: 8 , Cooking time: 25 minutes

Ingredients:

- 1 cup dried lentils, rinsed
- 2 cups water
- 2 cups sliced fresh mushrooms
- 1 medium cucumber, cubed
- 1 medium zucchini, cubed
- 1 small red onion, chopped
- 1/2 cup chopped soft sun-dried tomato halves (not packed in oil)
- 1/2 cup rice vinegar
- 1/4 cup minced fresh mint
- 1 tablespoon olive oil
- 2 teaspoons honey
- 1 teaspoon dried basil
- 1 teaspoon dried oregano
- 4 cups fresh baby spinach, chopped
- 1 cup (4 ounces) crumbled feta cheese

Directions for Cooking:

1. On high fire, add lentils and water in a saucepan. Cover and bring to a boil. Once boiling lower fire to a simmer and cook until tender around 25 minutes.
2. Drain lentils, wash in cold water to cool, and drain well.
3. Transfer lentils to a big salad bowl.
4. Except for cheese and spinach, add all ingredients and toss well to coat and mix.
5. To serve, evenly divide spinach on to 8 serving plates, top with 1/8 of the lentil mixture, and then sprinkle with 1/8 of the feta cheese.
6. Enjoy!

Nutrition Information:
Calories per Serving: 280.3; Carbs: 10.4g; Protein: 7g; Fats: 6.3g; Saturated Fat: 3g; Sodium: 242mg

Chicken Teriyaki Lettuce Wraps

Serves: 4 , Cooking time: 10 minutes

Ingredients:

- ¾-pound boneless skinless chicken breasts, cut into ¾-inch cubes
- 1 teaspoon ground ginger
- ¼ teaspoon pepper
- 2 teaspoons olive oil
- 1 tablespoon honey
- 2 tablespoons reduced-sodium teriyaki sauce
- 2 tablespoons rice vinegar
- 1-1/2 cups shredded carrots
- 1-1/4 cups coarsely chopped pitted fresh sweet cherries
- 4 green onions, chopped
- 1/3 cup coarsely chopped almonds
- 8 Bibb or Boston lettuce leaves

Directions for Cooking:

1. In a bowl, season chicken with ginger and pepper.
2. On medium high fire, place a nonstick pan and heat oil. Sauté chicken for 5 minutes or until no longer pink. Turn off fire.
3. In pan, stir in honey, teriyaki sauce, rice vinegar, and carrots. Leave in warm pan.
4. In a large salad bowl, toss well to mix almonds, green onions, and cherries. Pour chicken mixture from pan and mix well.
5. To serve, place 1/8 of the mixture in a lettuce leaf, roll like a lumpia, and enjoy.

Nutrition Information:

Calories per Serving: 195.6; Carbs: 15g; Protein: 22.2g; Fats: 5.2g; Saturated Fat: 1g; Sodium: 230mg

Cobb Salad with a Thai Twist

Serves: 6 , Cooking time: 15 minutes

Ingredients:

- 1 bunch romaine, torn
- 2 cups chicken breast, cooked and shredded
- 3 hard-boiled large eggs, coarsely chopped
- 1 medium ripe avocado, peeled and thinly sliced
- 1 medium carrot, shredded
- 1 medium sweet red pepper, julienned
- 1 cup fresh snow peas, halved
- 1/2 cup unsalted peanuts
- 1/4 cup fresh cilantro leaves
- 3/4 cup Asian toasted sesame salad dressing
- 1 tablespoon creamy peanut butter

Directions for Cooking:

1. Bring a small pot of water to boil. Slice chicken breast into four and place in pot. Boil chicken until cooked through, around 5 minutes. Leave in hot water for another 5 minutes. Drain well and cool to room temperature. Shred chicken with two forks and set aside.
2. In a large salad bowl, add lettuce on bottom. Evenly spread on top the chicken, then the eggs, then the avocado and carrots.
3. Sprinkle red pepper, snow peas, peanuts, and cilantro.
4. In a small bowl whisk well salad dressing and peanut butter until smooth and creamy. Drizzle over salad.
5. Serve and enjoy.

Nutrition Information:

Calories per Serving: 363.5; Carbs: 16.3g; Protein: 25.3g; Fats: 21.9g; Saturated Fat: 4g; Sodium: 263mg

Warm Salad of Pinto 'n Rice

Serves: 4 , Cooking time: 10 minutes

Ingredients:

- 1 teaspoon olive oil
- 1 cup frozen corn
- 1 small onion, chopped
- 2 garlic cloves, minced
- 1-1/2 teaspoons chili powder
- 1-1/2 teaspoons ground cumin
- 1 can (15 ounces) pinto beans, rinsed and drained
- 1 package (8.8 ounces) ready-to-serve brown rice
- 1 can (4 ounces) chopped green chilies
- 1/2 cup salsa

- 1/4 cup chopped fresh cilantro
- 1 bunch romaine, quartered lengthwise through the core
- 1/4 cup finely shredded cheddar cheese

Directions for Cooking:
1. On medium high fire, place a large nonstick pan and heat oil. Sauté garlic, onion, and corn for 5 minutes.
2. Season with cumin and chili powder. Mix well.
3. Add cilantro, salsa, green chilies, rice, and beans. Mix well and cook for 3 minutes. Turn off fire.
4. Evenly divide romaine lettuce on to four plates. Top with ¼ of the pinto-rice mixture, and evenly sprinkle each plate with cheese.
5. Enjoy.

Nutrition Information:
Calories per Serving: 422.5; Carbs: 77.8g; Protein: 15g; Fats: 5.7g; Saturated Fat: 2g; Sodium: 419mg

Steak-Blue Cheese 'n Fruits Salad

Serves: 4 , Cooking time: 15 minutes
Ingredients:
- 1 beef top sirloin steak (3/4-inch-thick and 1 pound)
- 1/4 teaspoon pepper
- 2 tablespoons lime juice
- 1 bunch romaine, torn (about 10 cups)
- 2 cups fresh strawberries, halved
- 1/4 cup thinly sliced red onion
- 1/4 cup crumbled blue cheese
- 1/4 cup chopped walnuts, toasted
- Reduced-fat balsamic vinaigrette

Directions for Cooking:
1. Season steak with pepper.
2. On medium high fire, heat a nonstick pan for 2 minutes. Add steak and pan fry for 2 to 3 minutes per side or to desired doneness. Transfer to a chopping board and let it sit for 5 minutes. Slice into thin strips, transfer to a bowl, add lime juice and toss to mix.
3. In a salad bowl, toss well to mix the onions, strawberries, and romaine lettuce.
4. Top with steak. Sprinkle walnuts and cheese. Drizzle vinaigrette.
5. Serve and enjoy.

Nutrition Information:
Calories per Serving: 416.4; Carbs: 13.5g; Protein: 35.9g; Fats: 23.2g; Saturated Fat: 8g; Sodium: 223mg

Sweet Potato, Rice, & Black Bean Salad

Serves: 4 , Cooking time: 35 minutes
Ingredients:
- 3/4 cup uncooked long grain rice
- 1/4 teaspoon garlic salt
- 1-1/2 cups water
- 1 tablespoon + 1 teaspoon olive oil, divided
- 1 large sweet potato, peeled and diced
- 1 medium red onion, finely chopped
- 4 cups chopped fresh kale (tough stems removed)
- 1 can (15 ounces) black beans, rinsed and drained
- 2 tablespoons sweet chili sauce
- Lime wedges, optional

Directions for Cooking:
1. In a large saucepan, add water, garlic salt, and rice. Cover and bring to a boil. Lower fire to a simmer and cook for 15 minutes or until water is fully absorbed. Turn off fire and let it rest for 5 minutes more.
2. On medium high fire, place a large frying pan and heat 1 tsp oil for a minute.
3. Sauté for 8 minutes the sweet potato.
4. Stir in onion and cook for 5 minutes.
5. Stir in kale and cook for 4 minutes.
6. Add beans and cook for 2 minutes or until heated through.
7. In a large salad bowl, toss well rice, remaining olive oil, and chili sauce. Mix in bean mixture and toss well to mix.
8. Serve and enjoy.

Nutrition Information:
Calories per Serving: 241.6; Carbs: 49.5g; Protein: 8.3g; Fats: 2.6g; Saturated Fat: 1g; Sodium: 140mg

Tabbouleh with Mint & Chickpea

Serves: 4 , Cooking time: 20 minutes

Ingredients:

- 1 cup bulgur
- 2 cups water
- 1 cup fresh or frozen peas (about 5 ounces), thawed
- 1 can (15 ounces) chickpeas or garbanzo beans, rinsed and drained well
- 1/2 cup minced fresh parsley
- 1/4 cup minced fresh mint
- 1 tbsp olive oil
- 2 tablespoons julienned soft sun-dried tomatoes (not packed in oil)
- 2 tablespoons lemon juice
- 1/4 teaspoon pepper

Directions for Cooking:

1. Bring to a boil water and bulgur in a large saucepan and cover. Lower fire to a simmer and cook for 10 minutes.
2. Mix in frozen peas and let it rest for 10 minutes.
3. Transfer bulgur and peas mixture into a bowl and mix in remaining ingredients and toss well to mix.
4. Place in the fridge for at least an hour to allow flavors to mix.
5. Toss well before serving.

Nutrition Information:

Calories per Serving: 167.6; Carbs: 24.5g; Protein: 6.6g; Fats: 4.8g; Saturated Fat: 1g; Sodium: 18mg

Shredded Pork Salad Southwest Style

Serves: 6 , Cooking time: 6 hours

Ingredients:

- 1 boneless pork loin roast (1 pound)
- 1-1/2 cups apple cider or juice
- 1 can (4 ounces) chopped green chiles, drained
- 3 garlic cloves, minced
- 1-1/2 teaspoons hot pepper sauce
- 1 teaspoon chili powder
- 1 teaspoon pepper
- 1/2 teaspoon ground cumin
- 1/2 teaspoon dried oregano
- 12 cups torn mixed salad greens
- 1 can (15 ounces) black beans, rinsed and drained
- 2 medium tomatoes, chopped
- 1 small red onion, chopped
- 1 cup fresh or frozen corn
- 1 cup crumbled cotija or shredded part-skim mozzarella cheese
- 6 tbsp low sodium Salad dressing of your choice

Directions for Cooking:

1. In a slow cooker, place pork.
2. In a small bowl, whisk well oregano, cumin, pepper, chili powder, pepper sauce, garlic, green chiles, and cider. Pour over pork.
3. Cover and cook pork on low settings for 6 hours.
4. Remove pork from slow cooker and shred with 2 forks. Let it sit to cool to room temperature.
5. Meanwhile, in a large salad bowl, mix well remaining ingredients except for cheese and dressing. Top with shredded pork. Drizzle with salad dressing and sprinkle cheese on top.
6. Serve and enjoy.

Nutrition Information:

Calories per Serving: 491; Carbs: 64.6g; Protein: 40.8g; Fats: 8.1g; Saturated Fat: 3.0g; Sodium: 304mg

Sesame-Ginger Dressing on Edamame Salad

Serves: 6 , Cooking time: 0 minutes

Ingredients:

- 6 cups baby kale salad blend (about 5 ounces)
- 1 can (15 ounces) garbanzo beans or chickpeas, rinsed and drained
- 2 cups frozen shelled edamame (about 10 ounces), thawed
- 3 clementines, peeled and segmented
- 1 cup fresh bean sprouts

- 1/2 cup salted peanuts
- 2 green onions, diagonally sliced
- 1/2 cup sesame ginger salad dressing

Directions for Cooking:
1. In a salad bowl, mix well all ingredients.

2. Serve and enjoy.

Nutrition Information:
Calories per Serving: 291.5; Carbs: 25.8g; Protein: 14g; Fats: 14.7g; Saturated Fat: 2g; Sodium: 283mg

Hearty Celery Chicken Salad

Serves: 5 , Cooking time: 0 minutes

Ingredients:
- 3 ¼ cups chicken breast (cooked, cubed, and skinless)
- 3 tbsp mayonnaise, low-fat
- ½ tsp onion powder
- 1 tbsp lemon juice
- ¼ cup celery, chopped
- 1 head lettuce, chopped

Directions for Cooking:

1. Except for chicken and lettuce, combine all ingredients in a bowl and whisk well.
2. Add chicken and toss well to coat.
3. Evenly divide chopped lettuce in 5 bowls and top evenly with chicken salad.
4. Enjoy!

Nutrition Information:
Calories per Serving: 237.5; Protein: 30.2g; Carbs: 15g; Fat: 6.3g; Saturated Fat: 1.2g; Sodium: 156mg

Olives 'n Orange Garden Salad

Serves: 4 , Cooking time: 15 minutes

Ingredients:
- 1 tbsp finely chopped celery
- 1 tbsp finely chopped red onion
- 1 tbsp extra virgin olive oil
- 4 garlic cloves, minced
- ½ cup red wine vinegar
- 4 boneless, skinless chicken breasts, 4-oz each
- 2 garlic cloves
- 8 cups leaf lettuce, washed and dried
- 2 navel oranges, peeled and segmented
- 16 large ripe black olives
- ¼ tsp freshly cracked black pepper or more to taste

Directions for Cooking:
1. Prepare the dressing by mixing pepper, celery, onion, olive oil, garlic and vinegar in a small bowl. Whisk well to combine.
2. Lightly grease grate and preheat grill to high.

3. Rub chicken with the garlic cloves and discard garlic.
4. Grill chicken for 5 minutes per side or until cooked through.
5. Remove from grill and let it stand for 5 minutes before cutting into ½-inch strips.
6. In 4 serving plates, evenly arrange two cups lettuce, ¼ of the sliced oranges and 4 olives per plate.
7. Top each plate with ¼ serving of grilled chicken, evenly drizzle with dressing, and topped with pepper.
8. Serve and enjoy.

Nutrition Information:
Calories per Serving: 133.9; Protein: 3.9g; Carbs: 18.1g; Fat: 5.1g; Saturated Fat: 1g; Sodium: 242mg

Strawberry Garden Salad

Serves: 6 , Cooking time: 0 minutes

Ingredients:
- 1 tbsp poppy seeds
- 1/8 cup distilled white vinegar
- ¼ cup milk
- ½ cup fat free creamy salad dressing
- ¼ cup red bell pepper, chopped

- ½ cup toasted pecans
- 1 cup sliced fresh strawberries
- ½ red onion, sliced
- 1 head romaine lettuce, torn into bite-size pieces

Directions for Cooking:
1. Whisk well poppy seeds, vinegar, milk, and salad dressing in a small bowl.
2. In a large salad bowl, mmix red bell pepper, pecans, strawberries, onion and lettuce.
3. Pour in dressing, toss to coat well.

4. Serve immediately.

Nutrition Information:
Calories per Serving: 130.5; Protein: 3g; Carbs: 12.3g; Fat: 7.7g; Saturated Fat: .9g; Sodium: 215mg

Meaty Wild Rice Salad

Serves: 4 , Cooking time: 20 minutes
Ingredients:
- 1 6-oz package wild rice
- Pepper to taste
- ¼ tsp coconut aminos
- 1 tsp white sugar
- 2 tsp vinegar
- ¾ cup light mayo
- 1 cup seedless red grapes
- ¼ cup diced green onion
- 2 cups cooked, cubed turkey meat

Directions for Cooking:
1. According to package directions, cook your wild rice. Once done, allow to cool.

2. Whisk well pepper, salt, sugar, vinegar and mayonnaise until smooth and creamy in a small bowl.
3. In a large salad bowl, mix grapes, onion, turkey, and cooled wild rice.
4. Pour in dressing and toss well to combine.
5. Place in the ref for at least an hour before serving.

Nutrition Information:
Calories per Serving: 228; Protein: 11g; Carbs: 41.5g; Fat: 2g; Saturated Fat: 1g; Sodium: 149mg

Caprese Salad with Tuna

Serves: 2 , Cooking time: 6 minutes
Ingredients:
- 1 tsp olive oil
- 6 oz fresh tuna steak
- 2 roma tomatoes, sliced thinly
- Pepper to taste
- 8 large fresh basil leaves
- 2 oz fresh mozzarella part-skim, sliced into ½-inch cubes
- 2 tsp balsamic vinegar
- 4 tsp extra virgin olive oil, divided

Directions for Cooking:
1. On medium high fire, place a large skillet and heat 1 tsp olive oil.

2. Once hot, pan fry tuna for 3 minutes per side. Transfer to a plate with paper towel and dab dry. Place in ref to cool for at least an hour.
3. To assemble, layer tomatoes and tuna on a plate.
4. Season with pepper. Sprinkle with basil and mozzarella,
5. Drizzle balsamic vinegar and olive oil before serving.

Nutrition Information:
Calories per Serving: 253.6; Protein: 29.0g; Carbs: 7.4g; Fat: 12g; Saturated Fat: 4g; Sodium: 340mg

Winter Fruit Salad with Lemon-Poppy Dressing

Serves: 12 , Cooking time: 0 minutes
Ingredients:
- ½ tsp salt
- 1 tsp Dijon-style prepared mustard
- 2 tsp diced onion
- ½ cup lemon juice
- ½ cup white sugar
- 2/3 cup olive oil
- 1 tbsp poppy seeds

- 1 pear, peeled, cored and diced
- 1 apple, peeled cored and diced
- ¼ cup dried cranberries
- 1 cup cashews
- 4 oz shredded Swiss cheese
- 1 head Romaine lettuce, torn into bite size pieces

Directions for Cooking:

1. In blender, process salt, mustard, onion, lemon juice, and sugar until smooth and creamy. Slowly pour in oil as blender is running. Continue blending until smooth and creamy. Add poppy seeds, blend one more time and set aside.

2. Mix well cubed pear, cubes apple, cranberries, cashews, Swiss cheese and lettuce in a large salad bowl.
3. Pour in dressing, toss well to coat.

Nutrition Information:
Calories per Serving: 341.9; Protein: 6.4g; Carbs: 26.2g; Fat: 23.5g; Saturated Fat: 5.2g; Sodium: 183mg

Almond-Cranberry Spinach Salad

Serves: 8 , Cooking time: 5 minutes

Ingredients:
- ¾ cup almonds, blanched and slivered
- 4 tbsp olive oil, divided
- ¼ cup cider vinegar
- ¼ cup white wine vinegar
- ¼ tsp paprika
- 2 tsp minced onion
- ½ cup white sugar
- 1 tbsp poppy seeds
- 2 tbsp toasted sesame seeds
- 1 cup dried cranberries
- 1 lb. spinach, rinsed and torn into bite-size pieces

Directions for Cooking:

1. On medium fire, heat 1 tbsp olive oil in a medium skillet. Add slivered almonds and toast lightly. Transfer to a plate and allow to cool.
2. Whisk well oil, cider vinegar, white wine vinegar, paprika, onion, sugar, poppy seeds, and sesame seeds in a medium bowl.
3. Mix well cranberries, cooled almonds, and spinach in a large salad bowl.
4. Pour in dressing, toss well to coat, and serve.

Nutrition Information:
Calories per Serving: 172.6; Protein: 3.2g; Carbs: 15.2g; Fat: 11g; Saturated Fat: 1.4g; Sodium: 66mg

Bell Pepper, Cilantro 'n Quinoa Salad

Serves: 6 , Cooking time: 20 minutes

Ingredients:
- 1 ½ cups water
- 1 cup uncooked quinoa, rinsed
- Pepper to taste
- ½ cup dried cranberries
- ½ cup minced carrots
- ¼ cup toasted sliced almonds
- 1 lime, juiced
- ¼ cup chopped fresh cilantro
- 1 ½ tsp curry powder
- 1 small red onion, finely chopped
- ¼ cup yellow bell pepper, chopped
- ¼ cup red bell pepper, chopped

Directions for Cooking:

1. In saucepan, bring water to a boil and add quinoa. Cover and lower fire to a simmer and cook until water is fully absorbed, around 15-20 minutes.
2. Transfer quinoa into a large salad bowl and allow to cool in the ref fully.
3. After an hour of cooling in the ref, add remaining ingredients and mix well.
4. Return bowl to ref and chill for another hour before serving.

Nutrition Information:
Calories per Serving: 132.9; Protein: 4.5g; Carbs: 24g; Fat: 2.1g; Saturated Fat: .3g; Sodium: 11mg

Tuscan White Beans & Spinach Salad

Serves: 4 , Cooking time: 15 minutes

Ingredients:

- 2 tbsp olive oil
- 1-pound large shrimp, peeled and deveined
- 2 tsp chopped fresh sage
- 4 cloves garlic, minced
- 1 medium onion, chopped
- 2 tbsp balsamic vinegar
- 5 cups baby spinach
- 15 ounces can no salt added cannellini beans, rinsed and drained
- 1 ½ ounces crumbled reduce-fat feta cheese

Directions for Cooking:

1. In a large non-stick skillet, heat 1 teaspoon oil. Heat it over medium-high.
2. Then for about 2 to 3 minutes, cook the shrimps using the heated skillet then place them on a plate.
3. Heat on the same skillet the sage, garlic, and onions then cook for about 4 minutes. Add and stir in vinegar for 30 seconds.
4. For about 2 minutes, add chicken broth. Then, add spinach and beans and cook for an additional 2 to 3 minutes.
5. Remove skillet then add and stir in cooked shrimps topped with feta cheese.
6. Serve and divide into 4 bowls. Enjoy!

Nutrition Information:
Calories per Serving: 167.3; Protein: 6.1g; Carbs: 13.9g; Fat: 9.7g; Saturated Fat: 2.4g; Sodium: 120mg

Almond-Pear Garden Salad with Yogurt Dressing

Serves: 4 , Cooking time: 0 minutes

Ingredients:

- ¼ tsp ground ginger
- ½ tsp prepared mustard
- 2 tbsp low fat mayonnaise
- ½ cup plain Greek yogurt
- ¼ cup diced celery
- ½ cup green bell pepper, sliced lengthwise
- 2 cups cooked boneless, skinless chicken breasts sliced into ½-inch cubes
- 2 fresh pears cut into 1-inch cubes
- 1 head lettuce, torn to bite sized pieces, reserving 4 large leaves
- 2 tbsp toasted slivered almonds

Directions for Cooking:

1. In a bowl mix ginger, mustard, mayonnaise and yogurt.
2. Mix in celery, bell pepper, and chicken. Toss well to coat in dressing.
3. Fold in pears and toss to mix.
4. Arrange 4 large lettuce leaves on 4 plates.
5. Evenly divide and spread torn lettuce leaves inside the large lettuce leaves.
6. Top it with ¼ of the chicken mixture and ¼ tbsp slivered almonds.
7. Serve and enjoy.

Nutrition Information:
Calories per Serving: 283.6; Protein: 22.5g; Carbs: 28.6g; Fat: 8.8g; Saturated Fat: 2g; Sodium: 363mg

Cherry Tomato & Pear Salad

Serves: 6 , Cooking time: 0 minutes

Ingredients:

- 2 tablespoons sherry vinegar or red wine vinegar
- 1 tablespoon minced shallot
- 1 tablespoon extra-virgin olive oil
- 1/4 teaspoon salt
- 1/8 teaspoon freshly ground black pepper
- 1 1/2 cups yellow pear tomatoes, halved
- 1 1/2 cups orange cherry tomatoes, halved
- 1 1/2 cups red cherry tomatoes, halved
- 4 large fresh basil leaves, cut into slender ribbons
- 2 cups cherry tomatoes, halved
- 2 pears, chopped into 1/2-inch cubes

Directions for Cooking:

1. In a bowl, add cherry tomatoes and Asian pears. Put in fridge and set aside.

2. In a small bowl, whisk well remaining ingredients and let it stand for 15 minutes.
3. Add dressing over tomato mixture and toss well to coat.

4. Serve and enjoy.
Nutrition Information:
Calories per Serving: 96.1; Carbs: 20.1g; Protein: 1g; Fats: 1.3g; Saturated Fat: .2g; Sodium: 127mg

Honey Dressing Over Warm Coleslaw

Serves: 6 , Cooking time: 20 minutes
Ingredients:
- 3 teaspoons olive oil
- 1 medium yellow onion, finely chopped (about 1/2 cup)
- 1 teaspoon dry mustard
- 1 large carrot, peeled and julienned (about 1 cup)
- 1/2 head Napa cabbage, cored and thinly sliced crosswise (about 5 cups)
- 3 tablespoons cider vinegar
- 1 tablespoon dark honey
- 1/4 teaspoon freshly ground black pepper
- 1/2 teaspoon caraway seed
- 1 tablespoon chopped fresh flat-leaf (Italian) parsley

Directions for Cooking:
1. On medium high fire, place large nonstick fry pan and heat a teaspoon of oil. Swirl to coat pan and heat for a minute.

2. Add onion and sauté for 5 minutes. Stir in mustard and cook for 2 minutes. Transfer to a large salad bowl.
3. In same pan, add another 1 teaspoon of oil and sauté carrot. Cook for 5 minutes or until crisp tender. Add to bowl of onions.
4. Add another teaspoon of oil and heat for a minute. Add cabbage and cook for 5 minutes until starting to wilt. Transfer to bowl of onions.
5. In same hot pan, turn off fire and add honey and vinegar stir well until melted and combined. Pour into bowl of veggies and toss well to coat.
6. Add remaining ingredients into bowl of salad and toss well to mix.
7. Serve and enjoy.
Nutrition Information:
Calories per Serving: 90.8; Carbs: 12g; Protein: 1.7g; Fats: 4g; Saturated Fat: 1g; Sodium: 40mg

Rosemary-Balsamic Dressing on Pasta-Veggie Salad

Serves: 6 , Cooking time: 20 minutes
Ingredients:
- 1 teaspoon dried rosemary or 1 tablespoon fresh rosemary
- 1/4 teaspoon ground cinnamon
- 1/4 teaspoon salt
- 3 tablespoons balsamic vinegar
- 3 tablespoons olive oil
- 4 ounces uncooked whole-wheat spiral pasta
- 6 cups mixed greens
- 2 large fresh pears, cored and sliced
- 1/2 cup sliced water chestnuts
- 1/2 cup golden raisins
- 3 tablespoons roasted unsalted soy nuts

Directions for Cooking:
1. On high fire, bring a pot of water to a boil. Once boiling cook pasta according to

manufacturer's instructions minus the oil and salt.
2. In a small bowl, whisk well rosemary, cinnamon, salt, balsamic, and oil. Let it stand for 10 minutes.
3. Once pasta is done cooking, drain well, cool completely with cold tap water, and drain thoroughly.
4. In a salad bowl, mix well remaining ingredients and the cold pasta. Drizzle with dressing and toss well to coat.
5. Serve and enjoy.
Nutrition Information:
Calories per Serving: 225.2; Carbs: 30.4g; Protein: 3.4g; Fats: 10g; Saturated Fat: 2g; Sodium: 232mg

Tasty Melon Salad

Serves: 4 , Cooking time: 0 minutes

Ingredients:

- 4 cups diced assorted melon, such as cantaloupe, honeydew or watermelon (or use any fruit you like)
- 1/2 cup plain or vanilla low-fat or nonfat yogurt
- 1/4 teaspoon nutmeg
- 1/4 teaspoon mace
- 1/8 teaspoon clove
- 1/8 teaspoon cinnamon
- 1 Orange zested and juiced

Directions for Cooking:

1. In a salad bowl, add assorted melon.
2. Sprinkle remaining ingredients on top and toss well to mix.
3. Serve and enjoy.

Nutrition Information:
Calories per Serving: 97; Carbs: 19g; Protein: 3g; Fats: 1g; Saturated Fat: 1g; Sodium: 49mg

Squash and Sunflower Seeds on Salad

Serves: 4 , Cooking time: minutes

Ingredients:

- 2 small acorn squash (about 2 pounds total)
- 2 tablespoons brown sugar
- 1 tablespoon olive oil
- 4 cups leaf lettuce, such as spring mix
- 2 tablespoons sunflower seeds
- 4 teaspoons honey

Directions for Cooking:

1. Place on a microwave safe bowl and Pierce all over with a knife.
2. Microwave one squash on high for 3 minutes. Turn squash over and microwave for another 3 minutes. Do the same for the other squash.
3. On cutting board, halve the squash and scrape out the pith and seeds. Discard.
4. Scrape squash meat into a bowl. Season with olive oil and brown sugar. Mix well and let it cool to room temperature.
5. Evenly divide salad greens on to 4 plates. Top each plate with ¼ of the squash mixture, 1 tsp honey, and ½ tablespoon sunflower seeds.
6. Serve and enjoy.

Nutrition Information:
Calories per Serving: 189.9; Carbs: 31.5g; Protein: 2.7g; Fats: 5.9g; Saturated Fat: .7g; Sodium: 9mg

Colorful Shredded Cabbage with Asian Peanut Sauce

Serves: 4 , Cooking time: 0 minutes

Ingredients:

- ¼ cup peanut butter, no salt
- ¼ teaspoon cayenne pepper
- ½ cup filtered water
- 1 tablespoon coconut aminos
- 1 packet Stevia
- 1 tablespoon lime juice
- 1 tablespoon toasted sesame oil
- 1 tablespoon low sodium soy sauce
- 1 teaspoon minced garlic
- 2 tablespoons minced ginger
- 3 cups shredded green cabbage
- 3 cups shredded red cabbage
- 1/4 cup chopped cilantro
- 1/4 cup chopped peanuts
- 1/4 cup chopped scallions

Directions for Cooking:

1. In a food processor, process peanut butter, cayenne pepper, water, coconut aminos, Stevia, lime juice, sesame oil, soy sauce, garlic, and ginger. Puree until smooth and creamy.
2. In a large salad bowl, toss well remaining ingredients.
3. Drizzle dressing all over and toss well to coat.
4. Serve and enjoy.

Nutrition Information:
Calories per Serving: 262.4; Carbs: 23.5g; Protein: 8.8g; Fats: 14.8g; Saturated Fat: 2.5g; Sodium: 811mg

Your Traditional Caesar Salad

Serves: 4 , Cooking time: 0 minutes

Ingredients:

- ¾ cup mayonnaise, low fat
- 1 head romaine lettuce, torn into bite sized pieces
- 1 tbsp lemon juice
- 1 tsp Dijon mustard
- 1 tsp Worcestershire sauce
- 3 cloves garlic, peeled and minced
- 6 tbsp grated Parmesan cheese, divided
- Ground black pepper to taste
- 1 cup croutons, low sodium

Directions for Cooking:

1. In a small bowl, whisk well mayonnaise, lemon juice, mustard, Worcestershire sauce, and peeled garlic. Whisk thoroughly until smooth. Season with pepper.
2. In a large bowl, add torn lettuce. Add dressing and toss well to coat.
3. Sprinkle cheese, croutons, and pepper.
4. Serve and enjoy.

Nutrition Information:

Calories per Serving: 205.4; Carbs: 21.3g; Protein: 5.3g; Fats: 11g; Saturated Fat: 2.7g; Sodium: 282mg

Grape 'n Arugula Salad with Honey-Mustard Dressing

Serves: 3 , Cooking time: 0 minutes

Ingredients:

- ¼ tsp ground black pepper
- ½ tsp stone-ground mustard
- 1 tsp chopped fresh thyme
- 1 tsp honey
- 1 tsp maple syrup
- 1 tsp grapeseed oil
- 3 tbsp red wine vinegar
- 7 cups loosely packed baby arugula
- 2 cups red grapes, halved
- 2 tbsp toasted sunflower seed kernels

Directions for Cooking:

1. In a large bowl, whisk well all ingredients except for arugula, grapes, and sunflower seeds. Mix thoroughly until smooth.
2. Toss in grapes and arugula and toss well to coat.
3. Sprinkle sunflower seeds.
4. Serve and enjoy

Nutrition Information:

Calories per Serving: 163; Carbs: 25.2g; Protein: 3.4g; Fats: 5.4g; Saturated Fat: .6g; Sodium: 18mg

Cranberry-Spinach Salad with Paprika Vinaigrette

Serves: 4 , Cooking time: 5 minutes

Ingredients:

- ¼ cup cider vinegar
- 2 tbsp honey
- ¼ cup white wine vinegar
- ¼ tsp paprika
- 2 tbsp olive oil
- ½ cup pumpkin seeds
- 2 tsp minced onion
- 1 cup dried cranberries
- 1 lb. spinach, rinsed and torn into bite sized pieces

Directions for Cooking:

1. In a large bowl, whisk well cider vinegar, honey, white wine vinegar, paprika, and olive oil. Mix thoroughly.
2. In a salad bowl place spinach leaves on bottom, sprinkle cranberries, onion, and pumpkin seeds.
3. Drizzle with dressing.
4. Serve and enjoy.

Nutrition Information:

Calories per Serving: 313; Carbs: 36.4g; Protein: 9g; Fats: 14.6g; Saturated Fat: 2.3g; Sodium: 144mg

Avocado 'n Cherry Tomato Salad

Serves: 4 , Cooking time: 0 minutes

Ingredients:

- ¼ tsp chipotle powder
- 1 bunch scallions, sliced
- 1 cup cherry tomatoes, halved
- 1 large avocado, diced
- 1 tbsp chili powder
- 1 tbsp lemon juice
- 2 tbsp olive oil
- 3 tbsp lime juice
- 4 cups carrots, spiralized

Directions for Cooking:

1. In a salad bowl, mix and arrange avocado, cherry tomatoes, scallions and spiralized carrots. Set aside.
2. In a small bowl, whisk salt, chipotle powder, chili powder, olive oil, lemon juice and lime juice thoroughly.
3. Pour dressing over noodle salad. Toss to coat well.
4. Serve and enjoy at room temperature.

Nutrition Information:

Calories per Serving: 214.7; Fat: 14.7g; Protein: 3g; Carbs: 17.6g; Saturated Fat: 2g; Sodium: 138mg

Greek Salad with English Cucumber and Tomatoes

Serves: 6 , Cooking time: 0 minutes

Ingredients:

- ¼ cup crumbled feta cheese
- ½ tsp garlic powder
- ¼ tsp salt
- ¾ tsp black pepper, divided
- 1 cup grape tomatoes, halved
- 1 cup peeled and chopped English cucumbers
- 1 cup plain fat-free yogurt
- 1-pound skinless, boneless chicken breast, cut into 1-inch cubes
- 1 tsp bottled minced garlic
- 1 tsp ground oregano
- 2 tsp sesame seed paste or tahini
- 5 tsp fresh lemon juice, divided
- 6 pitted kalamata olives, halved
- 8 cups chopped romaine lettuce
- Cooking spray

Directions for Cooking:

1. In a bowl, mix together ½ tsp pepper, garlic powder and oregano. Then on medium high heat place a skillet and coat with cooking spray and sauté together the spice mixture and chicken until chicken is cooked. Before transferring to bowl, drizzle with 3 tsp lemon juice.
2. In a small bowl, mix thoroughly the following: garlic, tahini, yogurt, ¼ tsp pepper, ¼ tsp salt, and 2 tsp lemon juice.
3. In another bowl, mix together olives, tomatoes, cucumber and lettuce.
4. To Serve salad, place 2 ½ cups of lettuce mixture on plate, topped with ½ cup chicken mixture, 3 tbsp yogurt mixture and 1 tbsp of cheese.

Nutrition Information:

Calories per Serving: 291.1; Fat: 5.5g; Protein: 20.7g; Carbs: 11.6g; Saturated Fat: 2g; Sodium: 265mg

Middle Eastern Style Tuna Salad

Serves: 6 , Cooking time: 0 minutes

Ingredients:

- ¼ cup chopped pitted ripe olives
- ¼ cup drained and chopped roasted red peppers
- ¼ cup Mayonnaise dressing, low fat
- 1 tbsp small capers, rinsed well and drained
- 2 green onions, sliced
- 2 pcs of 6-oz cans of tuna in water, drained and flaked
- 6 cups salad greens like lettuce

Directions for Cooking:

1. Except for salad greens, mix together all of the ingredients in a bowl.

2. Arrange salad greens on bottom of bowl and top with tun mixture.
3. Serve and enjoy.

Nutrition Information:

Calories per Serving: 38.7; Carbs: 4.3g; Protein: 2.9g; Fats: 1.1g; Saturated Fat: .2g; Sodium: 185mg

Savory Grilled Veggie with Balsamic Dressing

Serves: 2 , Cooking time: 8 minutes

Ingredients:
- 2 tbsp extra virgin olive oil, for brushing
- ¼ cup fresh basil leaves
- ¼ cup feta cheese
- ½ bunch asparagus, trimmed and cut into bite-size pieces
- 1 medium onion, cut into ½ inch thick rings
- 1-pint cherry tomatoes
- 1 red bell pepper, quartered, seeds and ribs removed
- 1 yellow bell pepper, quartered, seeds and ribs removed
- Pepper to taste

Directions for Cooking:

1. Toss olive oil and vegetables in a big bowl. Season with pepper.
2. Grill vegetables in a preheated griller for 4 minutes per side or until charred and tender.
3. Transfer veggies to a platter, add feta and basil.
4. In a separate small bowl, mix olive oil, balsamic vinegar, and garlic. Season with pepper.
5. Drizzle dressing over vegetables and serve.

Nutrition Information:
Calories per Serving: 207.3; Carbs: 7.5g; Protein: 4.5g; Fats: 17.7g; Saturated Fat: 4.2g; Sodium: 176mg

Pears and Fennel Salad

Serves: 6 , Cooking time: 0 minutes

Ingredients:
- ¼ cup chopped pistachios
- ¼ cup green onions, sliced
- 1 bunch watercress, trimmed
- 1 cup red bell pepper, diced
- 2 cups medium sized fennel bulb, thinly sliced
- 2 tbsp olive oil
- 3 cups Asian pears, cut into matchstick size
- 3 tbsp fresh lime juice
- Pepper to taste

Directions for Cooking:

1. In a large salad bowl, mix pistachios, green onions, bell pepper, fennel, watercress and pears.
2. In a small bowl, mix vegetable oil and lime juice. Season with pepper to taste.
3. Pour dressing over salad and gently mix before serving.

Nutrition Information:
Calories per Serving: 135.2; Carbs: 15.1g; Protein: 2.5g; Fats: 7.2g; Saturated Fat: 1g; Sodium: 42mg

Avocado & Nectarines Salad with Dijon-Lemon Dressing

Serves: 2 , Cooking time: 15 minutes

Ingredients:
- 2 tsp avocado oil
- 6 oz. wild caught salmon fillet with skin
- ¼ tsp Paleo Dijon style mustard
- 2 tsp fresh lemon juice
- 3 tsp olive oil
- Freshly ground black pepper to taste
- ½ avocado
- ½ cup cherry tomatoes
- ½ ripe nectarine
- 1/3 cup raw pecans
- 2 cups baby spinach leaves

Directions for Cooking:
1. Place a cast iron pan on medium high fire and melt avocado oil. Preheat oven to 400°F.
2. Once oil is hot sear salmon on both sides for 2 minutes per side. Pop in oven and bake for 10 minutes.

3. In a small bowl whisk well Dijon mustard, lemon juice, and olive oil until emulsified. Season with pepper to taste and set aside.
4. Chop pecans into small pieces. Chop avocado, tomatoes, and nectarines into bite-sized pieces and place in a large salad bowl.

5. Add spinach and chopped pecans in bowl. Pour dressing and toss to coat well.
6. Serve salad with roasted salmon on top.

Nutrition Information:
Calories per Serving: 388.4; Carbs: 23.7g; Protein: 4.1g; Fats: 30.8g; Saturated Fat: 3.5g; Sodium: 36mg

Tasty Broccoli Salad

Serves: 4 , Cooking time: 0 minutes
Ingredients:
- ¼ tsp ground cinnamon
- ½ tsp ground turmeric
- ¾ tsp ground ginger
- ½ tbsp extra virgin olive oil
- ½ tbsp apple cider vinegar
- 2 tbsp chopped green onion
- 1/3 cup coconut cream, low sodium
- ½ cup carrots, shredded
- 1 small head of broccoli, chopped

Directions for Cooking:

1. In a large salad bowl, mix well cinnamon, turmeric, ginger, olive oil, and vinegar.
2. Add remaining ingredients, tossing well to coat.
3. Pop in the ref for at least 30 to 60 minutes before serving.

Nutrition Information:
Calories per Serving: 90.5; Carbs: 4g; Protein: 1.3g; Fats: 7.7g; Saturated Fat: 6.2g; Sodium: 29mg

Cilantro-Mint Calamari Salad

Serves: 6 , Cooking time: 25 minutes
Ingredients:
- ¼ cup finely chopped cilantro leaves
- ¼ cup finely chopped mint leaves
- ¼ tsp freshly ground black pepper
- ½ cup finely chopped flat leaf parsley leaves
- 1 lb. cleaned and trimmed uncooked calamari rings and tentacles, defrosted
- 3 medium garlic cloves, smashed and minced
- 2 tbsp extra virgin olive oil
- A pinch of crushed red pepper flakes
- Juice of 1 large lemon
- Peel of 1 lemon, thinly sliced into strips

Directions for Cooking:
1. On a nonstick large fry pan, heat 1 tbsp olive oil. Once hot, sauté garlic until fragrant around a minute.

2. Add calamari, making sure that they are in one layer, if pan is too small then cook in batches.
3. Season with pepper, after 2 to 4 minutes of searing, remove calamari from pan with a slotted spoon and transfer to a large bowl. Continue cooking remainder of calamari.
4. Season cooked calamari with herbs, lemon rind, lemon juice, red pepper flakes, pepper, salt, and remaining olive oil.
5. Toss well to coat, serve and enjoy.

Nutrition Information:
Calories per Serving: 165.8; Carbs: 7.6g; Protein: 24.4g; Fats: 4.2g; Saturated Fat: 1g; Sodium: 375mg

Blueberry-Cucumber Quinoa Salad

Serves: 6 , Cooking time: 0 minutes
Ingredients:
- ¼ cup chopped parsley
- ¼ cup chopped scallions
- ¼ cup lime juice
- ¼ cup red onion, diced
- ½ cup diced carrots

- ½ cup diced celery
- ½ cup diced cucumber
- ½ cup diced red pepper
- ½ cup dried wild blueberries
- 2 tbsp olive oil

- ½ cup spicy pecans, chopped
- 1 tbsp chopped parsley
- 1 tsp honey
- 2 fresh pears, cut into chunks
- 3 cups cooked quinoa

Directions for Cooking:
1. In a small bowl mix well olive oil, lime juice, honey, and parsley. Set aside.

2. In large salad bowl, add remaining ingredients and toss to mix well.
3. Pour dressing and toss well to coat.
4. Serve and enjoy.

Nutrition Information:
Calories per Serving: 260.5; Carbs: 31.4g; Protein: 5.6g; Fats: 12.5g; Saturated Fat: 1.4g; Sodium: 23mg

Carrots 'n Beets Salad

Serves: 2 , Cooking time: 0 minutes

Ingredients:
- 4 cups mixed greens
- 2 tbsp lemon juice
- 2 tbsp pumpkin seed oil
- 1 tbsp chia seeds
- 2 tbsp almonds, chopped
- 1 large apple, diced
- 1 large carrot, coarsely grated
- 1 large beet, coarsely grated

Directions for Cooking:

1. In a medium salad bowl, except for mixed greens, combine all ingredients thoroughly.
2. Into 4 salad plates, divide the mixed greens.
3. Evenly top mixed greens with the salad bowl mixture.
4. Serve and enjoy.

Nutrition Information:
Calories per Serving: 132.7; Carbs: 27.4g; Protein: 3.3g; Fats: 1.1g; Saturated Fat: .1g; Sodium: 230mg

Arugula Salmon Filets Salad

Serves: 2 , Cooking time: 12 minutes

Ingredients:
- ¼ cup red onion, sliced thinly
- 1 ½ tbsp fresh lemon juice
- 1 tbsp olive oil
- 1 tbsp extra-virgin olive oil
- 1 tbsp red-wine vinegar
- 6-oz. center cut salmon fillet
- 2/3 cup cherry tomatoes, halved
- 3 cups baby arugula leaves
- Pepper to taste

Directions for Cooking:
1. In a shallow bowl, mix pepper, salt, 1 tbsp olive oil and lemon juice. Toss in salmon fillets and rub with the marinade. Allow to marinate for at least 15 minutes.

2. Grease a baking sheet and preheat oven to 350ºF.
3. Bake marinated salmon fillet for 10 to 12 minutes or until flaky with skin side touching the baking sheet.
4. Meanwhile, in a salad bowl mix onion, tomatoes and arugula.
5. Season with pepper. Drizzle with vinegar and oil. Toss to combine and serve right away with baked salmon on the side.

Nutrition Information:
Calories per Serving: 250.8; Carbs: 5.8g; Protein: 19.1g; Fats: 16.8g; Saturated Fat: 2.7g; Sodium: 239mg

Chapter 6 Bread & Sandwich Recipes

Sandwich with Spinach and Tuna Salad

Serves: 4 , Cooking time: 0 minutes

Ingredients:
- ½ tsp dill weed
- 2 ribs celery, diced
- ½ small onion, peeled and diced
- 1 can tuna flakes in water, low sodium
- 1 small cucumber, peeled and diced
- Juice of one lemon
- 1 tbsp olive oil
- 1 cup fresh baby spinach
- ¼ tsp freshly ground black pepper
- ½ tsp salt free seasoning blend
- 8 slices 100% whole wheat sandwich bread

Directions for Cooking:
1. In a medium bowl, mix well dill weed, celery, onion, cucumber and tuna.
2. Add lemon juice and olive oil and mix thoroughly.
3. Season with pepper and salt-free seasoning blend.
4. To assemble sandwich, you can toast bread slices, on top of one bread slice layer ½ cup tuna salad, top with ¼ cup spinach and cover with another slice of bread.
5. Repeat procedure to remaining ingredients, serve and enjoy.

Nutrition Information:
Calories per Serving: 244.2; Protein: 16.7g; Carbs: 30.4g; Fat: 6.2g; Saturated Fat: 1.2g; Sodium: 698mg

Whole Wheat, Cucumber and Tomato Sandwich

Serves: 1 , Cooking time: 2 minutes

Ingredients:
- 2 slices of whole wheat bread, toasted
- 2 slices of tomatoes
- 2 slices of cucumber

Directions for Cooking:
1. Put slices of tomatoes and cucumber in between two slices of toasted bread.
2. Slice diagonally before serving.

Nutrition Information:
Calories per Serving: 168; Carbs: 28.8g; Protein: 8.3g; Fats: 2.3g; Saturated Fat: 0.1g; Sodium: 249mg

Pesto, Avocado and Tomato Panini

Serves: 2 , Cooking time: 10 minutes

Ingredients:
- 2 slices of skim mozzarella cheese
- 4 tsp pesto
- 1 vine-ripened tomatoes cut into 4 equal slices
- 1 avocado, peeled, pitted, halved and cut into thin strips
- 4 ciabatta bread slices
- Pepper to taste

Directions for Cooking:
1. Lightly grease panini press with cooking spray and place on medium low fire.
2. On one side of each ciabatta bread slice slather 1 tsp pesto.
3. Top one slice with ½ of the avocado slices, ½ of the tomato slices, a dash of pepper. Top with a piece of bread slice.
4. Place sandwich on panini press and grill one side for 2 to 3 minutes. Turnover and grill the other side for 2 minutes. Meanwhile, repeat process of making sandwich and cook the same way.
5. Serve and enjoy.

Nutrition Information:
Calories per Serving: 346; Carbs: 29.5g; Protein: 8.4g; Fats: 23.1g; Saturated Fat: 4.2g; Sodium: 393mg

Lemon Aioli, Arugula and Swordfish Sandwich

Serves: 4 , Cooking time: 10 minutes

Ingredients:
- 1 cup fresh arugula greens
- 8 slices focaccia, toasted
- 2 cloves garlic, minced
- 1 tbsp herbes de Provence
- Pepper
- 1-lb swordfish fillet, cut into 4 equal pieces
- 1 tsp olive oil

Lemon Aioli Ingredients:
- ¼ tsp freshly ground black pepper
- 1 clove garlic, minced
- 2 tbsp fresh lemon juice
- 1 lemon, zested
- 1/3 cup low fat mayonnaise

Directions for Cooking:

1. In a small bowl, mix well all lemon Aioli ingredients and put aside.
2. Over medium high fire, heat olive oil in skillet. Season with pepper, minced garlic and herbs de Provence the swordfish. Then pan fry fish until golden brown on both sides, around 3 minutes per side.
3. Smear 1 tsp of lemon aioli on one side of each bread slice. Top with fish and arugula.
4. Serve and enjoy.

Nutrition Information:
Calories per Serving: 290; Carbs: 9.7g; Protein: 28.2g; Fats: 14.9g; Saturated Fat: 3.1g; Sodium: 212mg

Cheesy Mushroom Toast

Serves: 4 , Cooking time: 8 minutes

Ingredients:
- 8 slices focaccia bread
- 4 thin slices low fat swiss cheese
- 4 thin slices low sodium mozzarella
- 4 large portobello mushroom caps, stems removed
- 4 tbsp balsamic vinegar

Directions for Cooking:
1. Place a nonstick pan on medium high fire and spray lightly with cooking spray. Heat pan for 2 minutes.
2. Add mushroom caps. Add a tbsp of balsamic per cap and cook for 5 minutes in a covered pan. Turnover caps and cook for another 3 minutes the other side.
3. To make the sandwich, on top of a slice of bread place swiss cheese, followed by cooked mushroom cap, top with asiago cheese, and cover with another slice of focaccia bread.
4. Repeat process for remaining ingredients.
5. Serve and enjoy.

Nutrition Information:
Calories per Serving: 213; Carbs: 15.0g; Protein: 20.9g; Fats: 8.0g; Saturated Fat: 4.2g; Sodium: 157mg

Savory Crab Panini

Serves: 2 , Cooking time: 10 minutes

Ingredients:
- 4 slices whole grain bread
- 1/4-lb crab meat
- ½ cup celery
- ¼ cup green onion chopped
- 1 tsp lemon juice
- 1 tsp Dijon mustard
- 1/4 cup light mayonnaise

Directions for Cooking:
1. Lightly grease panini press with cooking spray and place on medium low fire.
2. In a bowl mix well crab meat, celery, green onion, lemon juice, Dijon mustard, and mayo.
3. On one side of each bread slather ½ of the crab mixture. Top with the other bread slice. Repeat process on remaining bread and crab mixture.
4. Place sandwich on panini press and grill one side for 2 to 3 minutes. Turnover and grill the other side for 2 minutes. Repeat grilling process on the other sandwich.
5. Serve and enjoy.

Nutrition Information:
Calories per Serving: 256; Carbs: 30.9g; Protein: 14.8g; Fats: 8.0; Saturated Fat: 1.5g; Sodium: 395mg

Lemon, Garlic, Buttered Shrimp Panini

Serves: 2 , Cooking time: minutes

Ingredients:
- 1 tbsp olive oil
- 1 6-inch baguette, sliced in half lengthwise
- 1 tsp hot sauce
- 1 tbsp parsley
- 2 tbsp lemon juice
- 2 garlic cloves, minced
- 1/4-lb shrimp peeled

Directions for Cooking:
1. Place a small nonstick fry pan on medium fire and heat oil. Add all ingredients except for baguette.
2. Sauté shrimps until pink, around 5 minutes. Turn off fire.
3. Lightly grease panini press with cooking spray and place on medium low fire.
4. To make the sandwich, on one baguette slice, carve out a hollowed portion. Evenly spread the shrimp mixture here. Top with the other bread slice. Cut in half.
5. Place sandwich on panini press and grill one side for 2 to 3 minutes. Turnover and grill the other side for 2 minutes. Repeat grilling process on the other sandwich.
6. Serve and enjoy.

Nutrition Information:
Calories per Serving: 286; Carbs: 29.6g; Protein: 21.9g; Fats: 9.2g; Saturated Fat: 1.4g; Sodium: 418mg

Tuna Melt Sandwich

Serves: 2 , Cooking time: 10 minutes

Ingredients:
- 1 6-oz can tuna in water, low sodium
- 2 stalks celery, diced
- ½ small onion, diced
- ¼ tsp pepper
- 1 tsp pickle relish
- 1 tbsp light mayo
- 6-inch Baguette, sliced in half lengthwise
- 2 slices low fat mozzarella

Directions for Cooking:
1. Drain tuna and place in a bowl. Whisk well with celery, onion, pepper, mayo, and pickle relish.
2. Lightly grease panini press with cooking spray and place on medium low fire.
3. Lay flat a slice of baguette and evenly spread tuna mixture, top with cheese, and cover with remaining slice of bread. Cut sandwich in half.
4. Place sandwich on panini press and grill one side for 2 to 3 minutes. Turnover and grill the other side for 2 minutes. Repeat grilling process on the other sandwich.
5. Serve and enjoy.

Nutrition Information:
Calories per Serving: 380; Carbs: 32.9g; Protein: 36.2g; Fats: 11.0g; Saturated Fat: 4.4g; Sodium: 381mg

Caramelized Onion and Thin Beef

Serves: 2 , Cooking time: 25 minutes

Ingredients:
- 6-inch Ciabatta loaf, sliced in half lengthwise
- ¼-lb thinly sliced beef
- 1 medium onions, sliced thinly
- 1 tsp olive oil
- 1 tsp pepper
- 2 slices of low-fat mozzarella

Directions for Cooking:
1. Place a nonstick pan on medium high fire and heat oil for 3 minutes. Stir in onions and sauté for 5 minutes or until soft and translucent.
2. Stir in beef and season with pepper, sauté for 5 minutes or until beef is browned. Turn off fire.
3. Lightly grease panini press with cooking spray and place on medium low fire.
4. Lay flat a slice of ciabatta and evenly beef mixture, top with cheese, and cover with

remaining slice of bread. Cut sandwich in half.
5. Place sandwich on panini press and grill one side for 2 to 3 minutes. Turnover and grill the other side for 2 minutes. Repeat grilling process on the other sandwich.

6. Serve and enjoy.
Nutrition Information:
Calories per Serving: 414; Carbs: 27.2g; Protein: 21.4g; Fats: 24.2g; Saturated Fat: 10.3g; Sodium: 217mg

Cheesy Eggplant Panini

Serves: 2 , Cooking time: 20 minutes
Ingredients:
- 6-inch Ciabatta loaf, sliced in half lengthwise
- 1 tsp olive oil
- 1 tsp pepper
- 2 slices of low-fat mozzarella
- 4 ¼-inch slices of eggplant
- ½ tsp Cajun seasoning

Directions for Cooking:
1. Place a nonstick large pan on medium high fire and heat for 2 minutes. Add oil and swirl to coat and heat for another 2 minutes.
2. Slice an eggplant lengthwise, around ¼-inch thick slices. Make 4 slices and place in heated pan and pan fry for 2 minutes per side. Season with pepper.

3. Lightly grease panini press with cooking spray and place on medium low fire.
4. Lay flat a slice of ciabatta and evenly spread 2 slices of eggplant, top with cheese, remaining eggplant slices, sprinkle with Cajun seasoning, and cover with remaining slice of bread. Cut sandwich in half.
5. Place sandwich on panini press and grill one side for 2 to 3 minutes. Turnover and grill the other side for 2 minutes. Repeat grilling process on the other sandwich.
6. Serve and enjoy.
Nutrition Information:
Calories per Serving: 252; Carbs: 30.4g; Protein: 12.5g; Fats: 9.0g; Saturated Fat: 3.8g; Sodium: 205mg

Sun Dried Tomatoes and Spinach Chicken Panini

Serves: 2 , Cooking time: 0 minutes
Ingredients:
- 4 slices whole wheat bread
- 2 ¼-inch thick slices of Rotisserie chicken breast, skin removed
- 1 cup baby spinach
- 2 tbsp sun dried tomatoes
- 2 tbsp balsamic vinegar

Directions for Cooking:
1. In a bowl, soak sun dried tomatoes in balsamic vinegar for 10 minutes.

2. Whisk well with celery, onion, pepper, mayo, and pickle relish.
3. Lay flat a slice of bread, add a slice of chicken, ½ of tomatoes, ½ of spinach, and cover with remaining slice of bread. Repeat process for remaining ingredients.
4. Serve and enjoy.
Nutrition Information:
Calories per Serving: 229; Carbs: 30.0g; Protein: 18.6g; Fats: 3.7g; Saturated Fat: 0.8g; Sodium: 330mg

Simple Pesto Chicken 'n Cheese

Serves: 2 , Cooking time: minutes
Ingredients:
- 4 slices whole wheat bread
- 2 slices of Pepper Jack cheese
- 2 tbsp pesto
- 2 ¼-inch thick slice of Rotisserie chicken breast, no skin

Directions for Cooking:
1. Place a slice of cheese on 1 bread and toast 4 slices of bread for 3 minutes.
2. Lay flat the slice of bread with cheese, top by chicken. Slather the pieces of bread without

cheese with 1/2 tbsp of pesto and place on top of chicken to make a sandwich. Repeat process for remaining ingredients.
3. Serve and enjoy.

Nutrition Information:
Calories per Serving: 310; Carbs: 26.0g; Protein: 23.3g; Fats: 12.4g; Saturated Fat: 4.5g; Sodium: 352mg

Egg 'n Cheese Panini

Serves: 2 , Cooking time: 20 minutes
Ingredients:
- 1 whole egg
- 2 egg whites
- ¼ tsp pepper
- A dash of salt
- 2 slices low sodium mozzarella
- 4 slices whole wheat toast
- 1 tsp olive oil
- 1 tbsp chopped green onions

Directions for Cooking:
1. In a small bowl, whisk well whole egg and egg whites. Season with pepper, green onions and salt.
2. Place a small nonstick saucepan on medium high fire and heat oil for 3 minutes. Add eggs and scramble for 4 minutes or to desired consistency.
3. Lightly grease panini press with cooking spray and place on medium low fire.
4. Lay flat a slice of bread, top with cheese, followed by ½ of scrambled egg and cover with remaining slice of bread.
5. Repeat process for remaining ingredients
6. Place sandwich on panini press and grill one side for 2 to 3 minutes. Turnover and grill the other side for 2 minutes. Repeat grilling process on the other sandwich.
7. Serve and enjoy.

Nutrition Information:
Calories per Serving: 315; Carbs: 26.8g; Protein: 19.9g; Fats: 13.7g; Saturated Fat: 5.0g; Sodium: 337mg

Omelet 'n Veggie Toast

Serves: 2 , Cooking time: 15 minutes
Ingredients:
- 1 whole egg
- 2 egg whites
- ¼ tsp pepper
- A dash of salt
- 2 slices low sodium mozzarella
- 4 slices whole wheat toast
- 1 tsp olive oil
- 1 tbsp chopped green onions
- 1 roma tomato sliced
- 4 button mushrooms sliced thinly
- 1 small onion, sliced thinly
- ½ cup spinach
- 1 clove garlic minced

Directions for Cooking:
1. Place a large nonstick pan on medium high fire and heat oil for 3 minutes.
2. Toast the bread slices.
3. Meanwhile, in a small bowl, whisk well whole egg and egg whites.
4. Stir in garlic, onion, and tomato. Sauté for 5 minutes. Add mushrooms and sauté for 5 minutes. Season with pepper and salt. Stir in spinach and sauté until wilted around 2 minutes.
5. Pour in egg and scramble for 4 minutes or until desired consistency is reached.
6. Lay flat a slice of bread, add 1 slice of cheese, ½ of omelet, and cover with remaining slice of bread.
7. Repeat process for remaining sandwich.
8. Serve and enjoy.

Nutrition Information:
Calories per Serving: 305; Carbs: 31.5g; Protein: 19.4g; Fats: 11.1g; Saturated Fat: 4.5g; Sodium: 326mg

Roast Beef Panini

Serves: 1 , Cooking time: 6 minutes

Ingredients:

- 1 tsp creamy horseradish sauce
- 1 slice Havarti cheese
- 2 slices whole wheat bread
- 2 slices deli roast beef

Directions for Cooking:

1. Lightly grease panini press with cooking spray and place on medium low fire.
2. Lay flat a slice of bread, add cheese, followed by roast beef, slather horseradish sauce, and cover with remaining slice of bread.
3. Place sandwich on panini press and grill one side for 2 minutes. Turnover and grill the other side for 2 minutes.
4. Serve and enjoy.

Nutrition Information:

Calories per Serving: 242; Carbs: 26.0g; Protein: 15.3g; Fats: 8.2g; Saturated Fat: 4.2g; Sodium: 328mg

Steak 'n Greens Toast

Serves: 2 , Cooking time: 10 minutes

Ingredients:

- 1 4-oz cut of ribeye steak, thinly sliced
- 2 slices of Havarti cheese
- 4 slices whole wheat bread
- ½ cup arugula
- 1 tsp pepper
- 1 tsp garlic powder
- 1 tsp olive oil

Directions for Cooking:

1. In a bowl, mix thinly sliced steak, pepper, and garlic powder.
2. Toast bread slices.
3. Place a nonstick pan on medium high fire and spray lightly with cooking spray. Heat pan for 2 minutes.
4. Stir fry steak for 5 minutes. Turn off fire.
5. To make the sandwich, on top of a slice of bread place cheese, followed by cooked steak, top with ½ of arugula, and cover with another slice of bread.
6. Repeat process for remaining ingredients.
7. Serve and enjoy.

Nutrition Information:

Calories per Serving: 305; Carbs: 27.2g; Protein: 20.0g; Fats: 12.9g; Saturated Fat: 5.4g; Sodium: 267mg

Rotisserie Chicken Sandwich

Serves: 2 , Cooking time: 0 minutes

Ingredients:

- 2 ¼-inch thick slices of Rotisserie Chicken breast, no skin
- 2 slices low sodium mozzarella
- 1 tbsp light mayo
- 1 tsp sriracha
- 1 tsp pickle relish
- ¼ tsp pepper
- 4 slices whole wheat bread

Directions for Cooking:

1. In a bowl, whisk well mayo sriracha, pickle relish, and pepper.
2. Place one bread slice on a flat surface, place 1 slice of cheese on top, 1 slice of chicken, ½ of mayo mixture slathered on chicken, followed by 1 slice of bread.
3. Repeat process for remaining ingredients.
4. Serve and enjoy.

Nutrition Information:

Calories per Serving: 28.1; Carbs: 28.1g; Protein: 22.7g; Fats: 9.6g; Saturated Fat: 4.0g; Sodium: 363mg

Healthy Caprese Sandwich

Serves: 2 , Cooking time: 0 minutes

Ingredients:
- 4 slices whole wheat bread
- 2 roma tomatoes, sliced in circles
- ¼ cup fresh basil leaves
- 4 slices low sodium mozzarella
- 1 tbsp balsamic vinegar
- Pepper to taste

Directions for Cooking:
1. In a bowl, soak tomato slices in balsamic vinegar for 10 minutes.
2. To make the sandwich, on top of a slice of bread place 1 slice of cheese, ¼ of basil leaves, ½ of the tomatoes, ¼ of the basil leaves, 1 slice of cheese, and top by 1 slice of bread.
3. Repeat process for remaining ingredients.
4. Serve and enjoy.

Nutrition Information:
Calories per Serving: 231; Carbs: 30.0g; Protein: 12.5g; Fats: 6.7g; Saturated Fat: 3.5g; Sodium: 159mg

Breakfast Egg Sandwich

Serves: 2 , Cooking time: 0 minutes

Ingredients:
- 4 slices of whole wheat bread
- 2 hardboiled egg, peeled
- ¼ tsp pepper
- 1 cup spinach
- 2 tbsp low fat mayo
- 1 tbsp pickle relish

Directions for Cooking:
1. In a bowl, add eggs and mash with a fork. Season with mayo, pickle relish, and pepper.
2. To make the sandwich, on top of a slice of bread place ½ of the egg mixture, ½ cup spinach, and top by 1 bread slice.
3. Repeat process for remaining ingredients.
4. Serve and enjoy.

Nutrition Information:
Calories per Serving: 229; Carbs: 30.0g; Protein: 10.5g; Fats: 7.5g; Saturated Fat: 2.0g; Sodium: 305mg

Simple Arugula and Cheese sandwich

Serves: 2 , Cooking time: 0 minutes

Ingredients:
- 1 cup arugula
- 4 bread slices
- 1 6-oz can tuna in water, low sodium
- 2 tbsp balsamic vinegar
- 2 slices low fat swiss cheese, low sodium

Directions for Cooking:
1. Drain well tuna and place in a bowl. Pour in balsamic and mix well.
2. To make the sandwich, on top of a slice of bread place 1 slice swiss cheese, followed by ½ of the tuna mixture, ½ cup arugula, and top by 1 bread slice.
3. Repeat process for remaining ingredients.
4. Serve and enjoy.

Nutrition Information:
Calories per Serving: 328; Carbs: 27.0g; Protein: 31.9g; Fats: 9.1g; Saturated Fat: 4.1g; Sodium: 198mg

Chapter 7 Pasta Recipes

Chicken Penne Pesto

Serves: 8 , Cooking time: 25 minutes

Ingredients:
- 1 16-oz package penne pasta
- 2 tbsp olive oil
- 2 cloves garlic, minced
- 4 skinless, boneless chicken breast halves, cut into thin strips
- 3 tbsp grated Parmesan cheese
- ¼ cup pesto
- 1 ¼ cups cottage cheese
- ¼ tsp pepper
- ½ tsp coconut aminos

Directions for Cooking:
1. Cook penne according to manufacturer's instructions, minus the salt and oil.
2. While penne are cooking, on medium fire, place a large saucepan and heat oil.
3. Add garlic and chicken, sauté for 7 minutes or until chicken strips are nearly cooked.
4. Lower fire and add Parmesan cheese, pesto, pepper and coconut aminos.
5. Continue cooking for 5-10 minutes more or until chicken is fully cooked. Stir frequently.
6. Once penne are cooked, drain well and pour into large saucepan, toss to coat.
7. Stir in cottage cheese and serve.

Nutrition Information:
Calories per Serving: 326; Protein: 34.0g; Carbs: 17.9g; Fat: 13.5g; Saturated Fat: 3.3g; Sodium: 391mg

Herby Pasta and Lentils

Serves: 7 , Cooking time: 45 minutes

Ingredients:
- 3 cups water
- 2 small dry red peppers, whole
- 1 tsp turmeric
- 1 tsp ground cumin
- 3 cloves garlic, minced
- 1 15-ounce can low sodium, diced tomatoes with juice
- 1 large onion, chopped
- ½ cup dry lentils, rinsed
- ½ cup orzo or tiny pasta
- ¼-½ cup fresh cilantro, chopped
- 3 tbsp low fat sour cream

Directions for Cooking:
1. In a skillet, combine all ingredients except for the cilantro then boil on medium-high heat.
2. Ensure to cover and slightly reduce heat to medium-low and simmer until pasta is tender for about 35 minutes.
3. Afterwards, take out the chili peppers then add cilantro and top it with low-fat sour cream. Enjoy!

Nutrition Information:
Calories per Serving: 157.7; Protein: 2.1g; Carbs: 32.5g; Fat: 2.1g; Saturated Fat: 0.2g; Sodium: 51 mg

Pasta with Cheesy Broccoli Sauce

Serves: 6 , Cooking time: 30 minutes

Ingredients:
- 12-oz uncooked whole wheat pasta
- 6 ½ cups fresh broccoli florets, no stems
- 1 tsp olive oil
- 5 cloves garlic, peeled, smashed and chopped
- ½ tsp pepper
- ¼ cup grated fat free Parmesan cheese

Directions for Cooking:
1. In a large pot of boiling water, cook pasta according to manufacturer's instructions minus oil and salt.
2. 5 minutes before pasta is done, add broccoli into pot, cover and cook until pasta is done.
3. Drain pasta and broccoli, while reserving 1 cup of liquid. Separate broccoli from pasta.

4. Return pot to high fire and heat oil.
5. Sauté garlic until lightly browned.
6. Lower fire to medium and add broccoli. Season with pepper.
7. Add cheese and water, mix until well combined.
8. Turn off fire and transfer broccoli mixture into blender. Puree until smooth and creamy.

9. Return to pot and turn on fire to medium and add pasta back.
10. Cook until well combined and heated through around 5 to 10 minutes.
11. Serve and enjoy.

Nutrition Information:
Calories per Serving: 111.9; Protein: 6.9g; Carbs: 13.2g; Fat: 3.5g; Saturated Fat: .8g; Sodium: 231mg

Tuna-Pasta Salad

Serves: 4 , Cooking time: 15 minutes
Ingredients:
- 2 cups whole wheat macaroni, uncooked
- 2 5-oz cans low-sodium tuna, water pack
- 1/3 cup diced onion
- ¼ cup sliced carrots
- ½ cup chopped zucchini
- ¼ cup fat free mayonnaise
- ¼ cup light sour cream
- ¼ tsp pepper

Directions for Cooking:
1. In a pot of boiling water, cook macaroni according to manufacturer's instructions minus the oil and salt.

2. Drain macaroni, run under cold tap water until cool and set aside.
3. Drain tuna and discard liquid.
4. Place tuna in a salad bowl.
5. Add zucchini, carrots, drained macaroni and onion. Toss to mix.
6. Add mayonnaise and sour cream. Mix well.
7. Season with pepper, serve and enjoy.
8. Serve and enjoy.

Nutrition Information:
Calories per Serving: 174.4; Protein: 5.1g; Carbs: 27.7g; Fat: 4.8g; Saturated Fat: 1.5g; Sodium: 54mg

Simple Pasta Limon

Serves: 2 , Cooking time: 15 minutes
Ingredients:
- 1/2-pound angel hair whole wheat spaghetti, cooked
- 1 lemon, juiced and zested
- 3 1/2 ounces low-sodium parmesan cheese
- Freshly ground black pepper
- 1 tablespoon olive oil
- ¼ cup packed fresh basil leaves, torn

Directions for Cooking:
1. Cook angel hair pasta according to manufacturer's instructions minus the oil and salt.

2. Meanwhile in a large bowl, mix well all remaining ingredients.
3. Once pasta is cooked, reserve ¼ cup of the boiling liquid, and drain pasta well.
4. Add pasta to bowl of cheese and swirl to coat. If needed, add a tbsp of the reserved boiling water to un-thicken sauce.
5. Serve and enjoy.

Nutrition Information:
Calories per Serving: 429; Protein: 26.8g; Carbs: 33.6g; Fat: 22.3g; Saturated Fat: 10.5g; Sodium: 35mg

Kale Pasta Pesto

Serves: 6 , Cooking time: 5 minutes
Ingredients:
- 3 cloves of garlic, minced
- 3 cups kale, rinsed
- ¾ cup hemp seeds or walnuts
- 2 tablespoons lemon juice, freshly squeezed

- ¾ teaspoon salt
- ¼ teaspoon ground pepper
- ¼ cup flaxseed oil

- 1-pound whole grain pasta, cooked according to package instructions minus the salt and oil

Directions for Cooking:
1. In a blender, place all ingredients except for the pasta.
2. Pulse until smooth.
3. Pour over cooked pasta and stir to combine everything.

Nutrition Information:
Calories per Serving: 249; Carbs: 24.2g; Protein: 4.4g; Fats: 16.2g; Saturated Fat: 2.3g; Sodium: 295mg

Seafood with Sundried Tomatoes Pasta

Serves: 8 , Cooking time: 10 minutes

Ingredients:
- ¼ cup olive oil
- 4 cloves of garlic, minced
- 1-pound scallops
- 1-pound shrimps, peeled and deveined
- 1/3 cup sun-dried tomatoes
- 2 ½ teaspoon lemon zest
- ½ tsp pepper
- 1 cup water
- 1-pound whole wheat linguine pasta, cooked
- ¼ cup parsley, chopped
- A dash of red pepper flakes

Directions for Cooking:
1. Heat the oil in a skillet and sauté the garlic until fragrant.
2. Add the scallop, shrimps, tomatoes, and lemon zest.
3. Season with pepper and pour in water.
4. Close the lid and bring to a boil.
5. Allow simmering for 6 minutes.
6. Stir in the pasta and cook for another 2 minutes.
7. Garnish with parsley and red pepper flakes.

Nutrition Information:
Calories per Serving: 241; Carbs: 14.6g; Protein: 22.5g; Fats: 10.3g; Saturated Fat: 3.8g; Sodium: 328mg

Chicken Pasta Florentine

Serves: 8 , Cooking time: 50 minutes

Ingredients:
- 1 tbsp Italian seasoning
- 4 tbsp Parmesan cheese
- 4-oz sliced Mozzarella cheese, low sodium
- 2 cloves garlic minced
- 16-oz ready to bake noodle pasta, broken in half
- 8 cups baby spinach
- 2 cans of cream of mushroom soup, low sodium
- 4 cups water
- 2 boneless skinless chicken breasts, cut into bite sized-pieces

Directions for Cooking:
1. Preheat oven to 400°F and lightly grease a large casserole dish with cooking spray.
2. Place chicken on bottom of dish and top with pasta noodles. Spread evenly.
3. In a blender, blend well mozzarella, garlic, cream of mushroom, and water. Pour over pasta and chicken. Making sure that pasta is submerged.
4. Cover dish with foil and bake in oven for 30 minutes.
5. Remove foil, stir in baby spinach. Sprinkle top with parmesan and Italian seasoning.
6. Return to oven and continue baking for another 10 minutes.
7. Let it rest for 10 minutes before serving.

Nutrition Information:
Calories per Serving: 362.2; Carbs: 51.0g; Protein: 22.0g; Fats: 8.5g; Saturated Fat: 3.2g; Sodium: 377mg

Pasta Creole Style

Serves: 8 , Cooking time: 30 minutes

Ingredients:

- 16-oz pasta, whole wheat
- 1 28-oz jar Pasta sauce, low sodium
- 1 tsp Cajun seasoning
- 2 bell peppers, sliced
- 2 medium onions, sliced
- 1 link turkey smoked sausage, sliced
- 1 tbsp olive oil

Directions for Cooking:

1. Cook pasta according to manufacturer's instructions minus salt and oil. Drain and set aside.
2. Place a large pot on medium high fire and heat for 3 minutes.
3. Add oil and swirl to coat bottom and sides of pot.
4. Stir in sausage, crumble and cook for 5 minutes. Season with Cajun seasoning.
5. Stir in onions and bell peppers, cook for 5 minutes.
6. Add jar of pasta sauce and simmer while covered for 10 minutes.
7. Stir in pasta. Turn off fire.
8. Serve and enjoy

Nutrition Information:

Calories per Serving: 309; Carbs: 56.6g; Protein: 8.6g; Fats: 6.0g; Saturated Fat: 1.0g; Sodium: 174mg

Easy Ground Beef Stroganoff

Serves: 4 , Cooking time: 30 minutes

Ingredients:

- 1 cup sour cream
- 3 cups egg noodles, uncooked
- 3 cups water
- 1 tbsp flour
- 2 tbsp water
- 1 10.5-oz can cream of mushroom, low sodium
- ¼ tsp pepper
- 1-lb. ground beef
- 1 clove garlic, minced
- ½ cup minced onion

Directions for Cooking:

1. Cook pasta according to manufacturer's instructions minus salt and oil. Drain and set aside.
2. Place a large pot on medium high fire and heat for 3 minutes.
3. Add oil and swirl to coat bottom and sides of pot.
4. Add garlic and sauté for a minute. Add onions and sauté for 2 minutes.
5. Add beef and brown for 10 minutes. Season with pepper.
6. Pour in broth and cream of mushroom. Mix well and simmer for 10 minutes.
7. Meanwhile, in a bowl mix water and flour. Stir into pot and continue mixing until thickened.
8. Stir in sour cream, serve, and enjoy with pasta

Nutrition Information:

Calories per Serving: 511; Carbs: 47.8g; Protein: 39.1g; Fats: 17.3g; Saturated Fat: 6.4g; Sodium: 340mg

Yummy Pasta Bolognese

Serves: 8 , Cooking time: 25 minutes

Ingredients:

- 1 tbsp Worcestershire sauce
- 5.5-fl. oz. tomato paste
- 1 cup unsalted chicken stock
- 2 cups water
- 1 tsp olive oil
- Pepper to taste
- 1 tsp dried basil
- 1 tsp dried oregano
- 1 small onion, sliced
- 3 cloves garlic, minced
- 12 white mushrooms, sliced
- 1-lb penne rigate
- ½-lb ground beef

Directions for Cooking:

1. Cook pasta according to manufacturer's instructions minus salt and oil. Drain and set aside.
2. Place a large pot on medium high fire and heat for 3 minutes.
3. Add oil and swirl to coat bottom and sides of pot.
4. Add garlic and sauté for a minute. Add onions and sauté for 3 minutes. Add dried basil and oregano and sauté for a minute.
5. Add beef and brown for 8 minutes, while pounding to separate the pieces.
6. Add mushrooms. Season with pepper and salt. Mix well.
7. Mix in tomato paste, Worcestershire sauce, fish sauce, light soy sauce, water, and chicken stock. Mix well.
8. Cover, bring to a simmer, and cook for 10 minutes.
9. Serve and enjoy with pasta.

Nutrition Information:
Calories per Serving: 312; Carbs: 51.8g; Protein: 12.9g; Fats: 6.7g; Saturated Fat: 2.0g; Sodium: 56mg

Traditional American Mac and Cheese

Serves: 6 , Cooking time: 30 minutes

Ingredients:
- 1 tsp ground mustard
- 1 tsp Sriracha
- 12-oz skim milk
- 2 large eggs, beaten
- Pepper to taste
- 8-oz cream cheese fat free
- 6-oz sharp cheddar, grated, low sodium
- ½ cup water
- 16-oz elbow macaroni

Directions for Cooking:
1. In a small bowl whisk well mustard, sriracha, milk, and eggs. Set aside.
2. Cook pasta according to manufacturer's instructions minus salt and oil. Drain and set aside.
3. Place a large pot on medium high fire and heat for 3 minutes.
4. Add water and milk mixture. Continue cooking and mixing for 3 minutes until smooth and creamy. Add the cheeses. Cook for another 10 minutes while mixing constantly until smooth and creamy.
5. Season with pepper and stir in pasta.
6. Toss well to mix, serve and enjoy.

Nutrition Information:
Calories per Serving: 472; Carbs: 62.8g; Protein: 26.2g; Fats: 12.1g; Saturated Fat: 6.6g; Sodium: 323mg

Comfort Food: Traditional Spaghetti

Serves: 8 , Cooking time: 10 minutes

Ingredients:
- 1 14.5-oz can diced tomatoes
- 4 ½ cups water
- 1 24-oz Jar spaghetti sauce
- 1-lb whole wheat spaghetti noodles
- ½ tsp Italian seasoning
- ½ tsp onion powder
- ½ tsp garlic powder
- 1-lb lean ground beef

Directions for Cooking:
1. Cook pasta according to manufacturer's instructions minus salt and oil. Drain and set aside.
2. Place a large pot on medium high fire and heat for 3 minutes.
3. Add oil and swirl to coat bottom and sides of pot.
4. Brown ground beef for 8 minutes, while pounding to separate the pieces.
5. Season with Italian seasoning, onion powder, and garlic powder.
6. Pour in diced tomatoes and spaghetti sauce. Mix well.
7. Pour in water and mix. Cover and bring to a boil. Lower fire to a simmer and cook for 10 minutes.
8. Serve sauce on top of pasta.

Nutrition Information:
Calories per Serving: 372; Carbs: 51.6g; Protein: 25.1g; Fats: 8.5g; Saturated Fat: 2.8g; Sodium: 73mg

Lip-Smacking Tomato-Pesto Pasta

Serves: 6 , Cooking time: minutes
Ingredients:
- Pepper to taste
- 1 tsp Basil
- 2 tsp olive oil
- 1 cup cherry tomatoes, halved
- ¾ cups prepared pesto
- 16-oz whole wheat pasta

Directions for Cooking:
1. Cook pasta according to manufacturer's instructions minus salt and oil. Drain and set aside.
2. Place a large pot on medium high fire and heat for 3 minutes.
3. Add oil and swirl to coat bottom and sides of pot.
4. Stir in basil, cherry tomatoes, and pesto. Sauté for 2 minutes or until heated through.
5. Add pasta, toss well to coat, and turn off fire.
6. Serve with a sprinkle of pepper.

Nutrition Information:
Calories per Serving: 336; Carbs: 44.4g; Protein: 10.8g; Fats: 14.7g; Saturated Fat: 2.5g; Sodium: 215mg

Cannellini, Pasta and Escarole

Serves: 5 , Cooking time: 25 minutes
Ingredients:
- 1 ½ cups canned cannellini beans, rinsed well and drained
- 2 carrots, chopped into large pieces
- 2 celery stalks, chopped
- 1 bulb of garlic, minced
- 6 sprigs of parsley
- 1 sprig of rosemary
- 2 bay leaves
- 1 onion, chopped
- 3 roma tomatoes, chopped
- 1 cup water
- 3 ounces pasta of your choice
- Pepper to taste
- ½ small head of escarole, torn
- 1 tablespoon olive oil

Directions for Cooking:
1. Place a heavy bottomed pot on medium high fire and heat pot for 3 minutes.
2. Once hot, add oil and stir around to coat pot with oil.
3. Add garlic, bay leaves, onion, tomatoes and sauté for 10 minutes until tomatoes are crushed.
4. Add remaining ingredients to pot, except for escarole and parsley. Mix well.
5. Cover, bring to a boil, lower fire to a simmer, and simmer for 10 minutes.
6. Stir in escarole and let it sit for 5 minutes, until liquid is fully absorbed.
7. Serve and enjoy with a sprinkle of parsley.

Nutrition Information:
Calories per Serving: 154; Carbs: 28.3g; Protein: 4.6g; Fats: 3.6g; Saturated Fat: 0.5g; Sodium: 126mg

Hearty and Easy Lasagna Soup

Serves: 6 , Cooking time: 25 minutes
Ingredients:
- 1 tablespoon olive oil
- 1 onion, chopped
- ½ green pepper, chopped
- 2 carrots, peeled and chopped
- 1 small zucchini, chopped
- 1 can diced tomatoes
- 4 cups vegetable stock
- 2 cups water
- ½ box of lasagna noodles, broken into small pieces
- ½ teaspoon onion powder
- 1 teaspoon oregano
- Pepper

Directions for Cooking:
1. Place a heavy bottomed pot on medium high fire and heat pot for 3 minutes.

2. Once hot, add oil and stir around to coat pot with oil.
3. Add onions and sauté for 5 minutes.
4. Stir in the rest of the ingredients. Mix well.
5. Cover, bring to a boil, lower fire to a simmer and simmer for 10 minutes.
6. Serve and enjoy.

Nutrition Information:
Calories per Serving: 251; Carbs: 42.8g; Protein: 9.1g; Fats: 5.5g; Saturated Fat: 1.0g; Sodium: 406mg

Alfredo Chicken Noodles

Serves: 4 , Cooking time: 15 minutes
Ingredients:
- 1 tablespoon olive oil
- 1 chicken breast, boneless and skinless, sliced thinly
- Pepper
- 5 cloves of garlic, minced
- 2 tablespoons low fat butter
- ¼ cup heavy cream
- 2 cups chicken broth
- A pinch of ground nutmeg
- 8-oz dry fettuccini noodles
- ½ cup parmesan cheese, grated
- Fresh basil leaves for garnish

Directions for Cooking:
1. Cook noodles according to package instructions minus the oil and salt.
2. Place a heavy bottomed pot on medium high fire and heat for 3 minutes.
3. Add oil Pour the oil and sauté the chicken breasts. Season with pepper. Cook until lightly brown, around 5 minutes.
4. Stir in the garlic and cook for a minute.
5. Add the remaining ingredients and mix well to make a smooth sauce. Cook for 5 minutes.
6. Stir in noodles.
7. Serve and enjoy.

Nutrition Information:
Calories per Serving: 432; Carbs: 46.1g; Protein: 28.8g; Fats: 14.4g; Saturated Fat: 5.3g; Sodium: 273mg

Pecorino Pasta with Sausage and Fresh Tomato

Serves: 4 , Cooking time: 20 minutes
Ingredients:
- ¼ cup torn fresh basil leaves
- 1/8 tsp black pepper
- 6 tbsp grated fresh low sodium pecorino Romano cheese, divided
- 1 ¼ lbs. tomatoes, chopped
- 2 tsp minced garlic
- 1 cup vertically sliced onions
- 2 tsp olive oil
- 8 oz sweet Italian sausage
- 8-oz uncooked penne, cooked and drained

Directions for Cooking:
1. On medium high fire, place a nonstick fry pan with oil and cook for five minutes onion and sausage. Stir constantly to break sausage into pieces.
2. Stir in garlic and continue cooking for two minutes more.
3. Add tomatoes and cook for another two minutes.
4. Remove pan from fire, season with pepper. Mix well.
5. Stir in 2 tbsp cheese and pasta. Toss well.
6. Transfer to a serving dish, garnish with basil and remaining cheese before serving.

Nutrition Information:
Calories per Serving: 377; Carbs: 54.2g; Protein: 18.6g; Fats: 10.8g; Saturated Fat: 3.8g; Sodium: 391mg

Feta, Eggplant and Sausage Penne

Serves: 6 , Cooking time: 20 minutes

Ingredients:
- ¼ cup chopped fresh parsley
- ½ cup crumbled feta cheese
- 6 cups hot cooked penne
- 1 14.5-oz can dice tomatoes
- ¼ tsp ground black pepper
- 1 tsp dried oregano
- 2 tbsp tomato paste
- 4 garlic cloves, minced
- ½ lb. bulk pork breakfast sausage
- 4 ½ cups cubed peeled eggplant

Directions for Cooking:
1. On medium high fire, place a nonstick, big fry pan and cook for seven minutes garlic, sausage and eggplant or until eggplants are soft and sausage are lightly browned.
2. Stir in diced tomatoes, black pepper, oregano and tomato paste. Cover and simmer for five minutes while occasionally stirring.
3. Remove pan from fire, stir in pasta and mix well.
4. Transfer to a serving dish, garnish with parsley and cheese before serving.

Nutrition Information:
Calories per Serving: 368; Carbs: 48.3g; Protein: 14.1g; Fats: 14.3g; Saturated Fat: 5.4g; Sodium: 436mg

Pastitsio Wild Mushroom

Serves: 5 , Cooking time: 60 minutes

Ingredients:
- 4 cups fusilli pasta, cooked and drained
- 1 ½ cups shredded low fat mozzarella cheese, divided
- 2 cups skim milk
- 1 ½ tbsp All-purpose flour
- 3 tbsp chopped fresh parsley
- 2 large eggs, lightly beaten
- 1 8oz can tomato sauce
- 1/8 tsp ground nutmeg
- ¼ tsp black pepper
- 1 tbsp chopped fresh oregano
- 2 8oz packages pre-sliced exotic mushroom blend, chopped
- 2 garlic cloves, minced
- 1 cup chopped onion
- 4 tsp olive oil, divided

Directions for Cooking:
1. On medium high fire, place Dutch oven with 1 tbsp oil and for three minutes fry garlic and onion. Stir in mushroom and cook until liquid has evaporated around eight minutes. Add tomato sauce, nutmeg, pepper, and oregano. Stir constantly and cook for another two minutes before removing from fire and put aside.
2. In a large bowl mix parsley and eggs. In same pan, heat 1 tsp oil and cook for a minute the flour. While constantly mixing, pour in milk gradually and boil for two minutes and let it thicken. Remove from fire and allow to stand for four minutes before whisking in 1 cup cheese. While stirring vigorously, slowly pour in the egg mixture. Then toss in pasta and mix.
3. In a greased rectangular glass dish, evenly spread 2 cups pasta mixture, top with mushroom mixture and pour remaining pasta. With foil, cover the dish and bake in a preheated 350°F oven for 30 minutes.
4. Remove dish from oven and set oven to broiler. Remove foil and sprinkle ½ cup of cheese. Return to oven and broil for five minutes. Remove from oven and allow to stand for fifteen minutes before serving.

Nutrition Information:
Calories per Serving: 399; Carbs: 47.5g; Protein: 23.7g; Fats: 13.8g; Saturated Fat: 5.7g; Sodium: 98mg

Penne Anti-Pasto

Serves: 5 , Cooking time: 15 minutes

Ingredients:

- ¼ cup pine nuts, toasted
- ½ cup grated low fat Parmigiana-Reggiano cheese, divided
- 8-oz penne pasta, cooked and drained
- 1 6oz jar drained, sliced, marinated and quartered artichoke hearts
- 1 7 oz jar drained and chopped sun-dried tomato halves packed in oil
- 3 oz chopped prosciutto
- 1/3 cup pesto
- 1/4 cup pitted and chopped Kalamata olives
- 1 medium red bell pepper

Directions for Cooking:

1. Slice bell pepper, discard membranes, seeds and stem. On a foiled lined baking sheet, place bell pepper halves, press down by hand and broil in oven for eight minutes. Remove from oven, put in a sealed bag for 5 minutes before peeling and chopping.
2. Place chopped bell pepper in a bowl and mix in artichokes, tomatoes, prosciutto, pesto and olives.
3. Toss in ¼ cup cheese and pasta. Transfer to a serving dish and garnish with ¼ cup cheese and pine nuts. Serve and enjoy!

Nutrition Information:

Calories per Serving: 493.6; Carbs: 53.0g; Protein: 17.7g; Fats: 25.9g; Saturated Fat: 5.4g; Sodium: 340.8mg

Filling Mushroom Bolognese

Serves: 6 , Cooking time: 60 minutes

Ingredients:

- ¼ cup chopped fresh parsley
- ¼ cup low fat Parmigiano-Reggiano cheese, grated
- 10-oz whole wheat spaghetti, cooked and drained
- ¼ cup skim milk
- 1 14oz can whole peeled tomatoes
- ½ cup white wine
- 2 tbsp tomato paste
- 1 tbsp minced garlic
- 8 cups finely chopped cremini mushrooms
- ½ lb. ground pork
- ½ tsp freshly ground black pepper, divided
- 2 ½ cups chopped onion
- 1 tbsp olive oil
- 1 cup boiling water
- ½-oz dried porcini mushrooms

Directions for Cooking:

1. Let porcini stand in a boiling bowl of water for twenty minutes, drain (reserve liquid), rinse and chop. Set aside.
2. On medium high fire, place a Dutch oven with olive oil and cook for ten minutes pork, ¼ tsp pepper, and onions. Constantly mix to break ground pork pieces.
3. Stir in ¼ tsp pepper, garlic and cremini mushrooms. Continue cooking until liquid has evaporated, around fifteen minutes.
4. Stirring constantly, add porcini and sauté for a minute.
5. Stir in wine, porcini liquid, tomatoes and tomato paste. Let it simmer for forty minutes. Stir occasionally. Pour milk and cook for another two minutes before removing from fire.
6. Stir in pasta and transfer to a serving dish. Garnish with parsley and cheese before serving.

Nutrition Information:

Calories per Serving: 353; Carbs: 55.4g; Protein: 23.6g; Fats: 7.0g; Saturated Fat: 2.0g; Sodium: 78mg

Fresh Herbs and Clams Linguine

Serves: 4 , Cooking time: 15 minutes

Ingredients:

- ½ tsp freshly ground black pepper
- 1.5-lbs. littleneck clams
- ½ cup white wine
- 4 garlic cloves, sliced
- ¼ tsp crushed red pepper
- 2 cups vertically sliced red onion
- 2 tbsp olive oil
- 2 tsp grated lemon zest
- 1 tbsp chopped fresh oregano
- 1/3 cup parsley leaves
- 8-oz linguine, cooked and drained

Directions for Cooking:

1. Chop finely lemon rind, oregano and parsley. Set aside.
2. On medium high fire, place a nonstick fry pan with olive oil and fry for four minutes garlic, red pepper and onion.
3. Add clams and wine and cook until shells have opened, around five minutes. Throw any unopened clam.
4. Transfer mixture into a large serving bowl. Add pepper and pasta. Toss to mix well. Serve with parsley garnish.

Nutrition Information:

Calories per Serving: 335; Carbs: 54.2g; Protein: 12.3g; Fats: 8.5g; Saturated Fat: 1.2g; Sodium: 41mg

Pasta Shells Stuffed with Feta, Spinach and Artichoke

Serves: 10 , Cooking time: 40 minutes

Ingredients:

- Cooking spray
- 20 jumbo pasta shells, cooked and drained
- 2 garlic cloves, minced
- 5 oz frozen chopped spinach, thawed, drained and squeezed dry
- 1 9oz package frozen artichoke hearts, thawed and chopped
- ¼ tsp freshly ground black pepper
- ½ cup fat free cream cheese softened
- 1 cup crumbled feta cheese
- 1 cup shredded provolone cheese, divided
- 1 8oz can no salt added tomato sauce
- 1 28oz can fire roasted crushed tomatoes with added puree
- ¼ cup chopped pepperoncini peppers
- 1 tsp dried oregano

Directions for Cooking:

1. On medium fire, place a medium fry pan and for 12 minutes cook tomato sauce, crushed tomatoes, peppers and oregano. Put aside.
2. In a medium bowl, mix garlic, spinach, artichoke, black pepper, cream cheese, feta cheese and ½ cup provolone. Evenly stuff these to the cooked pasta shells.
3. Grease a rectangular glass dish and arrange all the pasta shells within. Cover with tomato mixture and top with provolone.
4. Bake for 25 minutes in a preheated 375°F oven.

Nutrition Information:

Calories per Serving: 224; Carbs: 31.8g; Protein: 12.3g; Fats: 6.5g; Saturated Fat: 4.0g; Sodium: 383mg

Creamy Alfredo Fettuccine

Serves: 4 , Cooking time: 5 minutes

Ingredients:

- 1 cup grated low fat, low sodium parmesan cheese
- 1/8 tsp freshly ground black pepper
- ½ tsp salt
- 1/4 cup whipping cream
- 1 tbsp olive oil
- 8 oz dried fettuccine, cooked and drained

Directions for Cooking:

1. On medium high fire, place a big fry pan and heat oil.
2. Add pepper, ¾ cup parmesan, and cream gently boil for three to five minutes.

3. Once thickened, turn off fire and quickly stir in 1/4 cup of parmesan cheese. Toss in pasta, mix well.
4. Serve and enjoy.

Nutrition Information:
Calories per Serving: 355; Carbs: 46.4g; Protein: 14.8g; Fats: 12.9g; Saturated Fat: 5.9g; Sodium: 309mg

Lip Smacking Chicken Tetrazzini

Serves: 10 , Cooking time: 3 hours
Ingredients:
- ¾ cup thinly sliced green onion
- 2/3 cup grated parmesan cheese
- 10 oz dried spaghetti or linguine, cooked and drained
- ¼ tsp ground nutmeg
- ¼ tsp ground black pepper
- ¼ cup chicken broth
- 1 16oz jar of Alfredo pasta sauce
- 2 4.5oz jars of sliced mushrooms, drained
- 1-lb skinless chicken breasts cut into ½ inch slices

Directions for Cooking:

1. In a slow cooker, mix mushrooms and chicken.
2. In a bowl, mix well nutmeg, pepper, broth and alfredo sauce before pouring over chicken and mushrooms.
3. Set on high heat, cover and cook for two to three hours.
4. Once chicken is cooked, pour over pasta, garnish with green onion and serve.

Nutrition Information:
Calories per Serving: 318; Carbs: 23.5g; Protein: 22.5g; Fats: 14.7g; Saturated Fat: 8.3g; Sodium: 403mg

Pasta Shells Stuffed with Scampi

Serves: 10 , Cooking time: 40 minutes
Ingredients:
- 1/3 cup grated fresh Parmigiano-Reggiano cheese
- 3 cups lower-sodium marinara sauce, divided
- Cooking spray
- 1 tbsp potato starch
- 1 lb. medium shrimp, peeled, deveined and chopped coarsely
- 1/3 cup chopped fresh basil
- ¼ tsp ground red pepper
- ¼ cup reduced fat milk
- ½ cup 1/3-less fat cream cheese
- 2 tbsp minced garlic
- ½ cup chopped shallots
- 1 ½ tbsp olive oil
- 20 jumbo pasta shells, cooked and drained

Directions for Cooking:
1. On medium fire, place a nonstick fry pan with oil and fry for four minutes the shallots while occasionally mixing. Stir in garlic and cook for another minute.
2. In a bowl, place shrimp and sprinkle with potato starch and set aside.
3. Add pepper, milk and cream cheese while stirring constantly and cooking until cheese is melted and well mixed. Remove from fire and quickly stir in shrimp and basil.
4. In a greased rectangular glass dish, pour a cup of marinara sauce and spread evenly. Then equally stuff the pasta shells with the shrimp mixture and arrange the shells in the glass dish. Pour remaining marinara sauce on top of shells and garnish with cheese.
5. Place the dish in a preheated 400°F oven and cook for 20 minutes.

Nutrition Information:
Calories per Serving: 165; Carbs: 16.1g; Protein: 10.3g; Fats: 6.5g; Saturated Fat: 2.2g; Sodium: 388mg

Veggies and Sun-Dried Tomato Alfredo

Serves: 6 , Cooking time: 40 minutes

Ingredients:

- 2 tsp finely shredded lemon peel
- ½ cup finely shredded Parmesan cheese
- 1 ¼ cups skim milk
- 2 tbsp all-purpose flour
- 8 fresh mushrooms, sliced
- 1 ½ cups fresh broccoli florets
- 4 oz fresh trimmed and quartered Brussels sprouts
- 4 oz trimmed fresh asparagus spears
- 1 tbsp olive oil
- 4 tbsp low fat butter
- ½ cup chopped dried tomatoes
- 8 oz dried fettuccine

Directions for Cooking:

1. In a boiling pot of water, add fettuccine and cook following manufacturer's instructions. Two minutes before the pasta is cooked, add the dried tomatoes. Drain pasta and tomatoes and return to pot to keep warm. Set aside.
2. On medium high fire, in a big fry pan with 1 tbsp butter, fry mushrooms, broccoli, Brussels sprouts and asparagus. Cook for eight minutes while covered, transfer to a plate and put aside.
3. Using same fry pan, add remaining butter and flour. Stirring vigorously, cook for a minute or until thickened. Add Parmesan cheese, milk and mix until cheese is melted around five minutes.
4. Toss in the pasta and mix. Transfer to serving dish. Garnish with Parmesan cheese and lemon peel before serving.

Nutrition Information:

Calories per Serving: 223; Carbs: 44.4g; Protein: 8.5g; Fats: 3.3g; Saturated Fat: 0.6g; Sodium: 142mg

Gorgonzola and Chicken Pasta

Serves: 6 , Cooking time: 30 minutes

Ingredients:

- 12 oz pasta, cooked and drained
- ¼ cup snipped fresh Italian parsley
- 2/3 cup Parmesan cheese
- 1 cup crumbled Gorgonzola cheese
- 2 cups whipping cream
- 8 oz stemmed fresh cremini or shiitake mushrooms
- 1 tbsp olive oil
- ½ tsp ground pepper
- 1-lb skinless chicken breast, cut into ½-inch slices

Directions for Cooking:

1. Season chicken breasts with ¼ tsp pepper.
2. On medium high fire, place a nonstick pan with 1 tbsp oil and stir fry half of the chicken until cooked and lightly browned. Transfer chicken to a clean dish and repeat procedure to remaining batch of uncooked chicken.
3. In same pan, stir fry mushroom until liquid is evaporated and mushrooms are soft, around eight minutes. Stir occasionally.
4. Add chicken back to the mushrooms along with cream and simmer for three minutes. Then add the remaining pepper, parmesan cheese and ½ cup of Gorgonzola cheese. Cook until mixture is uniform. Turn off fire.
5. Add pasta into the mixture, tossing to combine. Transfer to serving dish and garnish with remaining Gorgonzola cheese and serve.

Nutrition Information:

Calories per Serving: 337; Carbs: 25.2g; Protein: 29.3g; Fats: 13.2g; Saturated Fat: 4.2g; Sodium: 304mg

Creamy Artichoke Lasagna

Serves: 9 , Cooking time: 1 hour 30 minutes

Ingredients:

- 1 cup shredded mozzarella cheese
- 2 cups light cream
- ¼ cup all-purpose flour
- 1 cup vegetable broth
- 1 egg
- 1 cup snipped fresh basil

- 1 cup finely shredded Parmesan cheese
- 1 15oz carton ricotta cheese
- 4 cloves garlic, minced
- ½ cup pine nuts
- 3 tbsp olive oil
- 9 dried lasagna noodles, cooked, rinsed in cold water and drained
- 15 fresh baby artichokes
- ¼ cup lemon juice
- 3 cups water

Directions for Cooking:

1. Prepare in a medium bowl lemon juice and water. Put aside. Slice off artichoke base and remove yellowed outer leaves and cut into quarters. Immediately soak sliced artichokes in prepared liquid and drain after a minute.
2. Over medium fire, place a big saucepan with 2 tbsp oil and fry half of garlic, pine nuts and artichokes. Stir frequently and cook until artichokes are soft around ten minutes. Turn off fire and transfer mixture to a big bowl and quickly stir in egg, ½ cup of basil, ½ cup of parmesan cheese and ricotta cheese. Mix thoroughly.
3. In a small bowl mix flour and broth. In same pan, add 1 tbsp oil and fry remaining garlic for half a minute. Add light cream and flour mixture. Stir constantly and cook until thickened. Remove from fire and stir in ½ cup of basil.
4. In a separate bowl mix ½ cup parmesan and mozzarella cheese.
5. Assemble the lasagna by layering the following in a greased rectangular glass dish: lasagna, 1/3 of artichoke mixture, 1/3 of sauce, sprinkle with the dried cheeses and repeat layering procedure until all ingredients are used up.
6. For forty minutes, bake lasagna in a pre-heated oven of 350ºF. Remove lasagna from oven and before serving, let it stand for fifteen minutes.

Nutrition Information:

Calories per Serving: 388; Carbs: 23.7g; Protein: 23.6g; Fats: 22.1g; Saturated Fat: 5.0g; Sodium: 202mg

Pastitsio an Italian Pasta Dish

Serves: 4 , Cooking time: 30 minutes

Ingredients:

- 2 tbsp chopped fresh flat leaf parsley
- ¾ cup shredded low fat mozzarella cheese
- 1 3oz package of fat free cream cheese
- ½ cup less fat cream cheese
- 1 can 14.5oz of diced tomatoes, drained
- 2 cups fat free milk
- 1 tbsp all-purpose flour
- 5 garlic cloves, minced
- 1 ½ cups chopped onion
- 1 tbsp olive oil
- 1/2 lb. ground sirloin
- Cooking spray
- 8 oz uncooked penne, cooked and drained

Directions for Cooking:

1. On medium high fire, place a big nonstick saucepan and for five minutes sauté beef. Keep on stirring to break up the pieces of ground meat. Once cooked, remove from pan and drain fat.
2. Using same pan, heat oil and fry onions until soft around four minutes while occasionally stirring.
3. Add garlic and continue cooking for another minute while constantly stirring.
4. Stir in beef and flour, cook for another minute. Mix constantly.
5. Add the fat free cream cheese, less fat cream cheese, tomatoes and milk. Cook until mixture is smooth and heated. Toss in pasta and mix well.
6. Transfer pasta into a greased rectangular glass dish and top with mozzarella. Cook in a preheated broiler for four minutes. Remove from broiler and garnish with parsley before serving.

Nutrition Information:

Calories per Serving: 376; Carbs: 49.6g; Protein: 28.5g; Fats: 7.1g; Saturated Fat: 4.6g; Sodium: 365mg

Serves: 12 , Cooking time: 1 hour 30-minutes

Ingredients:

- Snipped fresh Italian parsley
- 1 cup finely shredded parmesan cheese
- 15 dried lasagna noodles, cooked, rinsed in cold water and drained
- ½ cup skim milk
- ¼ tsp ground black pepper
- 2 tsp dried oregano
- 1 tbsp dried basil
- 1 can of 6oz tomato paste
- 1 can of 28oz crushed tomatoes
- 4 cloves garlic, minced
- 3 oz bacon, chopped
- ¼ cup chopped celery
- ½ cup chopped green sweet pepper
- ½ cup finely chopped carrot
- 1 cup chopped onion
- ½-lb. ground beef

Directions for Cooking:

1. Meat Sauce: In a medium pot placed on medium high fire, cook garlic, bacon, celery, sweet pepper, carrot, onion, and ground beef until ground meat is cooked. Ensure to break up the ground meat while sautéing. Remove from fire and drain fat.

2. Return the meat to pot and stir in black pepper, oregano, dried basil, tomato paste and tomatoes. For thirty minutes, let the mixture simmer while covered as you stir occasionally. After thirty minutes add oregano, basil and milk.

3. Assemble lasagna in a greased rectangular glass dish (as long as the lasagna). On the bottom of dish, add 1 cup of meat sauce and spread, top with 3 lasagna noodles, top again with meat sauce, noodles, noodles, meat sauce, noodles and the last of the sauce and cheese.

4. Cover the lasagna with tin foil and for thirty minutes bake in a pre-heated 350ºF oven. After that, remove foil, add more parmesan cheese and continue baking for another twenty minutes. Turn off the oven and allow lasagna to stand inside oven for another half hour. Remove from oven and serve.

Nutrition Information:

Calories per Serving: 230; Carbs: 26.6g; Protein: 13.5g; Fats: 7.6g; Saturated Fat: 1.7g; Sodium: 374mg

Serves: 6 , Cooking time: 20 minutes

Ingredients:

- 12 oz pasta, cooked and drained
- 1 cup finely shredded Parmesan Cheese
- ¼ cup snipped fresh basil
- ½ cup whipping cream
- 1 12oz jar roasted red sweet peppers, drained and chopped
- ¼ tsp crushed red pepper
- 6 cloves garlic, minced
- 1/3 cup finely chopped onion
- 1 tbsp olive oil
- 1 ½ lbs. fresh, peeled, deveined, rinsed and drained medium shrimps

Directions for Cooking:

1. On medium high fire, heat oil in a big fry pan and add garlic and onions. Stir fry until onions are soft, around two minutes. Add crushed red pepper and shrimps, sauté for another two minutes before adding roasted peppers.

2. Allow mixture to boil before lowering heat to low fire and for two minutes, let the mixture simmer uncovered. Stirring occasionally, add cream once shrimps are cooked and simmer for a minute.

3. Add basil and remove from fire. Toss in the pasta and mix gently. Transfer to serving plates and top with cheese.

Nutrition Information:

Calories per Serving: 501; Carbs: 77.0g; Protein: 18.6g; Fats: 14.7g; Saturated Fat: 6.0g; Sodium: 383mg

Prosciutto e Fagioli

Serves: 6 , Cooking time: 20 minutes

Ingredients:
- 12 oz pasta, cooked and drained
- Pepper to taste
- 3 tbsp snipped fresh chives
- 3 cups arugula or watercress leaves, loosely packed
- ½ cup chicken broth, warm
- ½ cup shredded pecorino toscano
- 4 oz prosciutto, cut into bite sizes
- 2 cups cherry tomatoes, halved
- 16-oz white kidney beans, rinsed and drained
- 1 tsp olive oil

Directions for Cooking:

1. Heat over medium low fire olive oil, cheese, prosciutto, tomatoes and beans in a big saucepan. Once mixture is simmering, stir constantly to melt cheese while gradually stirring in the broth. Once cheese is fully melted and incorporated, add chives, arugula, pepper and salt.
2. Turn off the fire and toss in the cooked pasta. Serve and enjoy.

Nutrition Information:
Calories per Serving: 404; Carbs: 64.1g; Protein: 22.1g; Fats: 7.4g; Saturated Fat: 2.5g; Sodium: 370mg

3-Kind Mushroom Lasagna

Serves: 12 , Cooking time: 1 hour 30 minutes

Ingredients:
- ½ cup grated Parmigiano-Reggiano cheese
- No boil lasagna noodles
- Cooking spray
- ¼ cup all-purpose flour
- 3 cups reduced fat milk, divided
- 2 tbsp chopped fresh chives, divided
- 1/3 cup less fat cream cheese
- 6 garlic cloves, minced and divided
- 1 ½ tbsp chopped fresh thyme
- ½ tsp freshly ground black pepper, divided
- 1 package 4 oz pre-sliced exotic mushroom blend
- 1 package 8oz pre-sliced cremini mushrooms
- 1 ¼ cups chopped shallots
- 2 tbsp olive oil, divided
- 1 oz dried porcini mushrooms
- 1 cup boiling water

Directions for Cooking:

1. For 30 minutes, submerge porcini in 1 cup boiling hot water. With a sieve, strain mushroom and reserve liquid.
2. Over medium high fire, heat 1 tbsp oil and for three minutes fry shallots. Add ¼ tsp pepper, exotic mushrooms and cremini, cook for six minutes. Stir in 3 garlic cloves and thyme, cook for a minute. Bring to a boil as your pour wine by increasing fire to high and cook until liquid evaporates around a minute. Turn off fire and stir in porcini mushrooms, 1 tbsp chives and cream cheese. Mix well.
3. On medium high fire, place a separate medium sized pan with 1 tbsp oil. Sauté for half a minute 3 garlic cloves. Then bring to a boil as you pour 2 ¾ cups milk and reserved porcini liquid. Season with remaining pepper and salt. In a separate bowl whisk together flour and ¼ cup milk and pour into pan. Stir constantly and cook until mixture thickens.
4. In a greased rectangular glass dish, pour and spread ½ cup of sauce, top with lasagna, top with half of mushroom mixture and another layer of lasagna. Repeat the layering process and instead of lasagna layer, end with the mushroom mixture and cover with cheese.
5. For 45 minutes, bake the lasagna in a preheated 350ºF oven. Garnish with chives before serving.

Nutrition Information:
Calories per Serving: 243; Carbs: 39.2g; Protein: 7.8g; Fats: 6.7g; Saturated Fat: 2.1g; Sodium: 328mg

Light and Creamy Mac 'N Cheese

Serves: 12 , Cooking time: 75 minutes

Ingredients:

- 2 tbsp chopped fresh parsley
- 1/4 cup panko
- 1 tsp olive oil
- Cooking spray
- 1 lb. uncooked cavatappi
- ¼ cup finely grated fresh Parmigiano-Reggiano cheese, divided
- 1 cup grated pecorino Romano cheese
- 1 ¼ cups shredded Gruyere cheese
- ½ tsp freshly ground black pepper
- 2 tbsp plain fat free Greek yogurt
- 2 garlic cloves, peeled
- 1 ½ cups fat free milk
- 1 ¼ cups fat free chicken broth
- 3 cups butternut squash, cubed and peeled

Directions for Cooking:

1. In a boiling pot of water, cook pasta according to manufacturer's instructions, drain and set aside.
2. On medium high fire, boil milk, broth and squash in a medium sized pan. Once boiling, reduce fire and allow mixture to simmer for 25 minutes or until squash is soft. Remove from fire and transfer to a blender and puree. Add Greek yogurt, pepper and salt. Continue to puree mixture until smooth.
3. Transfer squash mixture into a bowl and mix in 2 tbsp Parmigiano-Reggiano, pecorino Romano and Gruyere. Thoroughly mix.
4. Then add the pasta to the squash and cheese mixture. Mix well. Transfer into a greased 13x9 inch glass dish.
5. On medium fire, place a medium fry pan with oil and for two minutes fry panko. Turn off the fire and stir in the remaining Parmigiano-Reggiano. Quickly pour on top of pasta and coat lightly with cooking spray.
6. Place dish in a preheated 375ºF oven and bake for 25 minutes.
7. Garnish with parsley before serving.

Nutrition Information:

Calories per Serving: 273; Carbs: 36.8g; Protein: 11.7g; Fats: 9.4g; Saturated Fat: 5.2g; Sodium: 128mg

Chard and Ricotta Orecchiette

Serves: 8 , Cooking time: 35 minutes

Ingredients:

- Freshly grated pecorino cheese or ricotta salata
- Pepper
- ¼ cup fresh, low fat ricotta cheese
- ground nutmeg
- 2 oz ricotta salata, grated
- Crushed red pepper – optional
- 2 tbsp olive oil
- ¾ lb. dried orecchiette
- 1 large bunch rainbow swiss chard

Directions for Cooking:

1. In a boiling pot of water, boil Orecchiette for ten minutes.
2. Meanwhile, remove the stems from the chard leaves. After ten minutes of boiling the pasta, add the chard leaves and continue to boil for another two minutes before draining (ensure that you reserve ¼ cup of the liquid). Set Aside.
3. On medium high fire and a big fry pan with olive oil, sauté chard stems until tender and crisp around three to five minutes.
4. Then return pasta and chard leaves to the pot and cook on low fire. Add sautéed chard stem with oil and all, reserved cooking liquid, and crushed red pepper. Mix well.
5. Add nutmeg, pepper and grated ricotta salata and toss.
6. Remove from fire, transfer to serving bowls and top with more ricotta salata or pecorino cheese.

Nutrition Information:

Calories per Serving: 138; Carbs: 15.2g; Protein: 5.1g; Fats: 6.7g; Saturated Fat: 2.3g; Sodium: 225mg

Serves: 8 , Cooking time: minutes

Ingredients:

- 3.5 oz black olives, pitted and chopped
- 1 lemon juice
- 2 garlic cloves, crushed
- 2 tbsp olive oil
- 10 oz Smoked Salmon
- 1 bunch rocket
- 2 tbsp pine nuts
- 1 leek, sliced thinly
- 1-lb Whole wheat spaghetti

Directions for Cooking:

1. In a boiling pot of water. Once water is in a rolling boil, add pasta and cook following manufacturer's instructions. Drain and put aside.

2. Meanwhile on a fry pan, toast pine nuts until lightly browned. Remove from pan and put aside.

3. In same pan, heat oil and sauté for five minutes the leeks. Mix in garlic and continue sautéing for another two minutes. Turn off fire and stir in the smoked salmon, pine nuts, olives, rocket, lemon juice and pasta. Mix until well combined and serve.

Nutrition Information:

Calories per Serving: 291; Carbs: 45.5g; Protein: 15.1g; Fats: 7.0g; Saturated Fat: 1.1g; Sodium: 336mg

Serves: 8 , Cooking time: 40 minutes

Ingredients:

- 1 can Borlotti Bean, drained and rinsed
- 1 onion diced
- 2 tbsp olive oil
- 1 ½ cup vegetable stock
- ½ cup tomato sauce
- 2 cups collard greens chopped
- ¼ cup fresh parsley chopped
- 6 cloves garlic peeled, thinly sliced
- 1 box Barilla medium shells, 12-oz

Directions for Cooking:

1. Bring a big pot of water to a boil. Once boiling add the medium shells and cook for two minutes less than manufacturer's cooking instructions. Drain and set aside.

2. Meanwhile, in a separate pot, sauté onions and garlic in olive oil for seven to eight minutes or until onions are soft over medium fire.

3. Add collard greens and parsley and continue cooking for ten more minutes while pot is covered.

4. Add vegetable stock, tomato sauce and beans. Increase fire to high until mixture is boiling then put back to medium low and for 15 minutes allow to simmer while covered.

5. Add pepper to taste before pouring in the cooked pasta shells and simmering for ten minutes.

6. Remove from fire and serve.

Nutrition Information:

Calories per Serving: 262; Carbs: 48.8g; Protein: 7.4g; Fats: 5.3g; Saturated Fat: 0.7g; Sodium: 96mg

Ricotta and Spinach Ravioli

Serves: 6 , Cooking time: 30 minutes

Ingredients:
- 1 cup chicken stock
- 1 cup frozen spinach, thawed
- 1 batch pasta dough
- 3 tbsp heavy cream
- 1 cup ricotta
- 1 ¾ cups baby spinach
- 1 small onion, finely chopped
- 2 tbsp low fat butter

Directions for Cooking:
1. Create the filling: In a fry pan, sauté onion and butter around five minutes. Add the baby spinach leaves and continue simmering for another four minutes. Remove from fire, drain liquid and mince the onion and leaves. Then combine with 2 tbsp cream and the ricotta ensuring that it is well combined. Add pepper and salt to taste.
2. With your pasta dough, divide it into four balls. Roll out one ball to ¼ inch thick rectangular spread. Cut a 1 ½ inch by 3-inch rectangles. Place filling on the middle of the rectangles, around 1 tablespoonful and brush filling with cold water. Fold the rectangles in half, ensuring that no air is trapped within and seal using a cookie cutter. Use up all the filling.
3. Create Pasta Sauce: Until smooth, puree chicken stock and spinach. Pour into heated fry pan and for two minutes cook it. Add 1 tbsp cream and season with pepper and salt. Continue cooking for a minute and turn of fire.
4. Cook the raviolis by submerging in a boiling pot of water with salt. Cook until al dente then drain. Then quickly transfer the cooked ravioli into the fry pan of pasta sauce, toss to mix and serve.

Nutrition Information:
Calories per Serving: 192; Carbs: 17.9g; Protein: 10.0g; Fats: 9.4g; Saturated Fat: 5.4g; Sodium: 157mg

Spaghetti in Lemon Avocado White Sauce

Serves: 6 , Cooking time: 30 minutes

Ingredients:
- Freshly ground black pepper
- Zest and juice of 1 lemon
- 1 avocado, pitted and peeled
- 12-oz whole wheat spaghetti
- Pepper to taste
- 2 tbsp Olive oil
- 8 oz small shrimp, shelled and deveined
- 1 large onion, finely sliced
- 2 tbsp water

Directions for Cooking:
1. Let a big pot of water boil. Once boiling add the spaghetti or pasta and cook following manufacturer's instructions until al dente. Drain and set aside.
2. In a large fry pan, over medium fire sauté wine and onions for ten minutes or until onions are translucent and soft.
3. Add the shrimps into the fry pan and increase fire to high while constantly sautéing until shrimps are cooked around five minutes. Turn the fire off. Season with pepper and add the oil right away. Then quickly toss in the cooked pasta, mix well.
4. In a blender, until smooth, puree the lemon juice, water, and avocado. Pour into the fry pan of pasta, combine well. Garnish with pepper and lemon zest then serve.

Nutrition Information:
Calories per Serving: 340; Carbs: 49.0g; Protein: 17.0g; Fats: 10.7g; Saturated Fat: 1.6g; Sodium: 54mg

Chapter 8 Vegetarian Recipes

Herbed and Spiced Grilled Eggplant

Serves: 4 , Cooking time: 20 minutes

Ingredients:

- 1 large aubergine eggplant, around 1 ½ lbs.
- Pinch of ground cloves
- Pinch of ground nutmeg
- Pinch of ground ginger
- ½ tsp curry powder
- ½ tsp ground coriander
- ½ tsp ground cumin
- 1 tsp mustard seed
- 1 tbsp olive oil
- ½ yellow onion, finely chopped
- 1 tbsp chopped fresh cilantro
- 1 tsp red wine vinegar
- 1 garlic clove, minced
- 1 tbsp light molasses
- 2 cups cherry tomatoes, halved
- ¼ tsp freshly ground black pepper
- 1 tsp coconut aminos

Directions for Cooking:

1. Grease grill grate with cooking spray and preheat grill to high heat.
2. Trim eggplant and slice in ¼-inch thick lengthwise strips.
3. Grill strips of eggplant for 5 minutes per side or until browned and tender.
4. Remove eggplants from fire and keep warm.
5. In a small bowl, mix cloves, nutmeg, ginger, curry, coriander, cumin and mustard seed.
6. On medium high fire, place a medium nonstick skillet and heat oil.
7. Sauté spice mixture for 30 seconds and add onions.
8. Sauté onions for 4 minutes or until soft and translucent.
9. Add vinegar, garlic, molasses and tomatoes. Sauté for 4 minutes or until thickened.
10. Season with pepper and coconut aminos. Turn off fire.
11. On four plates, evenly divide grilled eggplant.
12. Evenly top each plate of eggplant with herbed and spiced sauce.
13. Serve and enjoy while warm.

Nutrition Information:

Calories per Serving: 102.3; Protein: 1.5g; Carbs: 12.6g; Fat: 5.1g; Saturated Fat: .7g; Sodium: 8mg

Roasted Vegetables with Polenta

Serves: 6 , Cooking time: 35 minutes

Ingredients:

- 1 sweet red pepper, seeded, cored and cut into chunks
- 6 medium mushrooms, sliced
- 1 small green zucchini, cut into ¼-inch slices
- 1 small yellow zucchini, cut into ¼-inch slices
- 1 small eggplant, peeled and cut into ¼-inch slices
- 10-oz frozen spinach, thawed
- 1 ½ cups coarse polenta
- 6 cups water
- ¼ tsp cracked black pepper
- 1 tbsp + 1 tsp extra virgin olive oil, divided
- 10 ripe olives, chopped
- 6 dry-packed sun-dried tomatoes, soaked in water to rehydrate, drained and chopped
- 2 Roma tomatoes, sliced
- 2 tsp oregano

Directions for Cooking:

1. Grease a baking sheet and a 12-inch round baking dish, position oven rack 4-inches away from heat source and preheat broiler.
2. Place red pepper, mushrooms, zucchini and eggplant in prepared baking sheet in a single layer. Pop in the broiler and broil under low setting.
3. Turn the veggies after 5 minutes. Continue broiling until veggies are slightly browned and tender, another 3 minutes.
4. Wash and drain spinach. Set aside.
5. Preheat oven to 350oF.
6. Bring water to a boil in a medium saucepan.
7. Whisk in polenta and lower fire to a simmer. For 5 minutes, cook and stir.

8. Once polenta no longer sticks to pan, add 1/8 tsp pepper and 1 tbsp olive oil. Mix well and turn off fire.
9. Evenly spread polenta on base of prepped baking dish. Brush tops with 1 tsp olive oil and for ten minutes bake in the oven.
10. When done, remove polenta from oven and keep warm.
11. With paper towels remove excess water from spinach. Layer spinach on top of polenta followed by sliced tomatoes, olives, sun-dried tomatoes, and roasted veggies. Season with remaining pepper and oregano.
12. Bake for another 10 minutes.
13. Remove from oven, cut into equal servings and enjoy.

Nutrition Information:
Calories per Serving: 72.7; Protein: 3.9g; Carbs: 11.8g; Fat: 1.1g; Saturated Fat: .2g; Sodium: 114mg

American Cheese Over Herbed Portobello Mushrooms

Serves: 2 , Cooking time: 10 minutes
Ingredients:
- 2 Portobello mushrooms, stemmed and wiped clean
- 1 tsp minced garlic
- ¼ tsp dried rosemary
- 1 tbsp brown sugar
- ½ cup balsamic vinegar
- ¼ cup grated non-fat American cheese

Directions for Cooking:
1. In oven, position rack 4-inches away from the top and preheat broiler.
2. Prepare a baking dish by spraying with cooking spray lightly.
3. Stemless, place mushroom gill side up.
4. Mix well garlic, rosemary, brown sugar and vinegar in a small bowl.
5. Drizzle over mushrooms equally.
6. Marinate for at least 5 minutes before popping into the oven and broiling for 4 minutes per side or until tender.
7. Once cooked, remove from oven, sprinkle cheese, return to broiler and broil for a minute or two or until cheese melts.
8. Remove from oven and serve right away.

Nutrition Information:
Calories per Serving: 131.2; Protein: 8.7g; Carbs: 19.6; Fat: 2g; Saturated Fat: .9g; Sodium: 342mg

Red Lentil and Cauliflower Curry

Serves: 4 , Cooking time: 40 minutes
Ingredients:
- 1 ½ cups water
- 2/3 cup red lentils
- 1 tsp whole mustard seed
- 1 tsp whole cumin seed
- 1 tsp whole coriander seed
- 3 whole cardamom pods
- 1 tsp avocado oil
- 1/2 cup sliced shallot
- 1 ½ tbsp minced ginger
- 1 serrano pepper, seeds removed and diced
- 2 cloves garlic, minced
- 3 large ripe tomatoes, chopped
- 1 ½ cups peeled and chopped golden potato or sweet potato, ½-inch cubes
- 1 cup chopped cauliflower
- 1 cup chopped red bell pepper
- 1 tsp curry powder
- 1 ½ cups low sodium vegetable broth
- 2 tbsp coconut aminos
- 1 packet stevia
- 1/2 cup almond milk

Directions for Cooking:
1. In a small pot, bring water to a boil and add lentil. Cook uncovered until just tender, around 9 minutes. Drain and set aside.
2. Place a large nonstick pot on medium flame and toast mustard, cumin, coriander, and cardamom pods for 2 to 3 minutes or until fragrant and popping.
3. In same pot, add oil and swirl to coat pot. Stir in shallot, ginger, pepper, and garlic. Sauté for 5 minutes until shallots are soft and translucent.
4. Stir in chopped tomatoes. Cook for 5 minutes.
5. Add sweet potatoes and continue sautéing for 7 minutes until tomatoes are pureed looking.

If needed add a tablespoon of water to deglaze pot.

6. Stir in cauliflower, bell pepper, curry powder, coconut aminos, drained lentil, and stevia. Mix well and cook for 5 minutes.
7. Add vegetable broth and bring to a simmer. Continue cooking for 5 minutes or until veggies are tender.

8. Turn off fire and stir in almond milk.
9. Serve and enjoy.

Nutrition Information:
Calories per Serving: 234.6; Protein: 11.8g; Carbs: 39.2g; Fat: 3.4g; Saturated Fat: .5g; Sodium: 105mg

Crispy Crusted Cauliflower Steaks

Serves: 4 , Cooking time: 40 minutes
Ingredients:
- 1 large head cauliflower (or sub 2 small for 1 large)
- 1 cup unsweetened almond milk
- 1 tbsp lemon juice
- 1 tsp liquid aminos
- 1 ½ cups raw cashews
- 1/4 tsp cayenne pepper
- 3/4 tsp garlic powder
- 1 ½ tsp curry powder
- 1 ½ tsp smoked paprika
- 3 tbsp cornstarch

Directions for Cooking:
1. Prepare a baking sheet and place a stainless-steel rack on top. Lightly grease with cooking spray and preheat oven to 350oF.
2. Cut the cauliflower into ¾-inch thickness like a steak.

3. In a medium shallow bowl, whisk well almond milk, lemon juice and coconut aminos. Soak cauliflower steaks. Turning over once in a while.
4. Meanwhile, in a food processor, process the remaining ingredients until it resembles a coarse powder. Transfer to a large shallow dish.
5. Dip and coat cauliflower steaks in cashew powder. Transfer to prepared rack.
6. Bake cauliflower steaks for 40 minutes or until crisp tender.
7. Serve and enjoy.

Nutrition Information:
Calories per Serving: 503.4; Protein: 15g; Carbs: 37.5g; Fat: 32.6g; Saturated Fat: 5.9g; Sodium: 73mg

Quesadillas with a Pear-Twist

Serves: 4 , Cooking time: 15 minutes
Ingredients:
- 4 medium whole wheat tortillas
- 2 tbsp minced onion
- ½ cup finely chopped green peppers
- 1 cup fresh pear, cubed
- 1 cup grated low sodium cheddar cheese

Directions for Cooking:
1. On a clean cutting board, lay two tortillas. You may also use two plates depending on your preference.
2. In each tortilla, place or spread ¼ cheese then divide the onions, peppers, and pears between the two tortillas.
3. Spread the remaining cheese onto the 2 tortillas then top off with the remaining two other tortillas.

4. On medium heat, place a pan and cook for 3 minutes the first quesadilla. Once the bottom begins to turn brown, gently turn it to cook the other side for another 3 minutes until cheese is melted and tortilla is crisped.
5. Slide onto plate then cook the other or second quesadilla.
6. Once all quesadillas are cooked, cut each into 4 pieces and they are ready to serve.

Nutrition Information:
Calories per Serving: 280; Protein: 11.1g; Carbs: 31.2g; Fat: 13.0g; Saturated Fat: 7.6g; Sodium: 311mg

Stir-Fried Brussels Sprouts Korean Style

Serves: 8 , Cooking time: 15 minutes

Ingredients:

- 1/2 cup Korean Gochujang Sauce
- 1 tsp sesame oil
- 2 tsp coconut aminos, divided
- 1 tbsp maple syrup
- 2 - 3 tbsp water
- 7 heaped cups halved Brussels sprouts
- 1 stalk green onion, chopped

Directions for Cooking:

1. In a small bowl, whisk well gochujang sauce, sesame oil, 1 tsp coconut aminos, and maple syrup. Mix well and set aside.
2. Place a large nonstick saucepan on medium high fire.
3. Add Brussels sprouts and water. Cover and cook for 5 minutes.
4. Stir fry Brussels sprouts until water is fully evaporated.
5. Mix in sauce and stir fry until heated through and Brussels sprouts are crisp tender. If needed, add another tbsp of water to continue cooking.
6. Serve and enjoy.

Nutrition Information:

Calories per Serving: 58; Protein: 2.9g; Carbs: 9.8g; Fat: .8g; Saturated Fat: 1g; Sodium: 136mg

Pan-Fried Kale Falafel

Serves: 4 , Cooking time: 15 minutes

Ingredients:

- 4 large cloves garlic, peeled
- 3 tbsp fresh lemon juice
- 1 tsp coconut aminos
- 4 cups loosely packed kale, stems removed and torn
- 1 15-ounce can chickpeas, rinsed well and drained
- 1 ½ tbsp tahini
- 1/2 tsp ground cumin
- 1/3 cup oat flour
- 1 tbsp olive oil

Directions for Cooking:

1. In a blender, add garlic, lemon juice, and coconut aminos. Puree until smooth and creamy or garlic are chopped finely.
2. Add kale and blend until finely chopped, but not creamy.
3. Add chickpeas, tahini and cumin. Blend well until chickpeas finely crumbled.
4. With a spatula, scrape the side of blender. And blend one last time.
5. Transfer to a bowl. Fold in oat flour.
6. Evenly divide batter into 4. Form into a ¼ to ½-inch thick patty.
7. On medium low fire, place a large nonstick pan and heat oil. Swirl oil to coat pan. After 2 minutes of heating add the patties and cook for 3 to 4 minutes per side or until golden brown. Flip and cook the other side.
8. Serve and enjoy.

Nutrition Information:

Calories per Serving: 296.2; Protein: 11.9g; Carbs: 38.3g; Fat: 10.6g; Saturated Fat: 1.3g; Sodium: 319mg

Easy-Peasy Balsamic Brussels Sprouts

Serves: 2 , Cooking time: 15 minutes

Ingredients:

- 1 tablespoon balsamic vinegar
- 2 cups Brussels sprouts, halved
- 1 tablespoon olive oil

Directions for Cooking:

1. Place a medium nonstick saucepan on medium fire and heat pan for 2 minutes.
2. Add 1 tbsp oil and heat.
3. Stir in Brussels sprouts and sauté for 5 minutes.
4. Stir in balsamic and toss well to mix.
5. Cover and cook for another 5 minutes until tender.
6. Serve and enjoy.

Nutrition Information:

Calories per Serving: 112.2; Carbs: 9.3g; Protein: 3g; Fats: 7g; Saturated Fat: 1g; Sodium: 24mg

Serves: 2 , Cooking time: 40 minutes

Ingredients:

- a dollop of vegan cream cheese
- a dollop of vegan butter
- 1/8 teaspoon salt
- 1 teaspoon olive oil
- 1 tablespoon Kalamata olives
- 1 tablespoon chives, chopped
- 1 medium russet potato, scrubbed and peeled
- ¼ teaspoon onion powder

Directions for Cooking:

1. Boil potatoes in a pot of water for 30 minutes. Remove from pot, place on a baking sheet and broil on low for 5 minutes per side.

2. Remove from oven and place on serving plates.
3. Heat oil in a large skillet and sauté the garlic for 2 minutes. Add the kale until it wilts. Transfer to a large bowl.
4. Add olive oil, onion powder, and vegan butter. Mix well.
5. Top the potatoes with chives, olives, cream cheese, and the creamy kale.
6. Enjoy!

Nutrition Information:

Calories per Serving: 252.8; Carbs: 34.2g; Protein: 4.7g; Fats: 10.8g; Saturated Fat: 5.4g; Sodium: 274mg

Serves: 2 , Cooking time: 10 minutes

Ingredients:

- Pepper to taste
- 1 vegan pizza dough
- 1 shallot, julienned
- 1 cup mushrooms, sliced thinly
- ½ red bell pepper, julienned
- ¼ tsp Italian seasoning
- ¼ cup pizza sauce
- ¼ cup cheese

Directions for Cooking:

1. Preheat oven to 400ºF and lightly grease a baking sheet with cooking spray.

2. Slice the pizza dough into squares. Set aside.
3. In a mixing bowl, mix together the oyster mushroom, shallot, bell pepper and parsley.
4. Season with pepper to taste.
5. Place the topping on top of the pizza squares.
6. Place pizza squares on baking sheet an inch apart. Bake for 12 minutes in the oven.
7. Serve and enjoy.

Nutrition Information:

Calories per Serving: 222; Carbs: 26.0g; Protein: 8.8g; Fats: 9.4g; Saturated Fat: 2.5g; Sodium: 238 mg

Serves: 4 , Cooking time: 20 minutes

Ingredients:

- pepper to taste
- 3 tablespoon plain flour
- 2 teaspoons thyme
- 2 teaspoons parsley
- 2 teaspoons garlic, minced
- 2 teaspoons coconut oil melted
- 2 teaspoons chives
- 1 teaspoon mustard powder
- 1 flax egg (1 flaxseed egg + 3 tablespoon water)
- 1 cup breadcrumbs
- ½ pound cauliflower, steamed and diced
- ½ cup oats
- ¼ cup desiccated coconut

Directions for Cooking:

1. Preheat oven to 400ºF.
2. Place an oven safe wire rack on top of a baking sheet and lightly grease wire rack with cooking spray.
3. Place the cauliflower in a tea towel and ring out excess water. Place in a mixing bowl and add all ingredients except the breadcrumbs. Mix well until well combined.
4. Form 8 burger patties with the mixture using your hands.

5. Roll the patties in breadcrumbs and place on the wire rack.
6. Cook for 10 minutes. Turn over patties and cook for another 5 to 10 minutes or until lightly browned and crisp.

7. Serve and enjoy.

Nutrition Information:
Calories per Serving: 121; Carbs: 17.4g; Protein: 4.3g; Fats: 3.8g; Saturated Fat: 2.3g; Sodium: 49mg

Veggie Stir Fry

Serves: 3 , Cooking time: 6 minutes

Ingredients:
- 1 ½ teaspoon avocado oil
- 1 white onion, chopped
- 2 carrots, peeled and julienned
- 1 chayote, peeled and julienned
- 1 red bell pepper, deseeded and julienned
- ½ small head of cabbage, cut into strips
- A dash of salt
- ¼ tsp pepper

Directions for Cooking:
1. Heat oil in a nonstick skillet over medium-high flame and sauté the onion until fragrant.

2. Stir in chayote and sauté for 3 minutes. Add carrots and coo for another 3 minutes.
3. Add bell pepper and cook for 3 minutes.
4. Stir in cabbage and sauté for a minute. Season with salt and pepper.
5. Continue stirring for 4 minutes until the vegetables are done.
6. Serve and enjoy while hot.

Nutrition Information:
Calories per Serving: 91; Carbs: 16.8g; Protein: 2.9g; Fats: 2.7g; Saturated Fat: 0.4g; Sodium: 57mg

Broccoli 'n Quinoa Casserole

Serves: 3 , Cooking time: 30 minutes

Ingredients:
- 1 cup cooked quinoa
- 1 cup broccoli florets, chopped
- ½ tsp pepper
- A dash of salt
- 1 cup almond milk
- 1 clove of garlic, minced
- 1 slice of whole wheat bread, cubed

Directions for Cooking:
1. Place all ingredients in a casserole dish and mix until well-combined.

2. Allow to set in the fridge for at least 2 hours for the bread to soak in the milk.
3. Preheat the oven to 350°F.
4. Bake the casserole for 30 minutes or until the tops become golden brown.

Nutrition Information:
Calories per Serving: 136; Carbs: 24.8g; Protein: 5.0g; Fats: 2.2g; Saturated Fat: 0.3g; Sodium: 74mg

Bean 'n Avocado Burrito

Serves: 1 , Cooking time: 2 minutes

Ingredients:
- 1 large whole wheat tortilla
- ½ cup red kidney beans, rinsed and drained
- 2 romaine lettuce leaves
- ½ avocado, peeled and sliced
- 1 tablespoon lime juice
- A sprig of cilantro, chopped

Directions for Cooking:
1. Lay the tortilla wrap on a flat surface.

2. Place the beans, lettuce leaves, and avocado in the middle of the wrap.
3. Sprinkle with salt and drizzle with lime juice.
4. Put the chopped cilantro last before rolling the burrito.

Nutrition Information:
Calories per Serving: 400; Carbs: 48.6g; Protein: 13.1g; Fats: 19.3g; Saturated Fat: 3.4g; Sodium: 371mg

Healthy Curried Tofu

Serves: 6 , Cooking time: 15 minutes

Ingredients:

- 1 tablespoon olive oil
- 2 cloves of garlic, minced
- 1 onion, cubed
- 12-ounce firm tofu, drained and cubed
- 1 teaspoon curry powder
- 1 tablespoon lemon juice
- ¼ teaspoon red pepper flakes
- 1 tablespoon soy sauce

Directions for Cooking:

1. Heat the oil in a skillet over medium flame.
2. Sauté the garlic and onion until fragrant.
3. Stir in the tofu and stir for 3 minutes.
4. Add the rest of the ingredients and adjust the water.
5. Close the lid and allow simmering for 10 minutes.

Nutrition Information:

Calories per Serving: 90; Carbs: 4.4g; Protein: 6.2g; Fats: 6.1g; Saturated Fat: 2.1g; Sodium: 46mg

Vegan Quinoa Salad

Serves: 4 , Cooking time: 15 minutes

Ingredients:

- 1 cup uncooked quinoa, rinsed
- 2 cups water
- 1 can chickpeas, rinsed and drained
- 1 cucumber, seeded and chopped
- 1 red bell pepper, chopped
- ¾ cup red onion, chopped
- 1 cup flat-leaf parsley, chopped
- 2 tbsp olive oil
- ¼ cup lemon juice, freshly squeezed
- 2 cloves of garlic, minced
- ½ tsp black pepper

Directions for Cooking:

1. Place quinoa and water in a pot and bring to a boil. Adjust the heat to medium and allow simmering for 15 minutes until quinoa is cooked. Turn off the heat and allow to rest until cool. Once cool enough, fluff the quinoa with a fork.
2. In a mixing bowl, put the quinoa, chickpeas, cucumber, red pepper, onion, and parsley.
3. In a small bowl, combine the olive oil, lemon juice, garlic, and pepper.
4. Pour over the quinoa mixture.
5. Stir gently to coat the quinoa with the dressing.

Nutrition Information:

Calories per Serving: 339.4; Carbs: 47.3g; Protein: 11.9g; Fats: 11.4g; Saturated Fat: 1.4g; Sodium: 172mg

Black Bean and Couscous Salad

Serves: 4 , Cooking time: 15 minutes

Ingredients:

- 1 cup couscous, uncooked
- 1 ¼ cups water
- 2 tablespoons extra virgin olive oil
- 1 teaspoon lemon juice
- ½ teaspoon ground cumin
- 8 stalks of green onion, chopped
- 1 red bell pepper, seeded and chopped
- ¼ cup fresh cilantro, chopped
- 1 cup corn kernels, fresh
- 2 cans black beans, rinsed and drained well
- Pepper to taste

Directions for Cooking:

1. Put the couscous and water in a pot and bring to a boil. Once the water has boiled, reduce the heat to medium-low. Cook for 15 minutes. Once cooked, drain the excess liquid and allow to cool.
2. Meanwhile, mix the olive oil, lemon juice, and cumin in a small bowl. Set aside.
3. Assemble the salad by putting the couscous and the rest of the ingredients into a bowl. Mix gently and pour over the sauce.
4. Season with pepper to taste.

Nutrition Information:

Calories per Serving: 224; Carbs: 37.9g; Protein: 10.6g; Fats: 4.2g; Saturated Fat: 0.7g; Sodium: 356mg

Marinated Tofu Salad

Serves: 4 , Cooking time: 25 minutes

Ingredients:

- 3 tbsp olive oil
- 2 tablespoons lemon juice
- A dash of salt and pepper
- 1 teaspoon dried basil
- ½ teaspoon dried oregano
- 12-ounce firm tofu, cut into cubes
- 2 tablespoons capers
- 1 head lettuce, wash and torn
- 10 cherry tomatoes, halved
- ¼ red onion, sliced thinly

Directions for Cooking:

1. In a bowl, whisk together the olive oil, lemon juice, salt, pepper, dried basil, and oregano. Reserve half of the mixture for the salad dressing.

2. Marinate the tofu cubes for at least 3 hours inside the fridge.
3. Preheat the oven to 350⁰F.
4. Place the marinated tofu in a baking dish greased with oil.
5. Bake in the oven for25 minutes, stirring halfway through the cooking time for even cooking.
6. Allow to cool before assembling the salad.
7. To assemble the salad, toss the baked tofu and the rest of the ingredients.
8. Drizzle with the reserved sauce.

Nutrition Information:

Calories per Serving: 282.3; Carbs: 14.5g; Protein: 15.8g; Fats: 17.9g; Saturated Fat: 2.5g; Sodium: 133mg

Vegan Buddha Bowl

Serves: 4 , Cooking time: 25 minutes

Ingredients:

- 1 medium sweet potato, peeled and cut into chunks
- 2 tablespoons extra virgin olive oil, divided
- ½ teaspoon ground pepper, divided
- 2 tablespoons tahini
- 2 tablespoons water
- 1 tablespoon lemon juice
- 1 clove of garlic, minced
- 1 cup cooked quinoa
- 1 can chickpeas, rinsed and drained
- 1 ripe avocado, diced
- ¼ cup cilantro, chopped

Directions for Cooking:

1. Preheat the oven to 3500F.
2. In a mixing bowl, mix the sweet potato chunks, half of the olive oil, and half of the

pepper. Toss to combine and place on a baking sheet.
3. Bake the potatoes in the oven for 25 minutes.
4. Meanwhile, mix the sauce in a bowl the remaining oil, pepper, tahini, water, lemon juice, and garlic. Set aside.
5. Once the sweet potatoes are cooked, assemble the Buddha bowl.
6. Place the cooked quinoa in a bowl and top with chickpeas, avocado, and baked sweet potatoes.
7. Pour over the sauce and sprinkle with cilantro.

Nutrition Information:

Calories per Serving: 344; Carbs: 37.8g; Protein: 9.5g; Fats: 17.2g; Saturated Fat: 2.3g; Sodium: 242mg

Stir Fried Gingered Vegetable

Serves: 6 , Cooking time: 15 minutes

Ingredients:

- 1 head broccoli, cut into florets
- 1.5-oz can water chestnuts, drained
- 1 Chinese eggplant, cut into ½-inch slices
- 1 zucchini, cut into large wedges
- 4 garlic cloves, smashed, peeled, and minced
- 1 yellow bell pepper, cut into large chunks
- 1 red bell pepper, cut into large chunks

- 1 onion, cut into large chunks
- 2 tbsp vegetable oil
- 1 tbsp ginger, grated
- 2 tbsp sriracha, or to taste
- 2 tbsp cornstarch
- 2 tbsp brown sugar
- 2 tbsp low-sodium soy sauce

Directions for Cooking:

1. Place a large saucepan on high fire and heat pan for 3 minutes.
2. Meanwhile, in a medium bowl mix well ginger, sriracha, cornstarch, brown sugar, brandy, and soy sauce. Set aside.
3. Once hot add oil and stir to coat pot. Add garlic and cook for a minute.
4. Add bell peppers and onion. Sauté for 2 minutes.
5. Add eggplant and zucchini. Stir fry for 3 minutes.
6. Add broccoli and chestnuts. Stir fry for 2 minutes.
7. Pour in the ginger mixture and toss well to coat.
8. Continue cooking vegetables for another 5 minutes or until desired tenderness is reached. If sauce gets too thick, add a splash of water and stir well to mix.
9. Transfer to bowls and sprinkle with sesame seeds before enjoying.

Nutrition Information:
Calories per Serving: 43.2; Carbs: 14.4g; Protein: 2.1g; Fats: 4.8g; Saturated Fat: 3.7g; Sodium: 175mg

Stir Fried Peas and Cabbage

Serves: 3 , Cooking time: 15 minutes

Ingredients:

- ¼ tsp cayenne pepper or to taste
- 1 tsp coriander
- ¼ tsp turmeric
- 1 tomato medium sized, chopped
- 4 garlic cloves, smashed, peeled, and minced
- ½ tsp mustard seeds
- 1 tbsp oil
- 1/2 cup green peas, frozen
- 1 cabbage medium sized, chopped

Directions for Cooking:

1. Place a nonstick saucepan on medium high fire and heat for 3 minutes.
2. Add oil and swirl to coat bottom of pot.
3. Add garlic and sesame seeds. Sauté for a minute.
4. Add cayenne pepper, coriander, turmeric, and chopped tomato. Sauté for 2 minutes.
5. Add peas. Cook for a minute.
6. Add cabbage. Toss well to mix. Continue to stir fry for 8 minutes, until cabbage is wilted.
7. Serve and enjoy.

Nutrition Information:
Calories per Serving: 45.9; Carbs: 9g; Protein: 2.5g; Fats: 5.1g; Saturated Fat: 1g; Sodium: 91mg

Sautéed Portobello in Balsamic Sauce

Serves: 2 , Cooking time: 12 minutes

Ingredients:

- Pepper to taste
- 3 tbsp balsamic vinegar
- 1 lb. fresh Portobello mushrooms, sliced
- 3 garlic cloves, crushed and minced
- 1 tbsp extra virgin olive oil

Directions for Cooking:

1. Place a nonstick saucepan on medium high fire and heat for 3 minutes.
2. Add oil and swirl to coat bottom of pot.
3. Add garlic and cook for a minute.
4. Add mushrooms and season with pepper.
5. Sauté for 10 minutes or until mushrooms are soft and have changed color. Turn off fire.
6. Pour in balsamic vinegar and white wine if using.
7. Toss well to coat and mix. Let it sit in the pot for another minute or two.
8. Transfer to a serving bowl and enjoy.

Nutrition Information:
Calories per Serving: 150.3; Carbs: 17.8g; Protein: 8.3g; Fats: 5.1g; Saturated Fat: .6g; Sodium: 93mg

Blended Spice on Sautéed Brussels Sprouts

Serves: 3 , Cooking time: 15 minutes

Ingredients:

- Pepper and salt to taste
- ½ tbsp cayenne pepper
- 1 tbsp smoked paprika
- 1 tsp onion powder
- 2 tsp Garlic powder
- 1 tsp red pepper flakes
- 1 tbsp chopped almonds
- 1 tsp olive oil
- 1 tbsp rice vinegar
- 2 tbsp sriracha sauce
- 1 tbs coconut aminos
- 2 lbs. Brussels sprouts, halved

Directions for Cooking:

1. Place a nonstick saucepan on medium high fire and heat for 3 minutes.
2. Add oil and swirl to coat bottom of pot.
3. Add almonds and cook for 2 minutes.
4. Meanwhile, in a small bowl combine all spices, sesame oil, vinegar, sriracha sauce, and coconut aminos. Mix well.
5. Stir in Brussels sprouts. Sauté for 5 minutes.
6. Pour in spiced sauce from step 3 and toss well to coat. Continue sautéing for another 5 minutes or until sprouts are to desired tenderness.
7. Serve and enjoy.

Nutrition Information:
Calories per Serving: 216.4; Carbs: 34.9g; Protein: 12g; Fats: 3.2g; Saturated Fat: .5g; Sodium: 171mg

Nutritious Stir-Fried Green Beans

Serves: 4 , Cooking time: 15 minutes

Ingredients:

- Pepper to taste
- 3 cloves garlic, minced
- 1 tsp olive oil
- 1 tbsp water
- 1 tbsp oyster sauce
- 1 tbsp rice vinegar
- 1-lb green beans, cut into 2-inch length slices
- 1 tbsp cilantro, chopped, optional

Directions for Cooking:

1. Place a nonstick saucepan on medium high fire and heat for 3 minutes.
2. Add oil and swirl to coat bottom of pot.
3. Meanwhile, in a small bowl mix well water, oyster sauce, and rice vinegar. Set aside.
4. Add garlic and sauté for a minute.
5. Add beans and stir fry for 4 minutes.
6. Pour in sauce and toss well to coat. Continue tossing around while cooking for another 2 minutes.
7. Add pepper and chopped cilantro if using. Toss well and heat for a minute.
8. Transfer to serving bowls and enjoy.

Nutrition Information:
Calories per Serving: 54.9; Carbs: 7.3g; Protein: 1.7g; Fats: 2.1g; Saturated Fat: .3g; Sodium: 127mg

Steamed Mixed and Fresh Vegetables

Serves: 4 , Cooking time: 10 minutes

Ingredients:

- 1 head broccoli, cut into florets
- 1 head cauliflower, cut into florets
- A handful of French beans, cut into 1-inch lengths
- 1 yellow squash, rinsed
- 1 tsp pepper
- Rice wine vinegar, dipping sauce

Directions for Cooking:

1. Place a steamer on medium high fire and fill 2-inches with water. Bring to a boil.
2. In steamer basket, add squash. Steam for 4 minutes.
3. Add remaining vegetables and season with pepper.
4. Steam for 5 minutes.
5. Serve and enjoy with rice wine vinegar.

Nutrition Information:
Calories per Serving: 109.1; Carbs: 18.2g; Protein: 6.6g; Fats: 1.1g; Saturated Fat: .2g; Sodium: 251mg

Steamed Garlic-y Broccol-y

Serves: 2 , Cooking time: 5 minutes

Ingredients:

- 1 head of broccoli, cut into florets
- 2 cloves of garlic, with peel and smashed
- Pepper to taste
- 1 cup of water

Directions for Cooking:

1. Place a steamer on medium high fire and fill 2-inches with water. Add garlic and bring to a boil.
2. In steamer basket, add broccoli. Steam for 4 minutes.
3. Serve and enjoy with a sprinkle of pepper.

Nutrition Information:

Calories per Serving: 147.1; Carbs: 23.3g; Protein: 9.2g; Fats: 1.9g; Saturated Fat: .2g; Sodium: 105mg

Stewed Spicy Cannellini Beans

Serves: 8 , Cooking time: 60 minutes

Ingredients:

- 1-pound dried cannellini beans, soaked overnight and rinsed
- 1 onion, halved
- 1 bulb garlic, minced
- 1 fennel bulb, sliced
- 1 carrot, peeled then chopped
- 4 sprigs of thyme
- 2 dried chilies
- 1 tsp olive oil
- 6 cups low sodium vegetable broth
- Pepper to taste

Directions for Cooking:

1. Place a heavy bottomed pot on medium high fire and heat pot for 3 minutes.
2. Meanwhile rinse and drain beans.
3. Once hot, add oil and stir around to coat pot with oil.
4. Add onions, garlic, fennel bulb, chilies, and beans. Sauté for 5 minutes.
5. Add broth and season with pepper.
6. Cover, bring to a boil, boil for 10 minutes, lower fire to a simmer and simmer for another 10 minutes.
7. Turn off fire, stir in thyme and let it sit for 30 minutes to soften beans.
8. Turn on fire and bring pot to a boil and turn off.
9. Serve and enjoy.

Nutrition Information:

Calories per Serving: 81.1; Carbs: 13.9g; Protein: 3g; Fats: 1.5g; Saturated Fat: .3g; Sodium: 127mg

Hearty Italian Bean Stew

Serves: 9 , Cooking time: 60 minutes

Ingredients:

- 1 tbsp olive oil
- 4 cloves of garlic, chopped
- ½ teaspoon red pepper flakes
- 2 medium carrots, chopped
- 2 stalks of celery, chopped
- 1 leek white part, chopped
- 3 roma tomatoes, chopped
- 3 cans cannellini beans, rinsed
- 1 bay leaf
- 1 sprig thyme
- 5 cups vegetable broth, low sodium
- Pepper to taste
- 1 bunch collard greens, chopped
- ½ cup low fat parmesan cheese, grated

Directions for Cooking:

1. Place a heavy bottomed pot on medium high fire and heat pot for 3 minutes.
2. Meanwhile rinse and drain beans.
3. Once hot, add oil and stir around to coat pot with oil.
4. Add garlic, red pepper flakes, leek, bay leaf, tomatoes, and beans. Sauté for 5 minutes.
5. Add broth and season with pepper.
6. Cover, bring to a boil, boil for 10 minutes, lower fire to a simmer and simmer for another 10 minutes.
7. Turn off fire, stir in thyme, celery and carrots. Let it sit for 30 minutes to soften beans.
8. Turn on fire and bring pot to a boil. Add collard greens and simmer for 5 minutes.
9. Serve and enjoy with a sprinkle of parmesan.

Nutrition Information:

Calories per Serving: 76.7; Carbs: 8g; Protein: 3.3g; Fats: 3.5g; Saturated Fat: 1.3g; Sodium: 394mg

3-Bean Cilantro Salad

Serves: 6 , Cooking time: 60 minutes

Ingredients:

- 1 cup black beans, soaked in water overnight
- 1 cup kidney beans, soaked in water overnight
- 1 cup red beans, soaked in water overnight
- 6 cups low-sodium vegetable stock
- Pepper to taste
- 1 teaspoon oregano
- 5 plum tomatoes, chopped
- ½ red onion chopped
- 2 serrano chilies, chopped
- ½ cup cilantro leaves, chopped
- ¼ cup olive oil

Directions for Cooking:

1. Place a pot on medium high fire and add broth.
2. Meanwhile rinse and drain beans well and add to the pot of water. Season with pepper.
3. Bring to a boil and boil for 10 minutes. Cover, lower fire to a simmer and simmer for 10 minutes.
4. Turn off fire and let beans sit for at least 30 minutes or until soft and tender. If needed, boil again for another 10 minutes.
5. Drain beans and allow to cool completely.
6. In a large bowl, whisk well remaining ingredients. Add cooled beans and toss well to coat.
7. Refrigerate for at least 30 minutes to allow flavors to meld.
8. Serve and enjoy

Nutrition Information:

Calories per Serving: 417.4; Carbs: 59.6g; Protein: 17.3g; Fats: 12.2g; Saturated Fat: 2.2g; Sodium: 154mg

Chapter 9 Poultry Recipes

Tummy-Warming Chicken Casserole

Serves: 6 , Cooking time: 45 minutes
Ingredients:

- 4 garlic cloves, crushed and peeled
- ¼ cup jalapeno pepper slices (optional)
- 1 cup chopped Poblano pepper
- 1 cup chopped red bell pepper
- 1 tbsp cumin
- 1 tbsp chili powder
- 1 (15 ounces) can black beans (no salt added, drained, and rinsed)
- 1 cup frozen yellow corn kernels
- 2 (14.5 ounces) cans tomatoes (no salt added, diced or crushed)
- 1 ½ cups cooked brown rice
- 1-pound skinless, boneless chicken breast, and cut into bite-sized pieces

Directions for Cooking:
1. Ensure to preheat first the oven to 400ºF.
2. In a bowl, combine garlic, peppers, seasonings, beans, corns, and tomatoes.
3. Then in shallow 3-quart casserole, spread the rice topped with chicken.
4. Pour over chicken casserole the garlic mixture and bake for 45 minutes.
5. Remove from oven and let it stand for 10 minutes.
6. Enjoy!

Nutrition Information:
Calories per Serving: 410; Protein: 28.9g; Carbs: 63.3g; Fat: 4.6g; Saturated Fat: .9g; Sodium: 84mg

Baked Chicken Pesto

Serves: 4 , Cooking time: 25 minutes
Ingredients:

- 2 small boneless, skinless chicken breast halves
- 4 tsp basil pesto
- 4 tsp grated parmesan cheese
- 6 tbsp shredded reduced fat mozzarella cheese
- 2 medium tomato (thinly sliced)

Directions for Cooking:
1. In cold water, wash chicken and dry using a paper towel. Create 4 thin slices out of chicken breasts by slicing horizontally.
2. In 400 º Fahrenheit, preheat oven then line a baking sheet with foil.
3. Put into the baking sheet the slices of chicken and spread at least 1 teaspoon of pesto on each chicken slice.
4. For 15 minutes, bake the chicken and ensure that the center is no longer pink. After which remove the baking sheet from the oven and top the chicken with parmesan cheese, mozzarella, and tomatoes.
5. Put into oven once again and heat for another 5 minutes to melt the cheese
6. Serve and enjoy.

Nutrition Information:
Calories per Serving: 163; Protein: 23.9g; Carbs: 3.26g; Fat: 5.9g; Saturated Fat: 1.3g; Sodium: 468mg

Avocado-Orange Grilled Chicken

Serves: 4 , Cooking time: 15 minutes
Ingredients:

- 1 tbsp honey
- 2 tbsp chopped cilantro
- ¼ cup minced red onion
- 1 cup low fat yogurt
- 1-lb boneless, skinless chicken breasts
- ½ tsp pepper
- ¼ tsp salt
- ¼ cup fresh lime juice
- 1 avocado
- 1 small red onion, sliced thinly
- 2 oranges, peeled and sectioned

Directions for Cooking:

1. In a large bowl mix honey, cilantro, minced red onion and yogurt.
2. Marinate chicken in mixture for at least 30 minutes.
3. Grease grate and preheat grill to medium high fire.
4. Remove chicken from marinade and season with pepper and salt.
5. Grill for 6 minutes per side or until chicken is cooked and juices run clear.
6. Meanwhile, peel avocado and discard seed. Chop avocados and place in bowl. Quickly add lime juice and toss avocado to coat well with juice.
7. Add cilantro, thinly sliced onions and oranges into bowl of avocado, mix well.
8. Serve grilled chicken and avocado dressing on the side.

Nutrition Information:
Calories per Serving: 356.8; Protein: 15.2g; Carbs: 40.7g; Fat: 14.8g; Saturated Fat: 3.5g; Sodium: 497mg

Herbs and Lemony Roasted Chicken

Serves: 8 , Cooking time: 1 hour and 30 minutes

Ingredients:
- ½ tsp ground black pepper
- 1 tsp garlic powder
- ½ tsp mustard powder
- ½ tsp salt
- 1 3-lb whole chicken
- 2 tsp Italian seasoning
- 2 tbsp olive oil
- 2 lemons

Directions for Cooking:
1. In small bowl, mix well black pepper, garlic powder, mustard powder, and salt.
2. Rinse chicken well and slice off giblets.
3. In a greased 9 x 13 baking dish, place chicken and add 1 ½ tsp of seasoning made earlier inside the chicken and rub the remaining seasoning all over chicken.
4. In small bowl, mix olive oil and juice from 2 lemons. Drizzle over chicken.
5. Bake chicken in a preheated 350oF oven until juices run clear, around 1 ½ hours. Every once in a while, baste chicken with its juices.
6. Once done, turn off oven, leave oven door open and let chicken rest for 10 minutes.
7. Serve and enjoy.

Nutrition Information:
Calories per Serving: 213.8; Protein: 38g; Carbs: 1.5g; Fat: 6.2g; Saturated Fat: 1.1g; Sodium: 250mg

Mexican Baked Beans and Rice

Serves: 6 , Cooking time: 45 minutes

Ingredients:
- 1 ½ cups cooked brown rice
- 1 lb. skinless, boneless chicken breast cut into bite sized pieces
- 4 garlic cloves, crushed
- 1 tbsp cumin
- 1 tbsp chili powder
- 1 cup chopped poblano pepper
- 1 cup chopped red bell pepper
- 1 cup frozen yellow corn
- 1 15-oz can no-salt added black beans, drained and rinsed
- 2 14.5-oz cans no salt added tomatoes, diced or crushed
- 1 cup shredded reduced fat Monterey Jack cheese

Directions for Cooking:
1. With cooking spray grease a 3-quart shallow casserole and preheat oven to 400oF.
2. Spread cooked brown rice in bottom of casserole.
3. Layer chicken on top of brown rice.
4. Mix well garlic, seasonings, peppers, corn, beans and tomatoes in a medium bowl.
5. Evenly spread bean mixture on top of chicken.
6. Sprinkle cheese on top of beans and pop into the oven.
7. Bake for 45 minutes, remove from oven and serve.

Nutrition Information:
Calories per Serving: 292.1; Protein: 27.5g; Carbs: 26.4g; Fat: 8.5g; Saturated Fat: 3.8g; Sodium: 260mg

Turkey Meatballs in Cranberry Sauce

Serves: 4 , Cooking time: 25 minutes

Ingredients:

- 1-lb ground turkey
- 2 cloves garlic, peeled
- 1 small onion, peeled and quartered
- 1 stalk green onions
- 1 tsp pepper
- 1 tsp dried rosemary
- 1 egg
- 1 cup cranberry
- 3 packets Stevia
- ½ cup water

Directions for Cooking:

1. In food processor, process garlic, onion, green onions, pepper, and rosemary until finely chopped. Pour into a bowl, add turkey and eggs. Mash with hands until thoroughly mixed, around 5 minutes.
2. Preheat oven to 400ºF and lightly grease a baking sheet with cooking spray.
3. Evenly divide into 4 portions. Divide each portion into 4 parts and form into balls. You will have a total of 16 meatballs.
4. Place meatballs on baking sheet without touching one another and bake in oven for 15 minutes or until lightly browned.
5. Meanwhile, place remaining ingredients in a small pot and bring to a boil. Continue simmering until cranberry has popped and desired consistency is reached.
6. Serve meatballs drizzled with cranberry sauce.

Nutrition Information:

Calories per Serving: 249; Carbs: 12.2g; Protein: 25.1g; Fats: 11.2g; Saturated Fat: 2.9g; Sodium: 95mg

Garlic Rosemary Roasted Cornish Hen

Serves: 2 , Cooking time: 45 minutes

Ingredients:

- 2 tsp rosemary
- 1 whole Cornish game hen
- 4 cloves of garlic, smashed
- ½ small onion, sliced
- 2 bay leaf
- 1/2 tsp pepper, divided
- 1 lemon

Directions for Cooking:

1. Place an oven safe wire rack on a baking pan and lightly grease rack with cooking spray. Preheat oven to 350ºF.
2. Slice lemon in half. Squeeze half of a lemon all over chicken. Slice the other half in circles.
3. In cavity of chicken add garlic, onion, bay leaf, sliced lemon, and ½ tsp pepper.
4. Rub rosemary and remaining pepper on outside of the chicken.
5. Place chicken on top of the rack and bake for 45 minutes.
6. Let chicken rest for 10 minutes. Slice in half and serve.

Nutrition Information:

Calories per Serving: 165; Carbs: 6.5g; Protein: 24.8g; Fats: 4.1g; Saturated Fat: 1.1g; Sodium: 84mg

Ginger, Chicken, And Spinach Stir Fry

Serves: 4 , Cooking time: 10 minutes

Ingredients:

- 1 tablespoon olive oil
- 2 cloves of garlic, minced
- 1 tablespoon fresh ginger, grated
- 1 ¼ pounds boneless chicken breasts, cut into strips
- 2 tablespoons yellow miso, diluted in water
- 2 cups baby spinach

Directions for Cooking:

1. Heat oil in a skillet over medium-high heat and sauté the garlic for 30 seconds until fragrant.
2. Stir in the ginger and chicken breasts.
3. Cook for 5 minutes while stirring constantly.
4. Stir in the diluted miso paste.

5. Continue cooking for 3 more minutes before adding spinach.
6. Cook for another minute or until the spinach leaves have wilted.

Nutrition Information:
Calories per Serving: 207; Carbs: 1.3g; Protein: 32.4g; Fats: 7.2g; Saturated Fat: 1.3g; Sodium: 76mg

Chicken and Mushrooms Sauté

Serves: 8 , Cooking time: 5 minutes
Ingredients:
- 1 tablespoon olive oil
- 1 large shallot, diced
- 2-lbs chicken breast, cubed
- 4 large cremini mushrooms, sliced
- ½ cup water
- ¼ cup yogurt
- ½ tsp pepper

Directions for Cooking:
1. Heat oil in a skillet over medium flame and sauté the shallot until fragrant.
2. Stir in the chicken breasts and continue cooking for 3 minutes while stirring constantly.
3. Add the mushrooms, water, and yogurt.
4. Season with salt and pepper to taste.
5. Close the lid and bring to a boil.
6. Reduce the heat to medium-low and allow simmering for 10 minutes.
7. Serve and enjoy.

Nutrition Information:
Calories per Serving: 218; Carbs: 1.0g; Protein: 24.3g; Fats: 12.5g; Saturated Fat: 3.4g; Sodium: 76mg

Chicken Ala Cubana

Serves: 4 , Cooking time: 15 minutes
Ingredients:
- 1 tablespoon olive oil
- 1 onion, chopped
- 3 cloves of garlic, chopped
- 2 chicken breasts, cut into chunks
- 1 cup diced tomatoes
- ½ cup chopped red bell pepper
- ½ cup raisins
- 1 tablespoon lemon juice, freshly squeezed
- 1 teaspoon ground oregano
- ¼ teaspoon ground cumin
- 2 bay leaves

Directions for Cooking:
1. Heat the olive oil in a skillet over medium-high flame and sauté the onion and garlic until fragrant.
2. Add the chicken breasts and stir for 2 minutes.
3. Stir in the rest of the ingredients.
4. Cover with lid and adjust the flame to medium.
5. Allow simmering for 10 minutes.

Nutrition Information:
Calories per Serving: 305; Carbs: 5.8g; Protein: 31.2g; Fats: 17.0g; Saturated Fat: 4.3g; Sodium: 95mg

Tasty Curried Chicken

Serves: 6 , Cooking time: 30 minutes
Ingredients:
- 1 tablespoon olive oil
- 2 cloves of garlic, minced
- 1 onion, chopped
- 1-lb boneless, skinless chicken thighs
- ¼ tsp pepper
- 1 tsp coconut aminos
- 1-inch ginger, peeled and sliced thinly
- 2 medium carrots, peeled and cut into 1-inch circles
- 2 small potato, quartered
- 1 tablespoon paprika
- 1 tablespoon curry powder
- 1 tsp turmeric
- ½ cup water
- 2 bay leaves

- 1 cup coconut milk, divided

Directions for Cooking:
1. Heat the olive oil in a skillet over medium flame and sauté the garlic, ginger and onion until fragrant, around 5 minutes.
2. Stir in the chicken and sauté for 7 minutes until no longer pink.
3. Stir in pepper, coconut aminos, paprika, curry powder, turmeric, and bay leaves. Sauté for 3 minutes.
4. Add water and deglaze pot. Add potatoes, carrots, and half of coconut milk. Cover and simmer for 10 minutes.
5. Once veggies are tender, stir in remaining coconut milk and cook until heated through.
6. Serve and enjoy.

Nutrition Information:
Calories per Serving: 365; Carbs: 45.3g; Protein: 11.3g; Fats: 16.6g; Saturated Fat: 5.0g; Sodium: 233mg

Basil Avocado Grilled Chicken Salad

Serves: 4 , Cooking time: 5 minutes

Ingredients:
- 2 ripe avocados, peeled, pitted, and mashed
- 1 lime, juiced
- 2 tablespoons fresh basil, chopped
- ½ teaspoon garlic powder
- ½ teaspoon ground black pepper
- 2 heads Bibb lettuce, leaves separated
- 1 large chicken breast, grilled and shredded
- ¼ cup raisins
- ¼ cup walnuts, chopped

Directions for Cooking:
1. In a mixing bowl, combine the avocado, lime juice and fresh basil. Season with salt, garlic powder, and black pepper to taste.
2. Place the bib in a salad bowl and pour over the avocado cream inside.
3. Arrange the chicken, raisins, and walnuts.
4. Chill before serving.

Nutrition Information:
Calories per Serving: 253; Carbs: 22.3g; Protein: 6.4g; Fats: 18.5g; Saturated Fat: 2.5g; Sodium: 46mg

Chicken Cheddar and Avocado Buns

Serves: 4 , Cooking time: 10 minutes

Ingredients:
- 1-pound ground chicken
- ½ cup yellow onion, minced
- 2 cloves of garlic, minced
- 1/3 cup cilantro, chopped
- 1 jalapeno pepper, seeded and minced
- ½ lime, juiced
- 1 teaspoon ground cumin
- 1 teaspoon paprika
- 1/3 cup low-fat cheddar cheese, shredded
- ½ teaspoon black pepper
- 4 slices low fat cheddar cheese
- 4 whole wheat hamburger buns
- 1 large tomato, cut into 4 slices
- 1 whole avocado, pitted and flesh scooped out

Directions for Cooking:
1. Preheat the grill to medium.
2. In a mixing bowl, combine the chicken, onion, garlic, cilantro, jalapeno pepper, cumin, paprika, shredded cheese, and pepper.
3. Make 4 patties using your hands and cook on the grill for 4 minutes on each side or until the inside is fully cooked.
4. Assemble the burger by putting the burger patties in sliced burger buns and topped with a slice of tomatoes and avocado.

Nutrition Information:
Calories per Serving: 403; Carbs: 23.8g; Protein: 29.0g; Fats: 21.3g; Saturated Fat: 4.3g; Sodium: 268mg

Simple Chicken Salad

Serves: 4 , Cooking time: 5 minutes

Ingredients:

- 12-oz skinless chicken breasts, grilled
- 1 head iceberg lettuce
- 1 head romaine lettuce
- 2 bunches green onions
- 1 large tomato, chopped
- 1 cup cheddar cheese, shredded low fat and low sodium
- ¼ cup plain yogurt
- 2 tablespoons lemon juice
- 1 tablespoon olive oil
- ¼ tsp pepper

Directions for Cooking:

1. Place all ingredients in a big salad bowl.
2. Toss to coat all ingredients with the light dressing.
3. Place in the fridge to chill before serving.

Nutrition Information:

Calories per Serving: 364; Carbs: 27.4g; Protein: 31.1g; Fats: 15.7g; Saturated Fat: 6.9g; Sodium: 101mg

Garlicky Zucchini-Turkey Casserole

Serves: 4 , Cooking time: 40 minutes

Ingredients:

- 1 tablespoon oil
- 1 white onion, chopped
- 2 cloves of garlic, minced
- 1-pound cooked turkey meat, shredded
- A dash of rosemary
- 1 zucchini, chopped
- 1 carrot, peeled and chopped
- ½ cup water
- Pepper to taste

Directions for Cooking:

1. Preheat oven to 400ºF.
2. Grease an oven safe casserole dish with oil.
3. Mix onion, garlic, turkey, pepper, salt, and rosemary in a bowl.
4. Pour into prepared casserole dish.
5. Sprinkle carrot on top, followed by zucchini, and then pour water over mixture.
6. Cover dish with a foil and bake for 25 minutes or until bubbly hot.
7. Remove foil and return to oven and broil top for 2 minutes on high.
8. Let it rest for 10 minutes.
9. Serve and enjoy.

Nutrition Information:

Calories per Serving: 250; Carbs: 5.7g; Protein: 32.9g; Fats: 10.0g; Saturated Fat: 2.8g; Sodium: 88 mg

Casserole a La Chicken Enchilada

Serves: 10 , Cooking time: 6 hours

Ingredients:

- 5 pitted dates
- 3 tablespoons olive oil
- ¼ cup chili powder
- 1 cup water
- 1 cup tomato paste
- 1 teaspoon ground cumin
- 1 teaspoon dried oregano
- Salt and pepper to taste
- 2 pounds chicken breasts, cut into strips
- 1 sweet potato, scrubbed and chopped

Directions for Cooking:

1. In a blender or food processor, place the dates, olive oil, chili powder, water, tomato paste, cumin, and oregano. Season with salt and pepper to taste. Pulse until smooth. This will be the enchilada sauce.
2. On the Crock-Pot, place the chicken breasts and sweet potatoes on bottom of pot.
3. Pour over chicken the enchilada sauce.
4. Close the lid and press the low settings and adjust the cooking time to 6 hours.
5. Serve and enjoy.

Nutrition Information:

Calories per Serving: 240; Carbs: 12.2g; Protein: 30.2g; Fats: 8.0g; Saturated Fat: 2.7g; Sodium: 204mg

Cilantro-Coconut Chicken Stew

Serves: 8 , Cooking time: 30 minutes

Ingredients:

- 1 whole chicken, around 2-lbs
- 1 can light coconut milk
- 1 cup water
- ½ fresh cilantro, chopped
- 1 tablespoon ginger
- 1 teaspoon cumin
- 1 teaspoon coriander
- ½ teaspoon salt
- ½ teaspoon curry
- 1 lemon, juice extracted

Directions for Cooking:

1. Place a heavy bottomed pot on medium high fire.
2. Add all ingredients except for coconut milk. Mix well.
3. Bring to a boil. Once boiling, lower fire to a simmer and cook for 20 minutes.
4. Stir in coconut milk. Continue simmering for another 10 minutes.
5. Serve and enjoy.

Nutrition Information:

Calories per Serving: 194; Carbs: 2.3g; Protein: 23.8g; Fats: 9.9g; Saturated Fat: 6.7g; Sodium: 236mg

Turkey Legs in Thai Sauce

Serves: 6 , Cooking time: 30 minutes

Ingredients:

- 1 ½ pounds large turkey legs
- 1 can light coconut milk
- 1 cup water
- 1 ½ teaspoon lemon juice
- ¼ cup cilantro, chopped
- Pepper to taste

Directions for Cooking:

1. Place a heavy bottomed pot on medium high fire.
2. Add all ingredients except for coconut milk. Mix well.
3. Bring to a boil. Once boiling, lower fire to a simmer and cook for 20 minutes.
4. Stir in coconut milk. Continue simmering for another 10 minutes.
5. Serve and enjoy.

Nutrition Information:

Calories per Serving: 236; Carbs: 2.5g; Protein: 23.0g; Fats: 14.8g; Saturated Fat: 3.8g; Sodium: 90mg

Filling Turkey Chili Recipe

Serves: 6 , Cooking time: 25 minutes

Ingredients:

- 1 tablespoon olive oil
- 1-pound ground turkey
- 1 onion, chopped
- 1 green bell pepper, seeded and chopped
- 3 carrots, peeled and chopped
- 2 stalks of celery, sliced thinly
- 1 cup chopped tomatoes
- 3 poblano chilies, chopped
- ½ cup water
- 3 tablespoons chili powder
- 1 ½ teaspoons ground cumin
- Pepper to taste

Directions for Cooking:

1. Place a heavy bottomed pot on medium high fire and heat for 3 minutes.
2. Add oil, swirl to coat bottom and sides of pot, and heat for a minute.
3. Stir in turkey. Brown and crumble for 8 minutes. Season generously with pepper. Discard excess fat.
4. Add all ingredients. Mix well.
5. Bring to a boil. Once boiling, lower fire to a simmer and cook for 10 minutes.
6. Serve and enjoy.

Nutrition Information:

Calories per Serving: 175; Carbs: 8.7g; Protein: 16.4g; Fats: 9.1g; Saturated Fat: 2.0g; Sodium: 188mg

Chicken Meatloaf with a Tropical Twist

Serves: 4 , Cooking time: 45 minutes

Ingredients:

- 1/8 teaspoon salt
- 1/8 teaspoon pepper
- 2 eggs
- ¼ cup parsley, chopped
- ¼ cup coconut flakes
- ½ tablespoons jalapeno, seeded and diced
- ½ cups diced mango
- 1 cup yellow bell pepper, diced
- 1-pound ground chicken
- 1 tablespoon oil

Directions for Cooking:

1. Preheat oven to 400ºF and lightly grease a loaf pan with oil.
2. In a large bowl, mix remaining ingredients.
3. Evenly spread in prepared pan and cover pan with foil.
4. Pop in the oven and bake for 30 minutes.
5. Remove foil and broil top for 3 minutes.
6. Let it sit for 10 minutes.
7. Serve and enjoy.

Nutrition Information:
Calories per Serving: 301; Carbs: 8.0g; Protein: 25.0g; Fats: 19.0g; Saturated Fat: 4.6g; Sodium: 215mg

Chicken-Mushroom Casserole

Serves: 3 , Cooking time: 35 minutes

Ingredients:

- 2 tbsp chopped fresh parsley
- 4 slices Muenster cheese
- 1 garlic clove, minced
- 1-lb sliced fresh mushrooms
- 1 cup water
- 1 18-oz can creamy mushroom soup, low sodium
- 1 chicken breast, sliced thinly
- ¼ tsp pepper
- 2 tbsp all-purpose flour

Directions for Cooking:

1. Place a nonstick saucepan on medium high fire and heat for 3 minutes.
2. Add oil and swirl pan to coat sides and bottom with oil Heat for a minute.
3. Add chicken and sauté until no longer pink, around 5 minutes. Season with pepper and transfer to a plate.
4. In same pan, add flour and sauté for 3 minutes. Add garlic and sauté for a minute more.
5. Stir in mushrooms and cook for 5 minutes until water comes out of it.
6. Add remaining ingredients, except for cheese and parsley. Mix well. Return chicken to pan.
7. Bring to a simmer, cover and cook for 10 minutes while mixing frequently.
8. Place cheese on top and let it rest while covered for 5 minutes.
9. Serve and enjoy with a sprinkle of parsley.

Nutrition Information:
Calories per Serving: 346; Carbs: 14.7g; Protein: 36.4g; Fats: 16.3g; Saturated Fat: 6.8g; Sodium: 109mg

Pineapple Chicken Hawaiian Style

Serves: 6 , Cooking time: 40 minutes

Ingredients:

- 2 tbsp cornstarch
- 1 small yellow bell pepper, cut into 1-inch pieces
- 1 small red bell pepper, cut into 1-inch pieces
- 1 20-oz can pineapple chunks, drained and ¼ cup liquid reserved
- 1 cup honey BBQ sauce
- 2 cloves garlic, chopped finely
- 1.5-lbs boneless, skinless chicken thighs
- 1 tsp oil

Directions for Cooking:

1. Place a heavy bottomed pot on medium high fire and heat pot for 3 minutes.

2. Once hot, add oil and stir around to coat pot with oil.
3. Add chicken and cook for 4 minutes per side.
4. Meanwhile, in a bowl mix cornstarch with ¼ cup water and set aside
5. Add pineapple chunks to pot and sauté for 2 minutes.
6. Stir in reserved liquid form pineapple, BBQ sauce, and garlic. Mix well and bring to a boil.
7. Cover, lower fire to a simmer and simmer for 8 minutes.
8. Stir in bell peppers and cornstarch slurry. Continue mixing and cooking until sauce has thickened, around 5 minutes.
9. Serve and enjoy.

Nutrition Information:
Calories per Serving: 402; Carbs: 45.9g; Protein: 28.7g; Fats: 11.6g; Saturated Fat: 3.0g; Sodium: 285mg

Honey Sesame Chicken

Serves: 4 , Cooking time: 20 minutes

Ingredients:
- 1 tbsp toasted sesame seeds
- 2 green onions, chopped
- 3 tbsp water
- 2 tbsp cornstarch
- ¼ tsp red pepper flakes
- ½ cup honey
- 2 tsp sesame oil
- ¼ ketchup
- 2 tbsp soy sauce
- 2 garlic cloves, minced
- ½ cup onion, diced
- 1 tsp olive oil
- Pepper to taste
- 2 medium boneless, skinless chicken breasts, chopped into 1-inch cubes

Directions for Cooking:
1. Place a heavy bottomed pot on medium high fire and heat pot for 3 minutes.
2. Meanwhile season chicken generously with pepper.
3. Once hot, add oil and stir around to coat pot with oil.
4. Stir in garlic and onion. Cook for 3 minutes.
5. Add chicken and cook for 5 minutes.
6. Stir in red pepper flakes, ketchup, and soy sauce. Mix well.
7. Cover, bring to a boil, lower fire to a simmer, and simmer for 5 minutes.
8. Meanwhile, in a bowl mix cornstarch with water and set aside
9. Stir in honey and sesame oil. Pour the cornstarch slurry and continue mixing while cooking until sauce has thickened, around 5 minutes.
10. Serve and enjoy with a sprinkle of green onions.

Nutrition Information:
Calories per Serving: 228; Carbs: 44.7g; Protein: 3.9g; Fats: 5.4g; Saturated Fat: 0.8g; Sodium: 304mg

Chicken Cooked the Italian Way

Serves: 6 , Cooking time: 25 minutes

Ingredients:
- ¼ cup loosely packed fresh Italian parsley, chopped coarsely
- ½ cup loosely packed fresh basil leaves, sliced thinly
- ¼ tsp black pepper
- ½ cup pitted green olives
- 2 cups cherry tomatoes
- 1 tbsp tomato paste
- 3 garlic cloves, smashed and peeled
- ½-lb cremini mushroom, quartered
- 2 medium carrot, chopped coarsely
- 1 small onion, chopped coarsely
- 1 tsp olive oil
- 6 boneless, skinless chicken thighs

Directions for Cooking:
1. Place a heavy bottomed pot on medium high fire and heat pot for 3 minutes.
2. Meanwhile season chicken generously with pepper.
3. Once hot, add oil and stir around to coat pot with oil.

4. Pan fry chicken for 4 minutes per side and transfer to a plate.
5. Add mushrooms, carrots, and onions to pot. Season with pepper. Sauté for 5 minutes.
6. Add tomato paste and garlic. Sauté for 2 minutes.
7. Add olives, cherry tomatoes, and return chicken. Mix well.
8. Cover, bring to a boil, lower fire to a simmer, and simmer for 10 minutes.
9. Stir in the fresh herbs.
10. Serve and enjoy.

Nutrition Information:
Calories per Serving: 241; Carbs: 7.7g; Protein: 21.5g; Fats: 13.9g; Saturated Fat: 3.7g; Sodium: 403mg

Italian Chicken Cacciatore

Serves: 6 , Cooking time: 30-40minutes

Ingredients:
- ¼ cup balsamic vinegar
- 1 tsp fresh thyme
- 2 tbsp parsley
- 1 14.5-oz can low sodium diced tomatoes, pulsed in a blender
- 1 14.5-oz can low sodium diced tomatoes in juice
- 1 cup chicken broth
- 1 bay leaf
- 2 tbsp fresh basil, chopped
- ¼ tsp red pepper flakes
- 1 tsp dried oregano
- 2 large garlic cloves, minced
- ½-lb mushrooms, sliced
- 1 red bell pepper, diced
- 3 carrots, peeled and diced
- 1 medium onion, sliced thinly
- 1 tbsp extra virgin olive oil
- 2 tsp ground pepper
- 6 chicken thighs, pat dry with paper towels

Directions for Cooking:

1. Place a heavy bottomed pot on medium high fire and heat pot for 3 minutes.
2. Meanwhile season chicken generously with pepper.
3. Once hot, add oil and stir around to coat pot with oil.
4. Brown chicken for 5 minutes per side. If needed cook in batches and place on a plate.
5. Add mushroom and onion. Sauté for 5 minutes.
6. Stir in pepper flakes, oregano, and garlic. Cook for a minute.
7. Stir in thyme and bay leaf. Cook for another minute.
8. Pour in tomatoes, chicken broth, bell pepper, carrots, and the chicken. Mix well.
9. Cover, bring to a boil, lower fire to a simmer, and simmer for 10 minutes.
10. Serve and enjoy with a sprinkle of parsley.

Nutrition Information:
Calories per Serving: 412; Carbs: 43.0g; Protein: 37.0g; Fats: 13.0g; Saturated Fat: 3.6g; Sodium: 364mg

Oregano-Basil Chicken Breast

Serves: 4 , Cooking time: 25 minutes

Ingredients:
- 1/2 cup water
- 1/8 tsp dried basil
- 1/8 tsp dried oregano
- 2 tbsp balsamic vinegar
- Black pepper to taste
- 2 boneless, skinless chicken breasts
- 1 tbsp oil

Directions for Cooking:
1. Place a heavy bottomed pot on medium high fire and heat pot for 3 minutes.
2. Meanwhile season chicken generously with pepper.
3. Once hot, add oil and stir around to coat pot with oil.
4. Add chicken breasts to hot pot and cook for 5 minutes per side.
5. Add remaining ingredients to pot.
6. Cover, bring to a boil, lower fire to a simmer, and simmer for 10 minutes.
7. Serve and enjoy.

Nutrition Information:
Calories per Serving: 142; Carbs: 2.5g; Protein: 19.1g; Fats: 5.8g; Saturated Fat: 1.0g; Sodium: 305mg

Filipino Style Chicken Adobo

Serves: 8 , Cooking time: 35 minutes

Ingredients:

- 4 dried bay leaves
- 1 tsp ground black peppercorn
- 1 large sweet onion, chopped
- 10 cloves garlic, smashed
- ¼ cup vinegar
- 2 tbsp coconut aminos
- 1.5-lbs chicken breast, boneless and skinless, cut into 2-inch cubes

Directions for Cooking:

1. Place a heavy bottomed pot on medium high fire and heat pot for 3 minutes.
2. Once hot, add oil and stir around to coat pot with oil.
3. Add garlic and sauté for 2 minutes or until lightly browned.
4. Add half of onions and sauté until soft, around 4 minutes.
5. Stir in chicken and cook for 10 minutes.
6. Add remaining ingredients, except for onions.
7. Cover, bring to a boil, lower fire to a simmer, and simmer for 15 minutes.
8. Stir in remaining onions.
9. Serve and enjoy.

Nutrition Information:

Calories per Serving: 169; Carbs: 3.1g; Protein: 23.5g; Fats: 6.3g; Saturated Fat: 1.8g; Sodium: 328mg

Stewed Chicken & Dried Cherries

Serves: 6 , Cooking time: 25 minutes

Ingredients:

- 1 tablespoon olive oil
- 1 cup shredded chicken meat
- 1 onion, chopped
- 2 teaspoons chili powder
- 1 teaspoon sambal oelek
- 1 tablespoon coconut aminos
- 2 cans cannellini beans, drained and rinsed
- ½ cup dried cherries
- 2 cups chicken broth, low sodium
- Pepper to taste
- 2 tablespoons chopped parsley

Directions for Cooking:

1. Place a heavy bottomed pot on medium high fire and heat pot for 3 minutes.
2. Once hot, add oil and stir around to coat pot with oil. sauté the chicken meat, onions, chili powder, and sambal oelek for 5 minutes. Season with coconut aminos.
3. Stir in the cannellini beans and cherries.
4. Add the broth and season with pepper.
5. Cover, bring to a boil, lower fire to a simmer, and simmer for 15 minutes.
6. Serve and enjoy with a sprinkle of parsley.

Nutrition Information:

Calories per Serving: 278; Carbs: 33.1g; Protein: 16.8g; Fats: 9.0g; Saturated Fat: 1.6g; Sodium: 264mg

Chicken 'n Ginger Congee

Serves: 8 , Cooking time: 45 minutes

Ingredients:

- 8 cups water
- 3 boneless chicken thighs, sliced thinly
- 1 cup rice, uncooked
- 4 thick slices of ginger, smashed
- ½ teaspoon salt
- 4 cloves garlic, peeled and minced
- ½ cup scallions, chopped
- 3 tablespoons ginger, minced
- ½ cup cilantro leaves
- 1 tsp olive oil
- Pepper to taste

Directions for Cooking:

1. Place a heavy bottomed pot on medium high fire and heat pot for 3 minutes.
2. Meanwhile season chicken generously with pepper.
3. Once hot, add oil and stir around to coat pot with oil.
4. Sauté garlic and ginger for 3 minutes. Add chicken and sauté for 3 minutes.

5. Add 4 cups water and remaining ingredients except for cilantro and scallions. Mix well.
6. Cover, bring to a boil and boil for 5 minutes.
7. Stir in remaining water and bring to a simmer and simmer for 25 minutes. Continue cooking until rice is soft and tender.
8. Stir in cilantro.
9. Serve and enjoy with a sprinkle of pepper and scallions.

Nutrition Information:
Calories per Serving: 152; Carbs: 19.7g; Protein: 9.1g; Fats: 3.9g; Saturated Fat: 0.9g; Sodium: 280mg

Broccoli-Chicken Rice

Serves: 5 , Cooking time: 35 minutes
Ingredients:
- 1 tsp olive oil
- 1-pound boneless chicken breasts, sliced thinly
- 2 cloves of garlic, minced
- 1 onion, chopped
- Pepper to taste
- 1 1/3 cups long grain rice
- 1 1/3 cups chicken broth, low sodium
- ½ cup skim milk
- 1 cup broccoli florets
- ½ cup low fat cheddar cheese, grated

Directions for Cooking:
1. Place a heavy bottomed pot on medium high fire and heat pot for 3 minutes.
2. Meanwhile season chicken generously with pepper.
3. Once hot, add oil and stir around to coat pot with oil.
4. Sauté garlic and onion for 3 minutes. Add chicken and cook for another 3 minutes.
5. Add rice and stir fry for 3 minutes.
6. Stir in chicken broth and season with pepper. Cover and simmer for 10 minutes or until water is fully absorbed.
7. Add broccoli florets and skim milk. Cover and simmer for another 5 minutes.
8. Sprinkle cheese on top, cover and let it sit for 5 minutes.
9. Serve and enjoy.

Nutrition Information:
Calories per Serving: 462; Carbs: 43.3g; Protein: 43.0g; Fats: 12.0g; Saturated Fat: 3.8g; Sodium: 413mg

Cajun Chicken and Rice

Serves: 5 , Cooking time: 35 minutes
Ingredients:
- 1 tablespoon oil
- 1 onion, diced
- 3 cloves of garlic, minced
- 1-pound chicken breasts, sliced
- 1 tablespoon Cajun seasoning
- 1 tablespoon tomato paste
- 2 cups chicken broth, low sodium
- 1 ½ cups white rice, rinsed
- 1 bell pepper, chopped

Directions for Cooking:
1. Place a heavy bottomed pot on medium high fire and heat pot for 3 minutes.
2. Once hot, add oil and stir around to coat pot with oil.
3. Sauté the onion and garlic until fragrant, around 3 minutes.
4. Stir in the chicken breasts and tomato paste. Season with Cajun seasoning. Sauté for 5 minutes.
5. Add broth and deglaze pot. Stir in rice.
6. Cover, bring to a boil, lower fire to a simmer, and simmer for 5 minutes.
7. Stir in bell pepper. Continue simmering for another 10 minutes or until rice is absorbed.
8. Turn off fire and let rice sit for 5 minutes.
9. Serve and enjoy.

Nutrition Information:
Calories per Serving: 389; Carbs: 50.4g; Protein: 30.8g; Fats: 5.8g; Saturated Fat: 3.2g; Sodium: 189mg

Serves: 6 , Cooking time: 30 minutes

Ingredients:

- 2 cups uncooked rice, rinsed
- 2 ½ cups, chicken stock low sodium
- 1 tablespoon rice wine
- 1 teaspoon olive oil
- 1 cup leftover chicken meat
- 2 small potatoes, peeled and quartered
- 2 carrots, chopped
- 1-pound white mushrooms, halved
- 1-pound green beans, chopped
- 3 cups kale, chopped
- 2 tablespoons soy sauce
- 1 tablespoon oyster sauce

Directions for Cooking:

1. Place a heavy bottomed pot on medium high fire and heat pot for 3 minutes.
2. Once hot, add oil and stir around to coat pot with oil.
3. Sauté the rice wine, chicken meat, potatoes, carrots, mushrooms, green beans, soy sauce, and oyster sauce. Mix well and cook for 5 minutes.
4. Add rice and chicken stock.
5. Cover, bring to a boil, lower fire to a simmer, and simmer for 15 minutes or until water is absorbed.
6. Stir in kale and fluff rice. Let it rest for 5 minutes.
7. Serve and enjoy.

Nutrition Information:

Calories per Serving: 396; Carbs: 73.6g; Protein: 16.3g; Fats: 4.3g; Saturated Fat: 0.9g; Sodium: 204mg

Serves: 6 , Cooking time: 30 minutes

Ingredients:

- 1 tablespoon olive oil
- 3 small shallots, diced
- 2 cloves of garlic, minced
- 1-pound boneless, skinless chicken thighs, sliced thinly
- Pepper to taste
- 3 carrots, diced
- 1 ½ cups white jasmine rice, rinsed and drained
- 2 cups low sodium chicken stock
- 2 tablespoons thyme leaves

Directions for Cooking:

1. Place a heavy bottomed pot on medium high fire and heat pot for 3 minutes.
2. Once hot, add oil and stir around to coat pot with oil.
3. Sauté the shallots and garlic until fragrant, around 3 minutes.
4. Stir in the chicken breasts and thyme leaves. Season with pepper. Sauté for 5 minutes.
5. Add broth and deglaze pot. Stir in rice and carrots.
6. Cover, bring to a boil, lower fire to a simmer, and simmer for 12 minutes.
7. Turn off fire and let rice sit for 5 minutes.
8. Fluff rice, serve and enjoy.

Nutrition Information:

Calories per Serving: 213; Carbs: 27.1g; Protein: 10.1g; Fats: 7.9g; Saturated Fat: 1.8g; Sodium: 324mg

Serves: 6 , Cooking time: 20 minutes

Ingredients:

- 1 tablespoon coconut oil
- 1 onion, chopped
- 3 cloves of garlic, minced
- 1.5-pounds chicken breasts
- 1 green bell pepper, chopped
- 1 can jalapenos, chopped
- 1 can green chilies, chopped
- 1 can diced tomatoes, no salt added
- 1 can tomato sauce, no salt added
- 1 tablespoon cumin
- 1 tablespoon chili powder
- 2 teaspoons dried oregano

- Pepper to taste

Directions for Cooking:
1. Place a heavy bottomed pot on medium high fire and heat pot for 3 minutes.
2. Once hot, add oil and stir around to coat pot with oil.
3. Sauté the onion and garlic until fragrant, around 3 minutes.
4. Stir in the chicken. Season with pepper. Sauté for 5 minutes.
5. Add remaining ingredients and deglaze pot.
6. Cover, bring to a boil, lower fire to a simmer, and simmer for 12 minutes.
7. Serve and enjoy.

Nutrition Information:
Calories per Serving: 265; Carbs: 10.3g; Protein: 25.8g; Fats: 13.8g; Saturated Fat: 5.1g; Sodium: 159mg

Creamy Thai Coconut Chicken Soup

Serves: 4 , Cooking time: 35 minutes

Ingredients:
- 2 tablespoons oil
- 1 onion, quartered
- 1-pound chicken breasts, skin and bones removed
- 2 tablespoons Thai red curry paste
- 1 red bell pepper, cut into strips
- 6 slices ginger
- 6 kaffir lime leaves
- 3 cups chicken broth
- 1 tablespoon coconut aminos
- 1 tablespoon sugar
- ¾ cup coconut milk
- 2 ½ tablespoons lime juice
- Cilantro leaves for serving

Directions for Cooking:
1. Place a heavy bottomed pot on medium high fire and heat pot for 3 minutes.
2. Once hot, add oil and stir around to coat pot with oil.
3. Brown chicken for 5 minutes per side. Transfer to a chopping board and cut into 1-inch cubes.
4. Sauté the onion, garlic and chicken for 5 minutes.
5. Add the red curry paste, bell pepper, galangal, and kaffir limes.
6. After 30 seconds, add the chicken broth, fish sauce, and sugar.
7. Cover, bring to a boil, lower fire to a simmer, and simmer for 10 minutes.
8. Stir in lime juice and coconut milk. Cook for 5 minutes.
9. Serve and enjoy.

Nutrition Information:
Calories per Serving: 380; Carbs: 16.1g; Protein: 25.7g; Fats: 25.0g; Saturated Fat: 10.5g; Sodium: 85mg

Chicken Tortilla Soup

Serves: 4 , Cooking time: 20 minutes

Ingredients:
- 1 tablespoon olive oil
- 1 onion, chopped
- 2 cloves of garlic, minced
- 2 tablespoons fresh cilantro, chopped
- 1 large ripe tomato, chopped
- 1 can black beans, drained and rinsed
- 1 cup frozen corn
- 4 cups chicken broth, low sodium
- 2 teaspoons chili powder
- 1 teaspoon cumin powder
- 1 bay leaf
- Pepper to taste
- 3 cooked chicken breasts, shredded
- 2 cooked corn tortillas, crumbled

Directions for Cooking:
1. Place a heavy bottomed pot on medium high fire and heat pot for 3 minutes.
2. Once hot, add oil and stir around to coat pot with oil.
3. Sauté the onion, tomato and garlic for 5 minutes.
4. Stir in remaining ingredients except for tortillas.

5. Cover, bring to a boil, lower fire to a simmer, and simmer for 10 minutes.
6. Serve and enjoy with a sprinkle of crumbled tortillas.

Nutrition Information:
Calories per Serving: 453; Carbs: 40.1; Protein: 50.1g; Fats: 10.0g; Saturated Fat: 2.1g; Sodium: 303mg

Chipotle Beans 'n Chicken Soup

Serves: 8 , Cooking time: 20 minutes
Ingredients:
- 1 tablespoon coconut oil
- 1 onion, chopped
- 3 cloves of garlic, minced
- 1 teaspoon chipotle seasoning
- ½ taco seasoning
- 6 cups sweet potatoes, peeled and chopped
- 6 cups chicken soup
- 3 cans cannellini beans, drained and rinsed well
- 4 cups cooked chicken, shredded
- Pepper

Directions for Cooking:

1. Place a heavy bottomed pot on medium high fire and heat pot for 3 minutes.
2. Once hot, add oil and stir around to coat pot with oil.
3. Sauté the onion and garlic for 5 minutes.
4. Add remaining ingredients and mix well.
5. Cover, bring to a boil, lower fire to a simmer, and simmer for 10 minutes.
6. Serve and enjoy.

Nutrition Information:
Calories per Serving: 277; Carbs: 26.8g; Protein: 26.7g; Fats: 7.1g; Saturated Fat: 2.5g; Sodium: 305mg

Chicken 'n Potatoes the French Way

Serves: 8 , Cooking time: 25 minutes
Ingredients:
- 1 tablespoon olive oil
- 4 chicken thighs, skinless and boneless
- 2 cloves of garlic, minced
- 1 onion, chopped
- 1 teaspoon onion powder
- 1 teaspoon garlic powder
- 2 teaspoons white sugar
- ¼ cup Dijon mustard
- 1 teaspoon rosemary
- 1 teaspoon thyme
- ½ pound baby potatoes, scrubbed and halved
- Pepper to taste
- 1 cup chicken stock, low sodium
- 2 tablespoons flour + 2 tablespoons skim milk

Directions for Cooking:
1. Place a heavy bottomed pot on medium high fire and heat pot for 3 minutes.

2. Once hot, add oil and stir around to coat pot with oil.
3. Brown chicken for 5 minutes per side. Transfer to a chopping board and cut into 1-inch cubes.
4. Sauté the onion and garlic for 3 minutes.
5. Add onion powder, chicken, garlic powder, white sugar, rosemary, thyme, and pepper.
6. After 30 seconds, add the chicken broth and Dijon mustard.
7. Cover, bring to a boil, lower fire to a simmer, and simmer for 5 minutes.
8. Stir in the milk mixture and continue stirring until thickened, around 5 minutes.
9. Serve and enjoy.

Nutrition Information:
Calories per Serving: 285; Carbs: 9.6g; Protein: 18.4g; Fats: 19.0g; Saturated Fat: 5.0g; Sodium: 214mg

Balsamic Orange Chicken Drumsticks

Serves: 4 , Cooking time: 20 minutes

Ingredients:

- 4 chicken drumsticks
- 2 tablespoons balsamic vinegar
- 1/4 cup orange marmalade
- 1/4 cup orange juice, freshly squeezed
- 1 tablespoon honey
- ¼ cup water

Directions for Cooking:

1. Place a heavy bottomed pot on medium high fire and heat pot for 3 minutes.
2. Once hot, brown chicken for 5 minutes per side.
3. Add remaining ingredients and mix well.
4. Cover and simmer for 10 minutes, frequently stirring.
5. Let it rest for 5 minutes before serving and enjoy.

Nutrition Information:

Calories per Serving: 289; Carbs: 20.9g; Protein: 23.7g; Fats: 12.0g; Saturated Fat: 3.2g; Sodium: 152mg

Chicken Japanese Style

Serves: 6 , Cooking time: 20 minutes

Ingredients:

- ½ cup yakitori sauce
- 2 cloves of garlic, minced
- 1 thumb-size ginger, grated
- 6 boneless, skinless chicken thighs
- ½ cup water
- 1 green onion, chopped
- ½ teaspoon sesame seeds, toasted

Directions for Cooking:

1. Place a heavy bottomed pot on medium high fire and add all ingredients.
2. Cover, bring to a boil, lower fire to a simmer, and simmer for 15 minutes.
3. Let it rest for 5 minutes.
4. Serve and enjoy.

Nutrition Information:

Calories per Serving: 152; Carbs: 4.8g; Protein: 19.2g; Fats: 5.9g; Saturated Fat: 1.7g; Sodium: 352mg

Herbed Chicken and Rice

Serves: 4 , Cooking time: 20 minutes

Ingredients:

- 1 chicken breast, sliced thinly
- 1 tsp rosemary
- ½ tsp dill
- ½ tsp pepper
- 1 tbsp soy sauce, low sodium
- 1 cup long-grain rice
- 2 cups chicken broth, low sodium
- 2 tablespoons oregano leaves

Directions for Cooking:

1. Place a heavy bottomed pot on medium high fire and add all ingredients except for oregano. Mix well.
2. Cover, bring to a boil, lower fire to a simmer, and simmer for 15 minutes.
3. Fluff rice and stir in oregano leaves. Let it sit for 5 minutes.
4. Serve and enjoy.

Nutrition Information:

Calories per Serving: 312; Carbs: 37.8g; Protein: 19.3g; Fats: 8.9g; Saturated Fat: 2.3g; Sodium: 110mg

Chili Sticky Chicken

Serves: 8 , Cooking time: 25 minutes

Ingredients:

- 8 chicken thighs
- ¼ cup honey
- 1 ½ tablespoons chili paste
- ½ cup chicken broth
- 2 cloves of garlic, minced
- 2 tablespoons currants
- 1 tablespoon olive oil
- 2 tablespoons balsamic vinegar
- Rind from 1 small lemon

Directions for Cooking:

1. Place a nonstick saucepan on medium high fire and heat pot for 3 minutes.
2. Once hot, add oil and stir around to coat pot with oil.
3. Brown chicken for 5 minutes per side. Transfer to a chopping board and cut into 1-inch cubes.
4. Sauté the garlic, currants, chili paste, and chicken for 5 minutes.
5. Add remaining ingredients. Sauté for 10 minutes.
6. Serve and enjoy.

Nutrition Information:

Calories per Serving: 314; Carbs: 10.8g; Protein: 41.5g; Fats: 10.9g; Saturated Fat: 2.7g; Sodium: 263mg

Lip Smacking Good Hoisin Chicken

Serves: 6 , Cooking time: 30 minutes

Ingredients:

- 6 ounces snow peas
- 1 can water chestnuts, cut into quarters
- 1-pound chicken breasts, skinless and boneless
- Pepper to taste
- 3 tablespoons hoisin sauce
- 2 teaspoons sugar
- 2 tbsp soy sauce, low sodium
- 1 tablespoon cornstarch + 2 tablespoons water

Directions for Cooking:

1. Place a nonstick saucepan on medium high fire and heat pot for 3 minutes.
2. Once hot, add oil and stir around to coat pot with oil.
3. Brown chicken for 5 minutes per side. Transfer to a chopping board and cut into 1-inch cubes.
4. Sauté the snow peas, chestnuts, pepper, hoisin sauce, sugar, soy sauce, and chicken for 10 minutes.
5. Stir in cornstarch slurry and continue sautéing until sauce has thickened, around 5 minutes.
6. Serve and enjoy.

Nutrition Information:

Calories per Serving: 155; Carbs: 7.5g; Protein: 23.5g; Fats: 2.9g; Saturated Fat: 0.7g; Sodium: 349mg

Mustard Chicken 'n Mushroom

Serves: 4 , Cooking time: 30 minutes

Ingredients:

- 2 chicken breasts, skinless and boneless
- 2 tablespoons flour
- 2 tablespoons olive oil, divided
- 1 onion, chopped
- 1 cup mushrooms, sliced
- ½ cup light cream
- 1 tablespoon fresh parsley, chopped
- 1 tablespoon Dijon mustard
- 1 tablespoon lemon juice, freshly squeezed
- Pepper

Directions for Cooking:

1. Place a nonstick saucepan on medium high fire and heat pot for 3 minutes.
2. Once hot, add 1 tbsp oil and stir around to coat pot with oil.
3. Brown chicken for 5 minutes per side. Transfer to a chopping board and cut into 1-inch cubes.
4. Add remaining oil and sauté onion, mushrooms, mustard, lemon juice, pepper, and chicken for 10 minutes.

5. Stir in flour and sauté for 3 minutes.
6. Stir in light cream. Mix well until thoroughly incorporated.
7. Serve and enjoy.

Nutrition Information:
Calories per Serving: 295; Carbs: 8.3g; Protein: 29.5g; Fats: 15.7g; Saturated Fat: 5.4g; Sodium: 118mg

Chicken Piccata Stew

Serves: 6 , Cooking time: minutes
Ingredients:
- 1-pound chicken breasts, bones, and skin removed
- ½ cup all-purpose flour
- 1 tablespoon olive oil
- 3 cloves of garlic, minced
- ¾ cup chicken broth, low sodium
- 1/3 cup lemon juice, freshly squeezed
- 1 sprig of basil, chopped
- 3 ounces capers, drained
- ¼ cup sour cream

Directions for Cooking:
1. Place a nonstick saucepan on medium high fire and heat pot for 3 minutes.
2. Once hot, add oil and stir around to coat pot with oil.
3. Brown chicken for 5 minutes per side. Transfer to a chopping board and cut into 1-inch cubes.
4. Sauté the garlic, capers, and chicken for 10 minutes.
5. Whisk well flour, lemon juice, and chicken broth in a bowl.
6. Stir in chicken broth slurry and continue sautéing until sauce has thickened, around 5 minutes.
7. Serve and enjoy with sour cream.

Nutrition Information:
Calories per Serving: 194; Carbs: 10.8g; Protein: 23.8g; Fats: 5.8g; Saturated Fat: 1.6g; Sodium: 389mg

Chicken Stew the Creole Way

Serves: 6 , Cooking time: 35 minutes
Ingredients:
- 1 tbsp butter
- 3 chicken breasts, boneless and skinless
- 1 cup chopped onion
- ½ cup chopped celery
- ½ cup green bell pepper, chopped
- 1 teaspoon coconut sugar
- ¼ teaspoon ground cloves
- 1 teaspoon garlic powder
- ½ teaspoon white pepper
- ½ teaspoon black pepper
- ½ teaspoon cayenne pepper
- ½ teaspoon dried basil
- 1 cup chopped tomatoes
- 1 cup tomato sauce, low sodium
- 1 cup chicken broth, low sodium

Directions for Cooking:
1. Place a nonstick saucepan on medium high fire and heat pot for 3 minutes.
2. Once hot, add butter and stir around to coat pot with oil.
3. Brown chicken for 5 minutes per side. Transfer to a chopping board and cut into 1-inch cubes.
4. Sauté the onion, celery, tomatoes, coconut sugar, cloves, garlic powder, white pepper, black pepper, cayenned, dried basil, and chicken for 10 minutes.
5. Stir in remaining ingredients. Cook for another 10 minutes.
6. Serve and enjoy.

Nutrition Information:
Calories per Serving: 190; Carbs: 6.7g; Protein: 28.8g; Fats: 5.1g; Saturated Fat: 2.0g; Sodium: 74mg

Grilled Jamaican Jerk Chicken

Serves: 6 , Cooking time: 15 minutes

Ingredients:

- 6 chicken drumsticks
- ½ cup ketchup
- ¼ cup dark brown sugar
- ¼ cup red wine vinegar
- 1 tablespoons soy sauce, low sodium
- 2 tablespoons Jamaican jerk seasoning
- Salt and pepper to taste

Directions for Cooking:

1. In a zip lock bag, combine all ingredients except for chicken. Mix well.
2. Add chicken and marinate for at least 30 minutes. For best results, marinate overnight. Turning chicken once in a while.
3. When ready to cook, preheat grill to 350°F.
4. Grease grate and grill chicken for 7 minutes per side.
5. Serve and enjoy.

Nutrition Information:

Calories per Serving: 130; Carbs: 12.2g; Protein: 13.3g; Fats: 2.7g; Saturated Fat: 0.7g; Sodium: 333mg

Chicken with White Wine Mushroom Sauce

Serves: 6 , Cooking time: 30 minutes

Ingredients:

- 1 tablespoon olive oil
- 2 chicken breasts, boneless and skinless
- 1 onion, chopped
- 4 cloves of garlic, minced
- 1-pound cremini mushrooms, sliced
- ½ cup dry white wine
- 2 cups chicken broth, low sodium
- 1 tablespoon thyme
- 2 bay leaves
- 1 tablespoon lemon juice, freshly squeezed
- Pepper
- 2 tablespoons cornstarch + 2 tablespoons water

Directions for Cooking:

1. Place a nonstick saucepan on medium high fire and heat pot for 3 minutes.
2. Once hot, add oil and stir around to coat pot with oil.
3. Brown chicken for 5 minutes per side. Transfer to a chopping board and cut into 1-inch cubes.
4. Sauté the onion, garlic, bay leaves, thyme, mushrooms, and chicken for 10 minutes.
5. Stir in remaining ingredients except for cornstarch slurry and mix well.
6. Stir in cornstarch slurry and continue sautéing until sauce has thickened, around 5 minutes.
7. Serve and enjoy.

Nutrition Information:

Calories per Serving: 152; Carbs: 7.6g; Protein: 20.6g; Fats: 4.6g; Saturated Fat: 0.9g; Sodium: 45mg

Serves: 8 , Cooking time: 25 minutes

Ingredients:

- 1 tablespoon coconut oil
- 1 onion, sliced
- 3 cloves of garlic, minced
- 4 chicken thighs, boneless and skinless
- 2 tablespoons achiote seasoning
- 2 tablespoons white vinegar
- 3 tablespoons Worcestershire sauce
- 1 teaspoon ground cumin
- 1 teaspoon dried oregano
- Salt and pepper to taste
- 1 tablespoon granulated sugar
- 2 cups chicken stock, low sodium

Directions for Cooking:

1. Place a nonstick saucepan on medium high fire and heat pot for 3 minutes.

2. Once hot, add oil and stir around to coat pot with oil.
3. Brown chicken for 5 minutes per side. Transfer to a chopping board and cut into 1-inch cubes.
4. Sauté the garlic, achiote, Worcestershire, white vinegar, cumin, oregano, sugar, and chicken for 5 minutes.
5. Stir in remaining ingredients and mix well. Simmer for 10 minutes.
6. Serve and enjoy.

Nutrition Information:

Calories per Serving: 90; Carbs: 4.7g; Protein: 7.2g; Fats: 4.5g; Saturated Fat: 2.2g; Sodium: 238mg

Serves: 6 , Cooking time: minutes

Ingredients:

- 1-pound chicken breasts, boneless, skinless
- 4 tablespoons honey
- 4 cloves of garlic, minced
- 2 tablespoons onion powder
- 1 tablespoon soy sauce, low sodium
- ½ tablespoon sriracha sauce
- ¼ cup water
- Green onions, chopped
- 1 tablespoon sesame oil

Directions for Cooking:

1. Place a nonstick saucepan on medium high fire and heat pot for 3 minutes.
2. Once hot, add oil and stir around to coat pot with oil.

3. Brown chicken for 5 minutes per side. Transfer to a chopping board and cut into 1-inch cubes.
4. Sauté the garlic, onion powder, soy sauce, sriracha sauce and chicken for 5 minutes.
5. Add water and deglaze pot. Continue cooking until liquid is rendered, around 5 to 8 minutes of sautéing.
6. Turn off fire. Add honey and toss well to mix.
7. Serve and enjoy with a sprinkle of green onions.

Nutrition Information:

Calories per Serving: 199; Carbs: 15.5g; Protein: 5.1g; Fats: 5.1g; Saturated Fat: 1.1g; Sodium: 103mg

Chapter 10 Meat Recipes

Grilled Flank Steak with Lime Vinaigrette

Serves:6 , Cook Time: 10 minutes

Ingredients:

- 2 tablespoons lime juice, freshly squeezed
- 2 tablespoons extra virgin olive oil
- ½ teaspoon ground black pepper
- ¼ cup chopped fresh cilantro
- 1 tablespoon ground cumin
- ¼ teaspoon red pepper flakes
- ¾ pound flank steak

Directions for Cooking:

1. Heat the grill to low medium heat
2. In a food processor, place all ingredients except for the cumin, red pepper flakes, and flank steak. Pulse until smooth. This will be the vinaigrette sauce. Set aside.
3. Season the flank steak with ground cumin and red pepper flakes and allow to marinate for at least 10 minutes.
4. Place the steak on the grill rack and cook for 5 minutes on each side. Cut into the center to check the doneness of the meat. You can also insert a meat thermometer to check the internal temperature.
5. Remove from the grill and allow to stand for 5 minutes.
6. Slice the steak to 2 inches long and toss the vinaigrette to flavor the meat.
7. Serve with salad if desired.

Nutrition Information:

Calories per Serving:103 ; Protein: 13g; Carbs: 1g; Fat: 5g; Saturated Fat: 1g; Sodium: 73mg

Asian Pork Tenderloin

Serves:4 , Cook Time: 15 minutes

Ingredients:

- 2 tablespoons sesame seeds
- 1 teaspoon ground coriander
- 1/8 teaspoon cayenne pepper
- 1/8 teaspoon celery seed
- ½ teaspoon minced onion
- ¼ teaspoon ground cumin
- 1/8 teaspoon ground cinnamon
- 1 tablespoon sesame oil
- 1-pound pork tenderloin sliced into 4 equal portions

Directions for Cooking:

1. Preheat the oven to 400⁰F.
2. In a skillet, toast the sesame seeds over low heat and set aside. Allow the sesame seeds to cool.
3. In a bowl, combine the rest of the ingredients expect for the pork tenderloin. Stir in the toasted sesame seeds.
4. Place the pork tenderloin in a baking dish and rub the spices on both sides.
5. Place the baking dish with the pork in the oven and bake for 15 minutes or until the internal temperature of the meat reaches to 170⁰F.
6. Serve warm.

Nutrition Information:

Calories per Serving: 248; Protein: 26g; Carbs: 0g; Fat: 16g; Saturated Fat: 5g; Sodium: 57mg

Simple Beef Brisket and Tomato Soup

Serves:8 , Cook Time: 3 hours

Ingredients:

- 1 tablespoon olive oil
- 2 ½ pounds beef brisket, trimmed of fat and cut into 8 equal parts
- A dash of ground black pepper
- 1 ½ cups chopped onions
- 4 cloves of garlic, smashed
- 1 teaspoon dried thyme
- 1 cup ripe roma tomatoes, chopped

- ¼ cup red wine vinegar
- 1 cup beef stock, low sodium or home made

Directions for Cooking:
1. In a heavy pot, heat the oil over medium-high heat.
2. Season the brisket with ground black pepper and place in the pot.
3. Cook while stirring constantly until the beef turns brown on all sides.
4. Stir in the onions and cook until fragrant. Add in the garlic and thyme and cook for another minute until fragrant.
5. Pour in the rest of the ingredients and bring to a boil.
6. Cook until the beef is tender. This may take about 3 hours or more.

Nutrition Information:
Calories per Serving: 229; Protein: 31g; Carbs: 6g; Fat: 9g; Saturated Fat: 3g; Sodium: 184mg

Beef Stew with Fennel And Shallots

Serves:6 , Cook Time: 40 minutes

Ingredients:
- 1 tablespoon olive oil
- 1-pound boneless lean beef stew meat, trimmed from fat and cut into cubes
- ½ fennel bulb, trimmed and sliced thinly
- 3 large shallots, chopped
- ¾ teaspoons ground black pepper
- 2 fresh thyme sprigs
- 1 bay leaf
- 3 cups low sodium beef broth
- ½ cup red wine
- 4 large carrots, peeled and cut into chunks
- 4 large white potatoes, peeled and cut into chunks
- 3 portobello mushrooms, cleaned and cut into chunks
- 1/3 cup Italian parsley, chopped

Directions for Cooking:
1. Heat oil in a pot over medium heat and stir in the beef cubes for 5 minutes or until all sides turn brown.
2. Stir in the fennel, shallots, black pepper, and thyme for one minute or until the ingredients become fragrant.
3. Stir in the bay leaf, broth, red wine, carrots, white potatoes and mushrooms.
4. Bring to a boil and cook for 30 minutes or until everything is tender.
5. Stir in the parsley last.

Nutrition Information:
Calories per Serving: 244; Protein: 21g; Carbs: 22g; Fat: 8g; Saturated Fat: 2g; Sodium: 184mg

Rustic Beef and Barley Soup

Serves:6 , Cook Time: 40 minutes

Ingredients:
- 1 teaspoon olive oil
- 1-pound beef round steak, sliced into strips
- 2 cups yellow onion, chopped
- 1 cup diced celery
- 4 cloves of garlic, chopped
- 1 cup diced roma tomatoes
- ½ cup diced sweet potato
- ½ cup diced mushrooms
- 1 cup diced carrots
- ¼ cup uncooked barley
- 3 cups low sodium vegetable stock
- 1 teaspoon dried sage
- 1 teaspoon dried oregano
- A dash of black pepper to taste
- 1 cup chopped kale

Directions for Cooking:
1. In a large pot, heat the oil over medium flame and stir in the beef. Cook for 5 minutes while stirring constantly until all sides turn brown.
2. Stir in the onion, celery, and garlic until fragrant.
3. Add in the rest of the ingredients except for the kale.
4. Bring to a boil and cook for 30 minutes until everything is tender.
5. Stir in the kale last and cook for another 5 minutes.

Nutrition Information:
Calories per Serving:246 ; Protein: 21g; Carbs: 24g; Fat: 4g; Saturated Fat: 1g; Sodium: 13mg

Beef Stroganoff

Serves:4 , Cook Time: 25 minutes

Ingredients:

- ½ cup chopped onion
- ½ pound boneless beef round steak, cut into ¾ inch thick
- 4 cups pasta noodles
- ½ cup fat-free cream of mushroom soup
- ½ cup water
- ½ teaspoon paprika
- ½ cup fat-free sour cream

Directions for Cooking:

1. In a non-stick frying pan, saute the onions over low to medium heat without oil while stirring constantly for about 5 minutes.
2. Stir in the beef and cook for another 5 minutes until the beef is tender and turn brown on all sides. Set aside.
3. In a large pot, fill it with water until ¾ full and bring to a boil. Cook the noodles until done according to package instructions. Drain the noodles and set aside.
4. In a saucepan, whisk the mushroom soup and water. Bring to a boil over medium heat and stir constantly until the sauce has reduced. Add in paprika and sour cream.
5. Assemble the stroganoff by placing the pasta in a bowl and pouring over the sauce. Top with the meat.
6. Serve warm.

Nutrition Information:

Calories per Serving: 273; Protein: 20g; Carbs: 37g; Fat: 5g; Saturated Fat: 2g; Sodium: 193mg

Curried Pork Tenderloin in Apple Cider

Serves:6 , Cook Time: 26 minutes

Ingredients:

- 16 ounces pork tenderloin, cut into 6 pieces
- 1 ½ tablespoons curry powder
- 1 tablespoon extra virgin olive oil
- 2 medium onions, chopped
- 2 cups apple cider, organic and unsweetened
- 1 tart apple, peeled and chopped into chunks

Directions for Cooking:

1. In a bowl, season the pork with the curry powder and set aside.
2. Heat oil in a pot over medium flame.
3. Saute the onions for one minute until fragrant.
4. Stir in the seasoned pork tenderloin and cook for 5 minutes or until lightly golden.
5. Add in the apple cider and apple chunks.
6. Close the lid and bring to a boil.
7. Allow to simmer for 20 minutes.

Nutrition Information:

Calories per Serving: 244; Protein: 24g; Carbs: 18g; Fat: 8g; Saturated Fat: 2g; Sodium: 70mg

Pork Medallions with Five Spice Powder

Serves:4 , Cook Time: 25 minutes

Ingredients:

- 1 tablespoon olive oil
- 3 cloves of garlic, minded
- 1-pound pork tenderloin, fat trimmed
- 2 tablespoon low-sodium soy sauce
- 1 tablespoon green onion, minced
- ¾ teaspoon five spice powder
- ½ cup water
- ¼ cup dry white wine
- 1/3 cup chopped onion
- ½ head green cabbage, thinly sliced and wilted
- 1 tablespoon chopped fresh parsley

Directions for Cooking:

1. In a bowl, combine the olive oil, garlic, pork tenderloin, soy sauce, green onion, and five spice powder. Mix until well combined and allow to marinate in the fridge for at least two hours.
2. Heat the oven to 400°F.
3. Remove the pork from the marinade and pat dry.
4. On a skillet, sear the meat on all sides until slightly brown before transferring into a heat-proof baking dish.
5. Place inside the oven and roast the pork for 20 minutes.

6. Meanwhile, pour the water, dry white wine, and onions in the skillet where you seared the pork and deglaze. Allow to simmer until the sauce has reduced.

7. Serve the pork medallions with wilted cabbages and drizzle the sauce on top.

Nutrition Information:
Calories per Serving: 219; Protein: 25g; Carbs: 5g; Fat: 11g; Saturated Fat: 2g; Sodium: 296mg

Grilled Pork Fajitas

Serves:8 , Cook Time: 15 minutes

Ingredients:
- ½ teaspoon paprika
- ½ teaspoon oregano
- ¼ teaspoon ground coriander
- ¼ teaspoon garlic powder
- 1 tablespoon chili powder
- 1-pound pork tenderloin, fat trimmed and cut into large strips
- 1 onion, sliced
- 8 whole wheat flour tortillas, warmed
- 4 medium tomatoes, chopped
- 4 cups shredded lettuce

Directions for Cooking:
1. In a bowl, mix the paprika, oregano, coriander, garlic powder, and chili powder.

2. Sprinkle the spice mixture on the pork tenderloin strips and toss to coat the meat with the spices.
3. Prepare the grill and heat to 400^{0}F.
4. Place the meat and onion in a grill basket and broil for 20 minutes or until all sides have browned.
5. Assemble the fajitas by placing in the center of the tortillas the grilled pork and onions. Add in the tomatoes and lettuce before rolling the fajitas.

Nutrition Information:
Calories per Serving: 250; Protein: 20g; Carbs: 29g; Fat: 6g; Saturated Fat: 2g; Sodium: 234mg

New York Strip Steak with Mushroom Sauce

Serves:2 , Cook Time: 20 minutes

Ingredients:
- 2 New York Strip steaks (4 ounces each), trimmed from fat
- 3 cloves of garlic, minced
- 2 ounces shiitake mushrooms, sliced
- 2 ounces button mushrooms, sliced
- ¼ teaspoon thyme
- ¼ teaspoon rosemary
- ¼ cup low sodium beef broth

Directions for Cooking:
1. Heat the grill to 350^{0}F.
2. Position the grill rack 6 inches from the heat source.

3. Grill the steaks for 10 minutes on each side or until slightly pink on the inside.
4. Meanwhile, prepare the sauce. In a small nonstick pan, water saute the garlic, mushrooms, thyme and rosemary for a minute. Pour in the broth and bring to a boil. Allow the sauce to simmer until the liquid is reduced.
5. Top the steaks with the mushroom sauce.
6. Serve warm.

Nutrition Information:
Calories per Serving: 270; Protein: 23g; Carbs: 4g; Fat: 6g; Saturated Fat: 2g; Sodium: 96 mg

Pork Chops with Black Currant Jam

Serves:6 , Cook Time: 20 minutes

Ingredients:
- ¼ cup black currant jam
- 2 tablespoons Dijon mustard
- 1 teaspoon olive oil
- 6 center cut pork loin chops, trimmed from fat
- 1/3 cup wine vinegar
- 1/8 teaspoon ground black pepper
- 6 orange slices

Directions for Cooking:
1. In a small bowl, mix together the jam and mustard. Set aside.

2. In a nonstick pan, heat the oil over medium flames and sear the pork chops for 5 minutes on each side or until all sides turn brown.
3. Brush the pork chops with the mustard mixture and turn the flame to low. Cook for two more minutes on each side. Set aside.
4. Using the same frying pan, pour in the wine vinegar to deglaze the pan. Season with ground black pepper and allow to simmer for at least 5 minutes or until the vinegar has reduced.
5. Pour over the pork chops and garnish with orange slices on top.

Nutrition Information:
Calories per Serving: 198; Protein: 25g; Carbs: 11g; Fat: 6g; Saturated Fat: 2g; Sodium: 188mg

Pork Medallion with Herbes de Provence

Serves:2 , Cook Time: 15 minutes
Ingredients:
- 8 ounces of pork medallion, trimmed from fat
- Freshly ground black pepper to taste
- ½ teaspoon Herbes de Provence
- ¼ cup dry white wine

Directions for Cooking:
1. Season the meat with black pepper.
2. Place the meat in between sheets of wax paper and pound on a mallet until about ¼ inch thick.
3. In a nonstick skillet, sear the pork over medium heat for 5 minutes on each side or until the meat is slightly brown.
4. Remove meat from the skillet and sprinkle with herbes de Provence.
5. Using the same skillet, pour the wine and scrape the sides to deglaze. Allow to simmer until the wine is reduced.
6. Pour the wine sauce over the pork.
7. Serve immediately.

Nutrition Information:
Calories per Serving: 120; Protein: 24g; Carbs: 1g; Fat: 2g; Saturated Fat: 0.5g; Sodium: 62mg

Pork Tenderloin with Apples And Balsamic Vinegar

Serves:4 , Cook Time: 25 minutes
Ingredients:
- 1 tablespoon olive oil
- 1-pound pork tenderloin, trimmed from fat
- Freshly ground black pepper
- 2 cups chopped onion
- 2 cups chopped apple
- 1 ½ tablespoons fresh rosemary, chopped
- 1 cup low sodium chicken broth
- 1 ½ tablespoons balsamic vinegar

Directions for Cooking:
1. Heat the oven to 450⁰F.
2. Heat the oil in a large skillet over medium flame.
3. Sear the pork and season with black pepper. Cook the pork for 3 minutes until all sides turn light brown. Remove from the heat and place in a baking pan.
4. Roast the pork for 15 minutes.
5. Meanwhile, place the onion, apples, and rosemary on the skillet where the pork is seared. Continue stirring for 5 minutes. Pour in broth and balsamic vinegar and allow to simmer until the sauce thickens.
6. Serve the roasted pork with the onion and apple sauce.

Nutrition Information:
Calories per Serving: 240; Protein: 26g; Carbs: 17g; Fat: 6g; Saturated Fat: 1g; Sodium: 83mg

Pork Tenderloin with Apples And Blue Cheese

Serves:4 , Cook Time: 25 minutes
Ingredients:
- 1-pound pork tenderloin, trimmed from fat
- ½ teaspoon white pepper
- 2 teaspoons black pepper
- ¼ teaspoon cayenne pepper
- 1 teaspoon paprika
- 2 apples, sliced

- ½ cup unsweetened apple juice
- ¼ cup crumbled blue cheese

Directions for Cooking:
1. Heat the oven to 350⁰F.
2. Season the tenderloin with white pepper, black pepper, cayenne pepper, and paprika.
3. Heat a non-stick pan over medium flame and sear the meat for 3 minutes on each side. Transfer to a baking dish and roast in the oven for 20 minutes or until the internal temperature is at 155⁰F. Remove from the oven to cool.
4. While the pork is roasting, prepare the sauce. Using the same skillet used to sear the meat, saute the apples for 3 minutes. Add the apple juice and allow the sauce to thicken for at least 10 minutes.
5. Serve the pork with the apple sauce and sprinkle with blue cheese on top.

Nutrition Information:
Calories per Serving: 235; Protein: 26g; Carbs: 17; Fat: 3g; Saturated Fat: 1g; Sodium: 145mg

Pork Tenderloin with Fennel Sauce

Serves:4 , Cook Time: 30 minutes

Ingredients:
- 4 pork tenderloin fillets, trimmed from fat and cut into 4 portions
- 1 tablespoon olive oil
- 1 teaspoon fennel seeds
- 1 fennel bulb, cored and sliced thinly
- 1 sweet onion, sliced thinly
- ½ cup dry white wine
- 12 ounces low sodium chicken broth
- 1 orange, sliced for garnish

Directions for Cooking:
1. Place the pork slices in between wax paper and pound with a mallet to about ¼-inch thick.
2. Heat oil in a skillet and fry the fennel seeds for 3 minutes or until fragrant.
3. Stir in the pork and cook on all sides for 3 minutes or until golden brown. Remove the pork from the skillet and set aside.
4. Using the same skillet, add the fennel bulb slices and onion. Saute for 5 minutes then set aside.
5. Add the wine and chicken broth in the skillet and bring to a boil until the sauce reduces in half.
6. Return the pork to the skillet and cook for another 5 minutes.
7. Serve the pork with sauce and vegetables.

Nutrition Information:
Calories per Serving: 276; Protein: 29g; Carbs: 13g; Fat: 12g; Saturated Fat:3 g; Sodium: 122mg

Spicy Beef Kebabs

Serves:8 , Cook Time: 10 minutes

Ingredients:
- 2 yellow onions, minced
- 2 tablespoons fresh lemon juice
- 1 ½ pounds lean ground beef, minced
- ¼ cup bulgur, soaked in water for 30 minutes then rinsed
- ¼ cup chopped pine nuts
- 2 cloves of garlic, minced
- 1 teaspoon ground cumin
- ½ teaspoon ground cinnamon
- ½ teaspoon ground cardamom
- ½ teaspoon freshly ground black pepper
- 16 wooden skewers, soaked in water for 30 minutes

Directions for Cooking:
1. In a mixing bowl, combine all ingredients except for the skewers. Mix well unt
2. Form a sausage from the meat mixture and thread it into the skewers. If the sausage is crumbly, add a tablespoon of water at a time until it holds well together. Refrigerate the skewered meat sausages until ready to cook.
3. Heat the grill to 350⁰F and place the grill rack 6 inches from the heat source.
4. Place the skewered kebabs on the grill and broil for 5 minutes on each side.
5. Serve with yogurt if desired.

Nutrition Information:
Calories per Serving: 219; Protein: 23g; Carbs: 3g; Fat: 12g; Saturated Fat: 3g; Sodium: 53mg

Spicy Beef Curry

Serves:6 , Cook Time: 40 minutes

Ingredients:

- 1 medium serrano pepper, cut into thirds
- 4 cloves of garlic, minced
- 1 2-inch piece ginger, peeled and chopped
- 1 yellow onion, chopped
- 2 tablespoon ground coriander
- 2 teaspoons ground cumin
- ½ teaspoon ground turmeric
- 2 teaspoons garam masala
- 1 tablespoon olive oil
- pounds beef, cut into chunks
- 1 cup ripe tomatoes, diced
- 2 cups water
- 1 cup fresh cilantro for garnish

Directions for Cooking:

1. In a food processor, pulse the serrano peppers, garlic, ginger, onion, coriander, cumin, turmeric, and garam masala until well-combined.
2. Heat oil over medium heat in a skillet and saute the spice mixture for 2 minutes or until fragrant.
3. Stir in the beef and allow to cook while stirring constantly for three minutes or until the beef turns brown.
4. Stir in the tomatoes and saute for another three minutes.
5. Add in the water and bring to a boil.
6. Once boiling, turn the heat to low and allow to simmer for thirty minutes or until the meat is tender.
7. Add cilantro last before serving.

Nutrition Information:
Calories per Serving: 181; Protein: 16g; Carbs: 5g; Fat: 8g; Saturated Fat: 2g; Sodium: 74mg

Pork Tenderloin with Apples And Sweet Potatoes

Serves:4 , Cook Time: 30 minutes

Ingredients:

- ¾ cup apple cider
- ¼ cup apple cider vinegar
- 2 tablespoons maple syrup
- ¼ teaspoon smoked paprika powder
- 1 teaspoon grated ginger
- ¼ teaspoon ground black pepper
- 2 teaspoons olive oil
- 1 12-ounce pork tenderloin
- 1 large sweet potato, cut into cubes
- 1 large apple, cored and into cubes

Directions for Cooking:

1. Preheat the oven to 375⁰F.
2. In a bowl, combine the apple cider, apple cider vinegar, maple syrup, smoked paprika, ginger, and black pepper. Set aside.
3. Heat the oil in a large skillet and sear the meat for 3 minutes on both sides.
4. Transfer the pork in a baking dish and place the sweet potatoes and apples around the pork. Pour in the apple cider sauce.
5. Place inside the oven and cook for 20 minutes.

Nutrition Information:
Calories per Serving: 267; Protein: 23.5g; Carbs:31 g; Fat: 5g; Saturated Fat: 0.5g; Sodium: 69mg

Mexican Beef and Veggie Skillet

Serves:4 , Cook Time:15 minutes

Ingredients:

- ½ pound lean ground beef
- ¾ cup chopped onion
- ½ cup bell pepper (any color), seeded and chopped
- ½ tablespoon chili powder
- 1 tablespoon oregano
- 1 cup tomatoes, chopped
- 1 cup frozen vegetable mix, chopped
- 2 cups water
- 1/2 cup shredded Mexican cheese blend

Directions for Cooking:

1. Place the beef in a large skillet and add onions. Sauté for 3 minutes or until the beef has slightly rendered its fat.
2. Stir in the bell pepper, chili powder, and oregano and cook for another minute.

3. Add in the tomatoes, vegetable mix and water.
4. Close the lid and bring to a simmer for 10 minutes.

5. Before serving, stir in cheese last.
Nutrition Information:
Calories per Serving: 222; Protein: 20g; Carbs11 g; Fat: 10g; Saturated Fat: 5g; Sodium: 132mg

Garlic Lime Marinated Pork Chops

Serves:4 , Cook Time: 10 minutes
Ingredients:
- 4 6-ounce lean boneless pork chops, trimmed from fat
- 4 cloves of garlic, crushed
- 1 teaspoon cumin
- 1 teaspoon chili powder
- 1 teaspoon paprika
- A dash of black pepper to taste
- Juice from ½ lime
- Zest from ½ lime

Directions for Cooking:

1. In a bowl, season the pork with the rest of the ingredients.
2. Allow to marinate inside the fridge for at least 2 hours.
3. Place the pork chops in a baking dish or broiler pan and grill for 5 minutes on each side until golden brown.
4. Serve with salad if desired.

Nutrition Information:
Calories per Serving: 233; Protein: 38.5g; Carbs: 4g; Fat: 6g; Saturated Fat: 1g; Sodium: 105mg

Oriental Stir Fry

Serves:4 , Cook Time: 20 minutes
Ingredients:
- 4 ounces pork loin, cut into thin strips
- 1 tablespoon ginger, minced
- 1 clove of garlic, chopped
- 1 ½ cups sliced onions
- 1 medium carrot, sliced thinly
- 2 medium green bell peppers, seeded and cut into thick strips
- 1 cup sliced celery
- 1 cup dried plums, pitted and halved
- 2 tablespoons low sodium soy sauce
- ¼ cup cold water + 2 tablespoons cornstarch

Directions for Cooking:
1. In a skillet, sauté the pork on medium heat until it has slightly rendered fat.

2. Stir in the ginger, garlic, and onions until fragrant.
3. Stir in the carrots, green bell peppers, celery, and plums.
4. Season with soy sauce.
5. Close the lid and adjust the flame to low. Cook for 10 minutes while stirring every 3 minutes.
6. Open the lid and adjust the flame to medium. Stir in the cornstarch slurry and cook for another 5 minutes until the sauce thickens.

Nutrition Information:
Calories per Serving: 145; Protein: 9g; Carbs: 21g; Fat: 3g; Saturated Fat: 0.4g; Sodium: 106mg

Cocoa-Crusted Pork Tenderloin

Serves:2 , Cook Time: 25 minutes
Ingredients:
- 1-pound pork tenderloin, trimmed from fat
- 1 tablespoon cocoa powder
- 1 teaspoon instant coffee powder
- ½ teaspoon ground cinnamon
- ½ teaspoon chili powder
- 1 tablespoon olive oil

Directions for Cooking:
1. In a bowl, dust the pork tenderloin with cocoa powder, coffee, cinnamon, and chili powder.

2. In a skillet, heat the oil and sear the meat for 5 minutes on both sides over low to medium flame.
3. Transfer the pork in a baking dish and cook in the oven for 15 minutes in a 350°F-preheated oven.

Nutrition Information:
Calories per Serving: 395; Protein: 60g; Carbs: 2g; Fat: 15g; Saturated Fat: 4g; Sodium: 150mg

Beef Kabobs with Pineapples

Serves:6 , Cook Time: 10 minutes

Ingredients:

- 1 ½ pounds beef shoulder steaks, cut into thick chunks
- A dash of ground black pepper
- 2 tablespoons olive oil
- 2 tablespoons lime juice
- 2 cloves of garlic, minced
- ½ teaspoon ground cumin
- 1 cup pineapple chunks
- 12 wooden skewers, soaked in water for 30 minutes

Directions for Cooking:

1. In a bowl, combine the beef, black pepper, olive oil, lime juice, garlic, and cumin until well-incorporated.
2. Place inside the fridge and allow to marinate for at least 3 hours.
3. Thread one chunk of beef and a chunk of pineapple alternately through the wooden skewer. Do two or three alternating layers.
4. Heat the grill to 350^0F and place the grill rack 6 inches away from the charcoal.
5. Grill the kabobs for 5 minutes on each side.

Nutrition Information:
Calories per Serving: 243; Protein: 24g; Carbs:11 g; Fat: 11g; Saturated Fat: 1g; Sodium: 71mg

Asian Beef and Zucchini Noodles

Serves:4 , Cook Time: 15 minutes

Ingredients:

- ½ pound lean ground beef
- 1 tablespoon minced ginger
- 2 cloves of garlic, minced
- 16 ounces Asian-style vegetable package, frozen
- 2 cups low sodium beef broth
- 1 large zucchini, spiralized or thinly sliced
- 2 green onions, sliced thinly

Directions for Cooking:

1. In a large skillet, saute the beef with minced ginger and garlic for three minutes while constantly stirring.
2. Stir in the vegetable package and the beef broth.
3. Bring to a boil for 10 minutes.
4. Assemble the dish by putting the zucchini in a bowl.
5. Pour in the soup and garnish with green onions.

Nutrition Information:
Calories per Serving: 271; Protein: 23g; Carbs:21 g; Fat: 5g; Saturated Fat: 3g; Sodium: 138mg

Exotic Thai Steak

Serves:4 , Cook Time: 20 minutes

Ingredients:

- 1-pound London broil, trimmed from fat
- 2 tablespoons light fish sauce
- 1 tablespoon olive oil
- 2 cloves of garlic, minced
- ½ teaspoon grated ginger
- ½ cup chopped coriander
- ¼ cup white vinegar
- 2 tablespoons honey

Directions for Cooking:

1. Place in a Ziploc bag all ingredients and allow to marinate in the fridge for at least 3 hours.
2. Heat the grill to low heat.
3. Place the meat on the grill rack and allow to cook for 10 minutes on each side or until the internal temperature reaches 175^0F.
4. Slice the London broil and serve with vegetables.

Nutrition Information:
Calories per Serving: 219; Protein: 23g; Carbs: 9g; Fat: 5g; Saturated Fat: 1g; Sodium: 100mg

Sweet and Spicy Edamame Beef Stew

Serves:6 , Cook Time: 20 minutes

Ingredients:

- 1 tablespoon olive oil
- 8 ounces sirloin steak, trimmed from fat
- 2 teaspoon ginger, finely chopped
- 3 cloves of garlic, minced
- 3 cups packaged vegetable of your choice
- 1 cup shelled sweet soybeans or edamame
- 3 tablespoons hoisin sauce
- 2 tablespoons rice vinegar
- 1 teaspoon red chili paste

Directions for Cooking:

1. In a non-stick pan, heat the oil over medium flame.
2. Saute the sirloin steak for 3 minutes while stirring constantly.
3. Stir in the ginger and garlic and saute for 1 minute.
4. Add in the rest of the ingredients.
5. Close the lid and allow to simmer for 10 minutes until the vegetables are cooked.

Nutrition Information:

Calories per Serving: 205; Protein: 14g; Carbs: 17g; Fat: 4g; Saturated Fat: 1g; Sodium: 146mg

Filling Sirloin Soup

Serves:4 , Cook Time: 15 minutes

Ingredients:

- 1 tablespoon oil
- 1 small onion, diced
- 3 cloves of garlic, minced
- 1-pound lean ground sirloin
- 3 cups low sodium beef broth
- 1 bag frozen vegetables of your choice
- Black pepper to taste

Directions for Cooking:

1. In a large saucepan, heat the oil over medium heat and saute the onion and garlic until fragrant.
2. Stir in the lean ground sirloin and cook for 3 minutes until lightly golden.
3. Add in the rest of the ingredients and bring the broth to a boil for 10 minutes.
4. Serve warm.

Nutrition Information:

Calories per Serving: 245; Protein: 29g; Carbs: 22g; Fat: 4g; Saturated Fat: 1g; Sodium: 152mg

Roast Rack of Lamb

Serves:8 , Cook Time: 30 minutes

Ingredients:

- 2 1-poundFrench-style lamb rib roast, trimmed from fat
- 1 cup dry red wine
- 2 cloves of garlic, minced
- 1 teaspoon freshly grated nutmeg
- 1 tablespoon olive oil
- 1 tablespoon chopped rosemary
- 3 tablespoons dried cranberries, chopped

Directions for Cooking:

1. In a resealable plastic, place the lamb and add in red wine, garlic, nutmeg, olive oil, and rosemary. Seal the bag and turn it to coat the lamb with the spices. Marinate inside the fridge for at least 4 hours while turning the bag occasionally.
2. Preheat the oven to 450^{0}F and remove the lamb from the marinade. Reserve the juices.
3. Place the lamb bone side down on a roasting pan lined with foil.
4. Pour the reserved marinade over the roasting pan.
5. Roast for 30 minutes until the lamb turns slightly golden. Turn the lamb every 10 minutes and baste with the sauce.
6. Once cooked, take out the lamb from the oven and slice.
7. Serve with chopped cranberries on top.

Nutrition Information:

Calories per Serving: 241; Protein: 25; Carbs: 1g; Fat: 12g; Saturated Fat: 3g; Sodium: 46mg

Pork Medallions with Pear Maple Sauce

Serves:4 , Cook Time: 10 minutes

Ingredients:

- 1 16-ounce pork tenderloin, trimmed from fat
- 2 teaspoons snipped fresh rosemary, crushed
- 1 teaspoon snipped fresh thyme, crushed
- A dash of black pepper to taste
- 1 tablespoon olive oil
- 2 medium pears, peeled and roughly chopped
- ¼ cup pure maple syrup
- 2 tablespoons dried tart red cherries, halved
- 2 tablespoons apple juice

Directions for Cooking:

1. Cut meat into ¼ inch slices and place in a bowl.
2. Add in the rosemary, thyme, and black pepper. Toss to coat the ingredients.
3. In the same skillet, heat the oil over medium flame and saute the meat for 5 minutes or until golden brown while stirring constantly. Set aside.
4. Using the same skillet, pour in the rest of the ingredients and cook on low heat. Boil gently uncovered for three minutes until the pears are tender and the sauce has slightly reduced.
5. Pour sauce over the pork.

Nutrition Information:

Calories per Serving: 305; Protein: 30g; Carbs: 29g; Fat: 8g; Saturated Fat: 1g; Sodium: 70mg

Mustard Maple Pork Roast

Serves:8 , Cook Time: 45 minutes

Ingredients:

- 2 ½ pounds boneless pork loin roast, trimmed from fat
- 2 tablespoon Dijon-style mustard
- 2 teaspoons dried sage, crushed
- 1 teaspoon shredded orange peel
- ¼ teaspoon ground black pepper
- 6 tiny potatoes, scrubbed
- 16 ounces packaged baby carrots, peeled
- 1 tablespoon olive oil

Directions for Cooking:

1. Preheat the oven to 325⁰F.
2. Place the pork in a baking dish.
3. In a bowl, combine the mustard, sage, orange peel, and black pepper.
4. Brush the meat with the spice mixture.
5. Roast uncovered for 45 minutes.
6. Meanwhile, cook the potatoes in boiling water for 5 minutes. Add the carrots and cook for another 5 minutes.
7. Drain the vegetables and coat with olive oil.
8. Place the vegetables around the pork until the end of cooking time.

Nutrition Information:

Calories per Serving: 324 Protein: 34g; Carbs28 g; Fat: 5g; Saturated Fat: 1g; Sodium: 164mg

Herbed Pepper Sirloin Steak

Serves:4 , Cook Time:10 minutes

Ingredients:

- ½ teaspoon coarse ground black pepper
- 1 ½ teaspoons fresh rosemary
- 1 ½ teaspoons snipped fresh basil
- 1/8 teaspoon garlic powder
- 1/8 teaspoon ground cardamom
- 1 ½ pounds boneless beef sirloin steak, cut into 1-inch thick
- ¼ cup low sodium beef broth
- Grilled sweet peppers, seeded and sliced

Directions for Cooking:

1. In a bowl, combine the black pepper, rosemary, basil, garlic, and cardamom. Stir to combine.
2. Sprinkle the spice mixture on to the sirloin steak. Set aside.
3. Heat non-stick skillet over medium flame and saute the seasoned sirloin steak for 5 minutes while stirring constantly.
4. Pour in the beef broth and allow to simmer for another 5 minutes.
5. Before serving, add in the roasted peppers.

Nutrition Information:

Calories per Serving: 235; Protein: 37g; Carbs:2 g; Fat: 6g; Saturated Fat: 2g; Sodium: 136mg

Grilled Marinated Flank Steak

Serves:4 , Cook Time: 20 minutes

Ingredients:

- 1 ½ pounds beef flank steak, trimmed from fat
- 1/3 cup red wine vinegar
- 2 cloves of garlic, minced
- 2 tablespoons Dijon-style mustard
- 2 tablespoons snipped fresh cilantro
- ¼ teaspoon crushed red pepper
- 1 head lettuce, shredded

Directions for Cooking:

1. In a large resealable bag, place all ingredients except for the shredded lettuce.
2. Allow to marinate in the fridge for at least 2 hours.
3. Heat the grill to medium.
4. Place the pork and grill for 5 to 10 minutes on each side.
5. Baste the pork with the marinade every three minutes.
6. Once cooked, slice the pork into strips.
7. Serve with shredded lettuce.

Nutrition Information:

Calories per Serving: 270; Protein: 38g; Carbs: 7g; Fat: 6g; Saturated Fat:1 g; Sodium: 197mg

Grilled Fennel Cumin Lamb Chops

Serves:6 , Cook Time: 20 minutes

Ingredients:

- 6 lamb rib chops
- 1 clove of garlic, minced
- ¾ teaspoon fennel seeds, crushed
- ¼ teaspoon ground coriander
- 1/8 teaspoon cracked black pepper

Directions for Cooking:

1. Place the lamb rib chops in a shallow dish and rub onto the surface the garlic, fennel seeds, coriander, and black pepper. Allow to marinate in the fridge for 4 hours.
2. Heat the grill to medium and place the grill rack 6 inches above the heat source.
3. Grill the lamb chops for 10 minutes on each side or until well-done. For medium rare lamb chops, cook for 6 to 8 minutes on each side.

Nutrition Information:

Calories per Serving: 126; Protein: 17g; Carbs: 0.5g; Fat: 5g; Saturated Fat:1 g; Sodium: 39mg

Caribbean Smoked Chops

Serves:4 , Cook Time: 2 hours

Ingredients:

- 8 pecans or cherry wood chunks
- 4 pork loin chops
- 3 teaspoon low sodium Jamaican jerk seasoning
- 1 medium mango, peeled and chopped
- ¼ cup sliced green onions
- ½ tablespoon chopped cilantro
- 1/2 teaspoon orange zest

Directions for Cooking:

1. Soak the wood chunks for at least an hour in water then drain before using.
2. Sprinkle the pork chops with the Jamaican jerk seasoning.
3. In a smoker, place the coals and the drained wood chunks. Place a pan with water around the wood chunks or according to the smoker's instruction. Place on the grill rack the pork.
4. Cover and allow to smoke for 2 hours until the juices run clear.
5. Meanwhile, prepare the side dish by combining the rest of the ingredients in a bowl. Toss to combine everything.
6. Serve the smoked pork with the side dish.

Nutrition Information:

Calories per Serving: 344; Protein: 40g; Carbs: 4g; Fat: 10g; Saturated Fat: 3g; Sodium: 88mg

Bistro Beef Tenderloin

Serves:7 , Cook Time: 45 minutes

Ingredients:

- 1 3-pound beef tenderloin, trimmed of fat
- 2 tablespoons extra virgin olive oil
- ½ teaspoon ground black pepper
- 2/3 cup chopped mixed herbs
- 2 tablespoons Dijon mustard

Directions for Cooking:

1. Preheat the oven to 400°F.
2. Secure the beef tenderloin with a string in three places so that it does not flatten while roasting.
3. Place the beef tenderloin in a dish and rub onto the meat the olive oil, black pepper, and mixed herb.
4. Place on a roasting pan and cook in the oven for 45 minutes.
5. Roast until the thermometer inserted into the thickest part of the meat until it registers 140°F for medium rare.
6. Place the tenderloin on a chopping board and remove the string. Slice into 1-inch thick slices and brush with Dijon mustard.

Nutrition Information:

Calories per Serving: 430; Protein: 59g; Carbs:0.6 g; Fat: 12g; Saturated Fat: 3g; Sodium:193 mg

Beef with Cucumber Raita

Serves:4 , Cook Time: 45 minutes

Ingredients:

- 1-pound beef sirloin steak, cut into 1-inch thick
- ½ teaspoon lemon-pepper seasoning.
- 1 8-ounce plain fat-free yogurt
- ¼ cup shredded unpeeled cucumber
- 1 tablespoon chopped red onion
- 1 tablespoon snipped fresh mint
- A pinch of salt

Directions for Cooking:

1. Preheat the oven to 400°F.
2. Sprinkle the meat with the lemon pepper seasoning.
3. Place the meat on a baking dish and allow to bake for 45 minutes.
4. Meanwhile, prepare the cucumber raita by mixing in a bowl the yogurt, cucumber, onion, and mint. Season with a pinch of salt.
5. Once the meat is cooked, place on a cutting board and slice.
6. Drizzle with cucumber yogurt on top.

Nutrition Information:

Calories per Serving: 297; Protein: 27g; Carbs:11 g; Fat: 13g; Saturated Fat:2 g; Sodium: 80mg

Marinated Pork Tenderloin

Serves:12 , Cook Time: 45 minutes

Ingredients:

- ¼ cup dry white wine
- ¼ cup worcestershire sauce
- ½ cups fresh parsley
- 1.4 cups nipped fresh basil
- 6 cloves of garlic, minced
- 2 tablespoons honey mustard
- 6 1-pound pork tenderloins

Directions for Cooking:

1. In a deep dish, combine the white wine, Worcestershire sauce, parsley, basil, garlic, and honey mustard sauce. Stir until well-combined.
2. Place the pork in a resealable plastic bag and pour over the sauce.
3. Allow to marinate in the fridge for at least 4 hours.
4. Preheat the oven to 4500F.
5. Drain the pork and discard the marinade.
6. Place the pork in a large roasting pan and roast uncovered for 35 minutes.
7. Once cooked, remove from the chopping board and slice thinly.

Nutrition Information:

Calories per Serving: 337; Protein: 60g; Carbs: 2g; Fat:5 g; Saturated Fat: 1g; Sodium: 103mg

Pork Tenderloin with Apples And Balsamic Vinegar

Serves:4 , Cook Time: 20 minutes

Ingredients:

- 1 tablespoon olive oil
- 1-pound pork tenderloin, trimmed from fat
- A dash of black pepper
- 1 cup chopped onion
- ½ cup chopped apple
- 1 ½ tablespoon fresh rosemary
- 1 cup low sodium chicken broth
- 1 ½ tablespoon balsamic vinegar

Directions for Cooking:

1. Preheat the oven to 405⁰F.
2. In a skillet, heat the olive oil over high heat and add the pork and sear on all sides for at least 3 minutes or until golden brown.
3. Remove the meat from the heat and place in a baking pan.
4. Roast the pork for at least 15 minutes or until the internal temperature reaches to 160⁰F.
5. Meanwhile, place the onion, apples, and rosemary in the skillet where the pork was seared. Saute over medium heat until everything is soft.
6. Pour in the broth and balsamic vinegar and cook for another 5 minutes or until the sauce has reduced.

Nutrition Information:
Calories per Serving: 185; Protein: 25g; Carbs: 6g; Fat: 6g; Saturated Fat: 1g; Sodium: 69mg

Pork Chops with Tomatoes And Green Beans

Serves:4 , Cook Time: 16 minutes

Ingredients:

- 4 bone-in pork chops
- ½ teaspoon pepper
- 1 tablespoon olive oil
- 2 cups green beans
- 1 ¼ cup cherry tomatoes

Directions for Cooking:

1. Season the pork with pepper.
2. Heat the oil in a skillet over medium heat and sear the pork chops for 8 minutes on each side or until all sides turn lightly golen.
3. Remove from pan and set aside.
4. In the same pan, add in the olive oil and stir in the green beans and cherry tomatoes for 5 minutes or until the vegetables are done.
5. Serve the pork chop with the vegetables.

Nutrition Information:
Calories per Serving: 379; Protein: g; Carbs: 41g; Fat: 21g; Saturated Fat: 15g; Sodium: 107mg

Curried Pork Tenderloin with Apples

Serves:6 , Cook Time: 20minutes

Ingredients:

- 16 ounces pork tenderloin, cut into 6 pieces
- 1 ½ tablespoons curry powder
- 1 tablespoon olive oil
- 2 medium yellow onions, chopped
- 2 cups low sodium beef broth
- 1 apple, peeled, cored, and chopped

Directions for Cooking:

1. Season the pork with curry powder and allow to marinate for 5 minutes.
2. Heat the oil in a skillet over medium heat and sear the meat for 5 minutes on each side.
3. Stir in the onions and cook until fragrant.
4. Add in the broth and apples.
5. Allow to simmer without closing the lid for 5 minutes or until the sauce thickens.

Nutrition Information:
Calories per Serving: 245; Protein: 23g; Carbs: 15g; Fat: 6g; Saturated Fat: 1g; Sodium: 69mg

Chapter 11 Seafood Recipes

Swordfish and Citrus Salsa Delight

Serves: 6 , Cooking time: 15 minutes
Ingredients:
- 1 tbsp chopped fresh cilantro
- 1 orange (peeled, sectioned, and cut into bite-size)
- 2 tsp white sugar
- ½ cup canned pineapple chunks (undrained)
- 1 tbsp diced red bell pepper
- 2 jalapeno peppers, seeded and minced
- ¼ cup diced fresh mango
- 3 tbsp orange juice
- 1 tbsp pineapple juice concentrate, thawed
- ¼ tsp cayenne pepper
- 1 tbsp olive oil
- ½ cup fresh orange juice
- 1 ½ pounds swordfish steaks

Directions for Cooking:
1. In a bowl, make the salsa by combining and mixing well the cilantro, oranges, sugar, pineapple chunks, diced red bell pepper, minced jalapenos, mango, and 3 tablespoons orange juice. Cover the bowl and refrigerate.
2. Mix the pineapple juice concentrate, cayenne pepper, olive oil and ½ cup orange juice in a non-reactive bowl.
3. Add swordfish steaks in the bowl of pineapple juice mixture. Coat and turn well. Ensure to marinate for about 30 minutes.
4. On a gas grill, set heat to medium-high or on an outside grill with oiled rack set 6 inches from the heat source.
5. For 7 minutes, grill the swordfish on each side then serve with salsa.

Nutrition Information:
Calories per Serving: 240.8; Protein: 23.1g; Carbs: 14.6g; Fat: 10g; Saturated Fat: 2.2g; Sodium: 94mg

Tilapia with Lemon Garlic Sauce

Serves: 4 , Cooking time: 20 minutes
Ingredients:
- 4 tilapia fillets
- 1 tbsp olive oil
- 3 tbsp fresh lemon juice
- Pepper to taste
- 1 tsp dried parsley flakes
- 1 clove garlic, finely chopped

Directions for Cooking:
1. First, spray baking dish with non-stick cooking spray then preheat oven at 375º F .
2. In cool water, rinse tilapia fillets and using paper towels pat dry.
3. Place tilapia fillets in the baking dish then pour olive oil and lemon juice and top off with pepper, parsley and garlic.
4. Bake tilapia in the preheated oven for 15 minutes.
5. Remove from oven and let it rest for 5 minutes.
6. Enjoy!

Nutrition Information:
Calories per Serving: 155; Protein: 23.7g; Carbs: 2.1g; Fat: 5.7g; Saturated Fat: 1.2g; Sodium: 62mg

Dill Relish on White Sea Bass

Serves: 4 , Cooking time: 17 minutes
Ingredients:
- 1 tsp lemon juice
- 1 tsp Dijon mustard
- 1 ½ tsp chopped fresh dill
- 1 tsp pickled baby capers, drained
- 1 ½ tbsp chopped white onion
- 1 lemon, quartered
- 4 pieces of 4-oz white sea bass fillets

Directions for Cooking:
1. Preheat oven to 375ºF.

2. Mix lemon juice, mustard, dill, capers and onions in a small bowl.
3. Prepare four aluminum foil squares and place 1 fillet per foil.
4. Squeeze a lemon wedge per fish.
5. Evenly divide into 4 the dill spread and drizzle over fillet.
6. Close the foil over the fish securely and pop in the oven.
7. Bake for 12 minutes. Remove from oven and let it rest for 5 minutes to continue cooking.
8. Remove from foil and transfer to a serving platter, serve and enjoy.

Nutrition Information:
Calories per Serving: 40.6; Protein: 5.6g; Carbs: 2.3g; Fat: 1g; Saturated Fat: .2g; Sodium: 306mg

Baked Cod Crusted with Herbs

Serves: 4 , Cooking time: 12 minutes
Ingredients:
- 1 tbsp extra virgin olive oil
- ½ cup panko
- 1 tsp rosemary
- ¼ tsp salt
- ½ tsp pepper
- 1 tsp dried parsley
- 1 tsp dried basil
- 4 pieces of 4-oz cod fillets
- 1 tbsp lemon juice
- 2 tbsp honey

Directions for Cooking:
1. With olive oil, grease a 9 x 13-inch baking pan and preheat oven to 375°F.
2. In a zip top bag mix panko, rosemary, salt, pepper, parsley and basil.
3. Evenly spread cod fillets in prepped dish and drizzle with lemon juice.
4. Then brush the fillets with honey on all sides.
5. Then evenly divide the panko mixture on top of cod fillets.
6. Pop in the oven and bake for ten minutes or until fish is cooked.
7. Broil top for 2 minutes until lightly browned.
8. Serve and enjoy.

Nutrition Information:
Calories per Serving: 75.3; Protein: 5g; Carbs: 10g; Fat: 1.7g; Saturated Fat: .3g; Sodium: 262mg

Dijon Mustard and Lime Marinated Shrimp

Serves: 4 , Cooking time: 10 minutes
Ingredients:
- ½ tsp hot sauce
- 1 tbsp capers
- 1 tbsp Dijon mustard
- ½ cup fresh lime juice, plus lime zest as garnish
- 1 medium red onion, chopped
- 1 bay leaf
- 3 whole cloves
- ½ cup rice vinegar
- 1 cup water
- 1 lb. uncooked shrimp, peeled and deveined

Directions for Cooking:
1. Mix hot sauce, mustard, capers, lime juice and onion in a shallow baking dish and set aside.
2. Bring to a boil in a large saucepan bay leaf, cloves, vinegar and water.
3. Once boiling, add shrimps and cook for a minute while stirring continuously.
4. Drain shrimps and pour shrimps into onion mixture.
5. For an hour, refrigerate while covered.
6. Then serve shrimps cold and garnished with lime zest.

Nutrition Information:
Calories per Serving: 118; Protein: 23.3g; Carbs: 3.7g; Fat: 1.7g; Saturated Fat: 0.1g; Sodium: 248mg

Serves: 6 , Cooking time: 10 minutes

Ingredients:

- 1 lb. cod or tilapia fish filets
- 2 tsp coconut aminos, divided
- 1 tsp chili powder
- 2 tbsp lime juice, divided
- ¼ cup + 1 tbsp chopped fresh cilantro, divided
- 3 round slices of fresh pineapple
- ¾ cup thinly shredded red cabbage
- ¼ cup finely diced red onion
- 6 medium corn tortillas

Directions for Cooking:

1. In a shallow bowl, mix well 1 tsp coconut aminos, chili powder, 1 tbsp lime juice, and 1 tbsp chopped fresh cilantro. Add fish filets and marinate for at least 10 minutes. Turning over once in a while.
2. In a medium mixing bowl, whisk well remaining coconut aminos, lime juice, and cilantro.
3. Mix in cabbage and red onions. Set aside.
4. On medium fire, place a nonstick pan and pan fry fish and pineapple for 3 minutes per side.
5. Chop up pineapple and toss into salad.
6. To serve, evenly divide fish in middle of 6 tortilla. Top with pineapple slaw and enjoy.
7. Best served with a dollop of the Chipotle Aioli Dip and Sauce found in the snack and appetizer recipes.

Nutrition Information:

Calories per Serving: 200.8; Protein: 15.8g; Carbs: 16.4g; Fat: 8g; Saturated Fat: 2.8g; Sodium: 78mg

Serves: 6 , Cooking time: 75 minutes

Ingredients:

- 5 cups water
- ½ lb. shrimp, peeled and deveined
- 3 tbsp garlic, minced
- 2 stalks celery, sliced
- 2 onions, chopped
- 2 chicken breast halves, skinless and boneless
- 1 link andouille sausage, sliced
- 2 cups long grain rice
- ¼ tsp cayenne
- ¼ tsp Thyme
- 2 tbsp Worcestershire
- 6 roma tomatoes, chopped
- 1 tbsp olive oil
- 2 tbsp Parsley, chopped

Directions for Cooking:

1. Bring a large saucepan, filled with 5 cups water, to a boil. Add shrimps and boil for 2 minutes. Drain shrimps, reserve liquid and transfer shrimps to a plate.
2. In same saucepan, add the reserved liquid from shrimp, 1/3 garlic, ½ of the celery, ½ of onions, and the 2 chicken breasts. Bring to a boil and once boiling, lower fire to a simmer.
3. Partially cover pan and simmer for 25 minutes or until chicken is cooked and juices run clear. Remove cooked chicken and chop coarsely once cool to handle. As for the liquid, strain and discard solids. Set aside 4 cups of the liquid, if not enough, just add more water to reach 4 cups.
4. In a Dutch oven placed on medium high fire, heat oil. Add sausage and sauté for 5 minutes or until browned.
5. Mix in cayenne, thyme, Worcestershire sauce, tomatoes and juice, and the reserved cooking liquid. Cook for 10 minutes while stirring constantly to break up the tomatoes.
6. Add rice and bring to a simmer, once simmering lower fire to medium low, cover and cook for 25 minutes or until water is fully absorbed by the rice.
7. Turn off fire. Mix in cooked chicken and shrimps. Cover pot and allow to stand for 5 minutes more to continue cooking.
8. To serve, transfer to serving bowls and sprinkle with parsley.

Nutrition Information:

Calories per Serving: 434; Protein: 34.4g; Carbs: 59.0g; Fat: 7.3g; Saturated Fat: 1.5g; Sodium: 187mg

Baked Salmon with Dill 'n Garlic

Serves: 4 , Cooking time: 15 minutes

Ingredients:
- 2 8-oz. salmon filets, skin on
- 1 tbsp avocado oil
- 1 pinch black pepper
- 4 tbsp fresh dill, chopped, divided
- 1 small lemon, thinly sliced into 1/8th-inch rounds
- 1/4 cup hummus
- 2 tbsp lemon juice
- 2 cloves garlic, minced

Directions for Cooking:
1. Lightly grease a non-stick baking dish with cooking spray and preheat oven to 400°F.
2. Place fish on baking sheet and drizzle with oil. Season with pepper and 2 tbsp fresh dill. Top fish with thinly sliced lemon.
3. Pop in the oven and roast for 15 minutes or until flaky.
4. Meanwhile, make the dill-garlic sauce by pulsing in a blender the garlic, remaining dill, and lemon juice until creamy. Stir in hummus.
5. Serve salmon topped with dill-garlic sauce.

Nutrition Information:
Calories per Serving: 486.4; Protein: 70.7g; Carbs: 8.6g; Fat: 18.8g; Saturated Fat: 3.6g; Sodium: 97mg

Chilean Sea Bass with Spinach and Avocado Pesto

Serves: 4 , Cooking time: 20 minutes

Ingredients:
- 1.5-lbs Chilean sea bass fillet, cut into 4 pieces
- ½ tsp pepper
- 2 cups spinach
- ½ cup parsley, chopped
- 1 clove of garlic, minced
- ¼ cup walnuts
- 2 teaspoons fresh lemon juice
- ¼ cup extra virgin olive oil

Directions for Cooking:
1. Preheat the oven to 350°F.
2. Season the sea bass fillets with pepper. Place in a baking tray.
3. In a blender, put the remaining ingredients and pulse until smooth.
4. Pour the pesto over the sea bass.
5. Place in the oven and cook for 20 minutes.

Nutrition Information:
Calories per Serving: 223; Carbs: 3.9g; Protein: 25.5g; Fats: 11.9g; Saturated Fat: 2.8g; Sodium: 221mg

Cilantro Lime Salmon Bowls

Serves: 4 , Cooking time: 15 minutes

Ingredients:
- 1 tablespoon olive oil
- 1-lb salmon fillet, sliced into 4 pieces
- 3 red bell peppers, seeded and julienned
- 1/3 cup lime juice
- 2 teaspoons honey, organic
- Salt and pepper to taste
- 4 cup brown rice
- 1 avocado, pitted and thinly sliced
- 2 tablespoons chopped cilantro
- Lime wedges

Directions for Cooking:
1. Heat oil in a skillet over medium-high heat and sear the salmon on all sides for 5 minutes each. Set aside.
2. Using the same skillet, sauté the bell peppers for 3 minutes then set aside.
3. Make the dressing by combining in a bowl the lime juice, honey, salt and pepper.
4. Assemble the salmon bowl.
5. Put a cup of rice on a bowl and add one fillet and bell peppers on top. Garnish with avocado slices, chopped cilantro, and lime wedges.
6. Drizzle with the dressing.

Nutrition Information:
Calories per Serving: 327; Carbs: 13.7g; Protein: 25.3g; Fats: 19g; Saturated Fat: 3.2g; Sodium: 339mg

Garlic and Lemon Mahi Mahi

Serves: 4 , Cooking time: 31 minutes

Ingredients:

- 1 tablespoon extra-virgin olive oil
- 3 cloves of garlic, minced
- 4 4-ounces mahi mahi or dolphinfish fillets
- ½ tsp pepper
- Zest from 1 lemon

Directions for Cooking:

1. Heat oil in a skillet over medium flame and sauté the garlic until fragrant.
2. Add the mahi mahi fillets and season with pepper, and lemon zest.
3. Place inside a 350°F preheated oven and cook for 30 minutes.

Nutrition Information:

Calories per Serving: 111.1; Carbs: 1.3g; Protein: 21.3g; Fats: 2.3g; Saturated Fat: .5g; Sodium: 131mg

Mediterranean Style Fish

Serves: 4 , Cooking time: 25 minutes

Ingredients:

- 2 tablespoons olive oil
- 4 6-ounce fish fillets
- 1 large tomato, chopped
- 1 onion, chopped
- ¼ cup pitted olives, low sodium
- 2 tbsp capers
- 1 tablespoon lemon juice
- Salt and pepper to taste

Directions for Cooking:

1. Preheat the oven to 350°F.
2. Place olive oil in the middle of a large aluminum foil.
3. Put the fish in the middle and top with tomato, onion, olives, and capers.
4. Season with lemon juice, salt and pepper.
5. Fold the aluminum foil and seal the edges by crimping.
6. Place inside the oven and cook for 25 minutes.

Nutrition Information:

Calories per Serving: 210.5; Carbs: 6.4g; Protein: 27.1g; Fats: 8.5g; Saturated Fat: 1.2g; Sodium: 282mg

Pan-Grilled Fish Steaks

Serves: 4 , Cooking time: 10 minutes

Ingredients:

- 1 tablespoon olive oil
- 1 clove of garlic, minced
- 2 fillets of halibut
- 1 teaspoon dried basil
- 1 teaspoon black pepper
- 1 tablespoon lemon juice, freshly squeezed
- 1 tablespoon fresh parsley, chopped

Directions for Cooking:

1. Heat oil in a skillet over medium heat and sauté the garlic until fragrant.
2. Stir in the halibut and sear all sides for 2 minutes each.
3. Add the basil, pepper, and lemon juice.
4. Continue cooking until the liquid almost evaporates. Flip the fillet.
5. Cook for 5 more minutes.
6. Garnish with parsley before serving.

Nutrition Information:

Calories per Serving: 407.7; Carbs: 1.1g; Protein: 29.5g; Fats: 31.7g; Saturated Fat: 5.4g; Sodium: 164mg

Pan-Grilled Tuna Burger

Serves: 2 , Cooking time: 10 minutes

Ingredients:

- 1 tail-end tuna fillet, without skin and chopped
- 1 tablespoon lemon juice
- ½ tsp pepper
- 1 small onion
- 1 tsp garlic powder

- ¼ tsp celery seeds
- ½ tsp Cajun seasoning
- ¼ teaspoon olive oil
- 2 whole wheat burger buns
- 1 tomato, sliced
- 2 lettuce leaf

Directions for Cooking:
1. Peel onions and slice in half widthwise. Slice half of the onion into two and set aside. Chop the other half of the onion.

2. In a bowl, mix well chopped tuna, lemon juice, pepper, chopped onion, garlic powder, celery seeds, and Cajun seasoning. Mix well and divide into two. Form into patties.
3. Heat pan with oil on medium high fire and pan fry patties for 3 minutes per side.
4. To serve, place pattie on a bun top with onion and tomato slices and a lettuce leaf.

Nutrition Information:
Calories per Serving: 110; Carbs: 6.9g; Protein: 14.3g; Fats: 3.5g; Saturated Fat: .8g; Sodium: 77mg

Indulgent Seafood Enchiladas

Serves: 6 , Cooking time: 5 minutes
Ingredients:
- ½ tablespoon olive oil
- 1 onion, chopped
- ½ pound crab meat
- ¼ pound shrimps, peeled and deveined
- Salt and pepper to taste
- 6 whole wheat tortillas
- ½ cup sour cream, low fat
- 8-ounce Colby cheese, low fat

Directions for Cooking:
1. Heat the oil in a skillet over medium heat and sauté the onion until fragrant.

2. Stir in the crab meat and shrimps.
3. Season with pepper to taste.
4. Continue stirring for 4 minutes. Set aside.
5. Assemble the enchiladas by putting the seafood mixture in tortilla wraps.
6. Add sour cream and cheese on top.

Nutrition Information:
Calories per Serving: 360; Carbs: 36.5g; Protein: 30.3g; Fats: 10.31g; Saturated Fat: 4.3g; Sodium: 324mg

Mouth-Watering Seafood Curry

Serves: 6 , Cooking time: 10 minutes
Ingredients:
- 1 tablespoon olive oil
- 1 onion, chopped
- 2 cloves of garlic, minced
- 1 teaspoon garam masala
- 1 teaspoon turmeric powder
- 1 teaspoon coriander powder
- 12-ounce cod fillets
- ½ pound shrimps, peeled and deveined
- ½ pound scallops
- 2 cups coconut milk
- 1 red bell pepper, seeded and sliced
- ¼ tsp pepper

Directions for Cooking:
1. Heat the oil in a pot over medium high flame and sauté the onion and garlic until fragrant, around 2 minutes.
2. Add the garam masala, turmeric, and coriander. Toast for 1 minute.
3. Stir in the rest of the ingredients.
4. Close the lid and bring to a boil.
5. Allow simmering for 6 minutes.

Nutrition Information:
Calories per Serving: 393.5; Carbs: 8.8g; Protein: 23.2g; Fats: 22.3g; Saturated Fat: 10.4g; Sodium: 305mg

Grilled Prawn Kebab

Serves: 3 , Cooking time: 6 minutes

Ingredients:

- 6 large prawns, peeled and deveined
- 2 tablespoons lemon juice
- Pepper to taste
- 1 teaspoon parsley leaves, chopped
- 3 pineapple slices

Directions for Cooking:

1. Marinate the prawns in lemon juice, salt and pepper for 30 minutes in the fridge.
2. Preheat the grill to medium.
3. Skewer 2 prawns and a pineapple slice on each bamboo skewer.
4. Grill for 3 minutes on each side.

Nutrition Information:

Calories per Serving: 104; Carbs: 21.6g; Protein: 3.8g; Fats: 0.9g; Saturated Fat: 0g; Sodium: 13mg

Summertime Crab with Napa Cabbage

Serves: 6 , Cooking time: 0 minutes

Ingredients:

- 2 tablespoons lemon juice
- 1 tablespoon olive oil
- 1 tablespoon maple syrup
- Salt and pepper to taste
- 1-pound crabmeat, shredded
- 1 ½ pounds Napa cabbage, shredded
- 5 stalks of celery, diced
- 6 radishes, sliced thinly
- 2 tbsp black olives, drained, rinsed and sliced
- 3 green onions, sliced thinly

Directions for Cooking:

1. In a small bowl, combine the lemon juice, olive oil, and maple syrup. Season with pepper to taste. Set aside.
2. Mix all ingredients in a bowl.
3. Drizzle with the sauce and toss to coat.
4. Chill before serving.

Nutrition Information:

Calories per Serving: 268; Carbs: 20.4g; Protein: 37.4g; Fats: 4.3g; Saturated Fat: 1.8g; Sodium: mg

Salmon Avocado Salad

Serves: 3 , Cooking time: 10 minutes

Ingredients:

- 12-ounce salmon fillet
- Salt and pepper to taste
- ½ avocado, thinly sliced
- ¼ cucumber, thinly sliced
- A dash of lemon juice
- A pinch of dill weed, chopped
- 2 teaspoons capers

Directions for Cooking:

1. Preheat the grill to medium.
2. Season the salmon with salt and pepper to taste.
3. Grill the salmon for 5 minutes on each side. Set aside and allow to cool.
4. Once cooled, flake the salmon using two forks.
5. Place in a bowl and toss together with the other ingredients.
6. Season with more salt and pepper if desired.

Nutrition Information:

Calories per Serving: 118; Carbs: 2.7g; Protein: 12.2g; Fats: 6.6g; Saturated Fat: 3.4g; Sodium: 247mg

Shrimp and Avocado Salad

Serves: 6 , Cooking time: 6 minutes

Ingredients:

- 1-pound shrimp, shelled and deveined
- 2 tomatoes, finely chopped
- 1 bunch cilantro, chopped
- 1 red onion, chopped finely
- 2 avocados, sliced thinly
- 2 tablespoons lemon juice

Directions for Cooking:

1. Steam the shrimps for 6 minutes. Set aside and allow to cool.
2. In a bowl, combine the rest of the ingredients.
3. Toss in the shrimps and gently stir.
4. Allow to chill in the fridge before serving

Nutrition Information:
Calories per Serving: 191; Carbs: 7.7g; Protein: 17.6g; Fats: 10.9g; Saturated Fat: 3.6g; Sodium: 185mg

Simple Tuna and Cucumber Salad

Serves: 5 , Cooking time: 6 minutes
Ingredients:
- ½ pound tuna fillet
- ¼ tsp pepper
- 1 large cucumber, peeled and sliced
- 1 radish, peeled and sliced
- 1 medium-sized tomato, cubed
- 1 red onion, cubed
- 2 tablespoons lemon juice
- 1 thumb-size ginger, grated

Directions for Cooking:
1. Season the tuna with pepper.
2. Heat a skillet over medium flame and sear the tuna fillet for 3 minutes each side. Slice the tuna into cubes and set aside.
3. In a mixing bowl, combine the rest of the ingredients and toss in the sliced tuna.
4. Season with pepper.

Nutrition Information:
Calories per Serving: 70; Carbs: 7.1g; Protein: 9.9g; Fats: 0.6g; Saturated Fat: 0.1g; Sodium: 89mg

Salmon with Dill and Lemon

Serves: 2 , Cooking time: 20 minutes
Ingredients:
- 1/2-pound salmon fillet, cut into 2 equal portions
- Pepper to taste
- 2 lemons, juice extracted
- 2 sprigs fresh dill, chopped
- Cooking spray

Directions for Cooking:
1. Preheat oven to 400ºF.
2. Lightly grease an oven safe dish with cooking spray.
3. Place salmon on dish skin side down.
4. Pour lemon juice, season generously with pepper, and top with dill.
5. Place in oven and bake for 12 to 15 minutes or until flaky.
6. Let salmon rest for 5 minutes.
7. Serve and enjoy.

Nutrition Information:
Calories per Serving: 199; Carbs: 5.5g; Protein: 24g; Fats: 9g; Saturated Fat: 1.8g; Sodium: 293mg

Cioppino – Seafood Stew A la San Francisco

Serves: 8 , Cooking time: 50 minutes
Ingredients:
- 3 celery sticks, chopped
- 1 red bell pepper, chopped
- 2 onions, chopped
- 2 cups fish stock, low sodium
- ½ cup water
- 2 large tomatoes, chopped
- 1 tablespoon garlic, minced
- 2 teaspoons Italian seasoning
- 1 bay leaf
- Pepper to taste
- 1-pound little neck clams
- 1-lb shrimps, shelled and deveined
- 1-lb cod fillet, cut into 1-inch pieces
- 2 tablespoons basil, chopped
- 1 tablespoon parsley, chopped
- red pepper flakes to taste

Directions for Cooking:
1. Place a heavy bottomed pot on medium high fire.
2. Add celery, bell pepper, onions, fish stock, tomatoes, garlic, Italian seasoning, pepper flakes, pepper, fish stock, Italian seasoning, water and bay leaf. Mix well.

3. Bring to a boil, lower fire to a simmer, cover and cook for 10 minutes.
4. Stir in shrimps and clams. Cover and cook for another 7 minutes.
5. Add fish and basil. Cook for 3 minutes. Let it rest for 5 minutes. Do not mix as the fish fillet will crumble.
6. Serve and enjoy with a sprinkle of parsley.

Nutrition Information:
Calories per Serving: 172.3; Carbs: 14.5g; Protein: 23.4g; Fats: 2.3g; Saturated Fat: .4g; Sodium: 351mg

Stir-Fried Sesame Shrimp

Serves: 3 , Cooking time: 15 minutes

Ingredients:
- ¾ cup chicken broth, low sodium
- 1/8 cup cornstarch
- 1/2 -pound sugar snap peas
- 1 tbsp teriyaki sauce
- 3 green onions, sliced
- 1 red bell pepper, sliced into thin strips
- 2 tsp sesame oil
- ¼ tsp ground black pepper
- 1 tbsp sesame seeds
- 1 clove garlic, minced
- ¼ tsp cayenne pepper
- ¼ tsp ground ginger
- 1-lb medium shrimp, peeled and deveined

Directions for Cooking:
1. In a large bowl mix black pepper, sesame seeds, cayenne pepper. Ginger, and shrimp. Mix well and let it marinate for at least 30 minutes.
2. When ready, place a nonstick saucepan on medium high fire and heat for 3 minutes.
3. Add oil and heat for a minute. Swirl to coat pot.
4. Add green onions and bell pepper. Stir fry for 4 minutes.
5. Add shrimp, peas, and teriyaki sauce. Stir fry for 5 minutes or until shrimps are slightly opaque.
6. In a bowl, mix broth and cornstarch. Pour into pot and mix well.
7. Continue mixing and cooking until sauce has thickened.
8. Serve and enjoy.

Nutrition Information:
Calories per Serving: 308.6; Carbs: 16.2g; Protein: 37.1g; Fats: 10.6g; Saturated Fat: 2.3g; Sodium: 216mg

Steamed Salmon Teriyaki

Serves: 4 , Cooking time: 15 minutes

Ingredients:
- 3 green onions, minced
- 2 packet Stevia
- 1 tbsp freshly grated ginger
- 1 clove garlic, minced
- 2 tsp sesame seeds
- 1 tbsp sesame oil
- ¼ cup mirin
- 2 tbsp low sodium soy sauce
- 1/2-lb salmon filet

Directions for Cooking:
1. Place a large saucepan on medium high fire. Place a trivet inside saucepan and fill pan halfway with water. Cover and bring to a boil.
2. Meanwhile in a heat-proof dish that fits inside saucepan, mix well stevia, ginger, garlic, oil, mirin, and soy sauce. Add salmon and cover well with sauce.
3. Top salmon with sesame seeds and green onions. Cover dish with foil.
4. Place on top of trivet. Cover and steam for 15 minutes.
5. Let it rest for 5 minutes in pan.
6. Serve and enjoy.

Nutrition Information:
Calories per Serving: 242.7; Carbs: 1.2g; Protein: 35.4g; Fats: 10.7g; Saturated Fat: 2.1g; Sodium: 285mg

Easy Steamed Alaskan Cod

Serves: 3 , Cooking time: 15 minutes

Ingredients:

- 2 tbsp butter
- Pepper to taste
- 1 cup cherry tomatoes, halved
- 1 large Wild Alaskan cod filet, cut into 3 smaller pieces

Directions for Cooking:

1. Place a large saucepan on medium high fire. Place a trivet inside saucepan and fill pan halfway with water. Cover and bring to a boil.

2. Meanwhile in a heat-proof dish that fits inside saucepan, add all ingredients.
3. Cover dish with a foil. Place on trivet and steam for 15 minutes.
4. Serve and enjoy.

Nutrition Information:
Calories per Serving: 132.9; Carbs: 1.9g; Protein: 12.2g; Fats: 8.5g; Saturated Fat: 4.9g; Sodium: 296mg

Dill and Lemon Cod Packets

Serves: 2 , Cooking time: 10 minutes

Ingredients:

- 2 tsp olive oil, divided
- 4 slices lemon, divided
- 2 sprigs fresh dill, divide
- ½ tsp garlic powder, divided
- Pepper to taste
- 1/2-lb cod filets

Directions for Cooking:

1. Place a large saucepan on medium high fire. Place a trivet inside saucepan and fill pan halfway with water. Cover and bring to a boil.
2. Cut two pieces of 15-inch lengths foil.

3. In one foil, place one filet in the middle. Season with pepper to taste. Sprinkle ¼ tsp garlic. Add a tsp of oil on top of filet. Top with 2 slices of lemon and a sprig of dill. Fold over the foil and seal the filet inside. Repeat process for remaining fish.
4. Place packet on trivet. Cover and steam for 10 minutes.
5. Serve and enjoy.

Nutrition Information:
Calories per Serving: 164.8; Carbs: 9.4g; Protein: 18.3g; Fats: 6g; Saturated Fat: 1g; Sodium: 347mg

Steamed Fish Mediterranean Style

Serves: 4 , Cooking time: 15 minutes

Ingredients:

- Pepper to taste
- 1 clove garlic, smashed
- 2 tsp olive oil
- 1 bunch fresh thyme
- 2 tbsp pickled capers
- 1 cup black salt-cured olives
- 1-lb cherry tomatoes, halved
- 1 ½-lbs. cod filets

Directions for Cooking:

1. Place a large saucepan on medium high fire. Place a trivet inside saucepan and fill pan halfway with water. Cover and bring to a boil.

2. Meanwhile in a heat-proof dish that fits inside saucepan, layer half of the halved cherry tomatoes. Season with pepper.
3. Add filets on top of tomatoes and season with pepper. Drizzle oil. Sprinkle 3/4s of thyme on top and the smashed garlic.
4. Cover top of fish with remaining cherry tomatoes and place dish on trivet. Cover dish with foil.
5. Cover pan and steam for 15 minutes.
6. Serve and enjoy.

Nutrition Information:
Calories per Serving: 263.2; Carbs: 21.8g; Protein: 27.8g; Fats: 7.2g; Saturated Fat: 1.1g; Sodium: 264mg

Steamed Veggie and Lemon Pepper Salmon

Serves: 4 , Cooking time: 15 minutes

Ingredients:
- 1 carrot, peeled and julienned
- 1 red bell pepper, julienned
- 1 zucchini, julienned
- ½ lemon, sliced thinly
- 1 tsp pepper
- ½ tsp salt
- 1/2-lb salmon filet with skin on
- A dash of tarragon

Directions for Cooking:
1. Place a large saucepan on medium high fire. Place a trivet inside saucepan and fill pan halfway with water. Cover and bring to a boil.
2. Meanwhile in a heat-proof dish that fits inside saucepan, add salmon with skin side down. Season with pepper. Add slices of lemon on top.
3. Place the julienned vegetables on top of salmon and season with tarragon. Cover top of fish with remaining cherry tomatoes and place dish on trivet. Cover dish with foil.
4. Cover pan and steam for 15 minutes.
5. Serve and enjoy.

Nutrition Information:
Calories per Serving: 216.2; Carbs: 4.1g; Protein: 35.1g; Fats: 6.6g; Saturated Fat: 1.5g; Sodium: 332mg

Steamed Fish with Scallions and Ginger

Serves: 3 , Cooking time: 15 minutes

Ingredients:
- ¼ cup chopped cilantro
- ¼ cup julienned scallions
- 2 tbsp julienned ginger
- 1 tbsp peanut oil
- 1-lb Tilapia filets
- 1 tsp garlic
- 1 tsp minced ginger
- 2 tbsp rice wine
- 1 tbsp low sodium soy sauce

Directions for Cooking:
1. In a heat-proof dish that fits inside saucepan, add garlic, minced ginger, rice wine, and soy sauce. Mix well. Add the Tilapia filet and marinate for half an hour, while turning over at half time.
2. Place a large saucepan on medium high fire. Place a trivet inside saucepan and fill pan halfway with water. Cover and bring to a boil.
3. Cover dish of fish with foil and place on trivet.
4. Cover pan and steam for 15 minutes.
5. Serve and enjoy.

Nutrition Information:
Calories per Serving: 219; Carbs: 4.5g; Protein: 31.8g; Fats: 8.2g; Saturated Fat: 1.9g; Sodium: 252mg

Steamed Tilapia with Green Chutney

Serves: 3 , Cooking time: 10 minutes

Ingredients:
- 1-pound tilapia fillets, divided into 3
- ½ cup green commercial chutney

Directions for Cooking:
1. Place a large saucepan on medium high fire. Place a trivet inside saucepan and fill pan halfway with water. Cover and bring to a boil.
2. Cut 3 pieces of 15-inch lengths foil.
3. In one foil, place one filet in the middle and 1/3 of chutney. Fold over the foil and seal the filet inside. Repeat process for remaining fish.
4. Place packet on trivet. Cover and steam for 10 minutes.
5. Serve and enjoy.

Nutrition Information:
Calories per Serving: 151.5; Carbs: 1.1g; Protein: 30.7g; Fats: 2.7g; Saturated Fat: .9g; Sodium: 79mg

Creamy Haddock with Kale

Serves: 5 , Cooking time: 10 minutes

Ingredients:
- 1 tbsp olive oil
- 1 onion, chopped
- 2 cloves of garlic, minced
- 2 cups chicken broth
- 1 teaspoon crushed red pepper flakes
- 1-pound wild Haddock fillets
- ½ cup heavy cream
- 1 tablespoons basil
- 1 cup kale leaves, chopped
- Pepper to taste

Directions for Cooking:
1. Place a heavy bottomed pot on medium high fire and heat pot for 3 minutes.
2. Once hot, add oil and stir around to coat pot with oil.
3. Sauté the onion and garlic for 5 minutes.
4. Add remaining ingredients, except for basil and mix well.
5. Cover, bring to a boil, lower fire to a simmer, and simmer for 5 minutes.
6. Serve and enjoy with a sprinkle of basil.

Nutrition Information:
Calories per Serving: 130.5; Carbs: 5.5g; Protein: 35.7g; Fats: 14.5g; Saturated Fat: 5.2g; Sodium: 278mg

Coconut Curry Sea Bass

Serves: 3 , Cooking time: 15 minutes

Ingredients:
- 1 can coconut milk
- Juice of 1 lime, freshly squeezed
- 1 tablespoon red curry paste
- 1 teaspoon coconut aminos
- 1 teaspoon honey
- 2 teaspoons sriracha
- 2 cloves of garlic, minced
- 1 teaspoon ground turmeric
- 1 tablespoon curry powder
- ¼ cup fresh cilantro
- Pepper

Directions for Cooking:
1. Place a heavy bottomed pot on medium high fire.
2. Mix in all ingredients.
3. Cover, bring to a boil, lower fire to a simmer, and simmer for 5 minutes.
4. Serve and enjoy.

Nutrition Information:
Calories per Serving: 241.8; Carbs: 12.8g; Protein: 3.1g; Fats: 19.8g; Saturated Fat: 17g; Sodium: 19mg

Stewed Cod Filet with tomatoes

Serves: 6 , Cooking time: 15 minutes

Ingredients:
- 1 tbsp olive oil
- 1 onion, sliced
- 1 ½ pounds fresh cod fillets
- Pepper
- 1 lemon juice, freshly squeezed
- 1 can diced tomatoes

Directions for Cooking:
1. Place a heavy bottomed pot on medium high fire and heat pot for 3 minutes.
2. Once hot, add oil and stir around to coat pot with oil.
3. Sauté the onion for 2 minutes. Stir in diced tomatoes and cook for 5 minutes.
4. Add cod filet and season with pepper.
5. Cover, bring to a boil, lower fire to a simmer, and simmer for 5 minutes.
6. Serve and enjoy with freshly squeezed lemon juice.

Nutrition Information:
Calories per Serving: 106.4; Carbs: 2.5g; Protein: 17.8g; Fats: 2.8g; Saturated Fat: .4g; Sodium: 381mg

Lemony Parmesan Shrimps

Serves: 4 , Cooking time: 15 minutes

Ingredients:
- 1 tablespoon olive oil
- ½ cup onion, chopped
- 3 cloves of garlic, minced
- 1-pound shrimps, peeled and deveined
- ½ cup parmesan cheese, low fat
- 1 cup spinach, shredded
- ½ cup chicken broth, low sodium
- ¼ cup water
- Pepper

Directions for Cooking:
1. Place a heavy bottomed pot on medium high fire and heat pot for 3 minutes.
2. Once hot, add oil and stir around to coat pot with oil.
3. Sauté the onion and garlic for 5 minutes. Stir in shrimps and cook for 2 minutes.
4. Add remaining ingredients, except for parmesan.
5. Cover, bring to a boil, lower fire to a simmer, and simmer for 5 minutes.
6. Serve and enjoy with a sprinkle of parmesan.

Nutrition Information:
Calories per Serving: 252.6; Carbs: 5.4g; Protein: 33.9g; Fats: 10.6g; Saturated Fat: 3.2g; Sodium: 344mg

Tuna 'n Carrots Casserole

Serves: 4 , Cooking time: 12 minutes

Ingredients:
- 2 carrots, peeled and chopped
- ¼ cup diced onions
- 1 cup frozen peas
- ¾ cup milk
- 2 cans tuna in water, drained
- 1 can cream of celery soup
- 1 tbsp olive oil
- ½ cup water
- 2 eggs beaten
- Pepper

Directions for Cooking:
1. Place a heavy bottomed pot on medium high fire and heat pot for 3 minutes.
2. Once hot, add oil and stir around to coat pot with oil.
3. Sauté the onion and carrots for 3 minutes.
4. Add remaining ingredients and mix well.
5. Bring to a boil while stirring constantly, cook until thickened around 5 minutes.
6. Serve and enjoy.

Nutrition Information:
Calories per Serving: 281.3; Carbs: 14.3g; Protein: 24.3g; Fats: 14.1g; Saturated Fat: 3.7g; Sodium: 275mg

Sweet-Ginger Scallops

Serves: 3 , Cooking time: 15 minutes

Ingredients:
- 1-pound sea scallops, shells removed
- ½ cup coconut aminos
- 3 tablespoons maple syrup
- ½ teaspoon garlic powder
- ½ teaspoon ground ginger

Directions for Cooking:
1. In a heat-proof dish that fits inside saucepan, add all ingredients. Mix well.
2. Place a large saucepan on medium high fire. Place a trivet inside saucepan and fill pan halfway with water. Cover and bring to a boil.
3. Cover dish of scallops with foil and place on trivet.
4. Cover pan and steam for 10 minutes. Let it rest in pan for another 5 minutes.
5. Serve and enjoy.

Nutrition Information:
Calories per Serving: 233.4; Carbs: 23.7g; Protein: 31.5g; Fats: 1.4g; Saturated Fat: .4g; Sodium: 153mg

Savory Lobster Roll

Serves: 6 , Cooking time: 20 minutes

Ingredients:

- 1 ½ cups chicken broth, low sodium
- 2 teaspoon old bay seasoning
- 2 pounds lobster tails, raw and in the shell
- 1 lemon, halved
- 3 scallions, chopped
- 1 teaspoon celery seeds

Directions for Cooking:

1. Place a heavy bottomed pot on medium high fire and add all ingredients and ½ of the lemon.
2. Cover, bring to a boil, lower fire to a simmer, and simmer for 15 minutes.
3. Let it rest for another 5 minutes.
4. Serve and enjoy with freshly squeezed lemon juice.

Nutrition Information:

Calories per Serving: 209; Carbs: 1.9g; Protein: 38.2g; Fats: 5.4g; Saturated Fat: 1.4g; Sodium: 288mg

Garlic 'n Tomatoes on Mussels

Serves: 6 , Cooking time: 15 minutes

Ingredients:

- ¼ cup white wine
- ½ cup water
- 3 Roma tomatoes, chopped
- 2 cloves of garlic, minced
- 1 bay leaf
- 2 pounds mussels, scrubbed
- ½ cup fresh parsley, chopped
- 1 tbsp oil
- Pepper

Directions for Cooking:

1. Place a heavy bottomed pot on medium high fire and heat pot for 3 minutes.
2. Once hot, add oil and stir around to coat pot with oil.
3. Sauté the garlic, bay leaf, and tomatoes for 5 minutes.
4. Add remaining ingredients, except for parsley and mussels. Mix well.
5. Add mussels.
6. Cover, bring to a boil, and boil for 5 minutes.
7. Serve and enjoy with a sprinkle of parsley and discard any unopened mussels.

Nutrition Information:

Calories per Serving: 172.8; Carbs: 10.2g; Protein: 19.5g; Fats: 6g; Saturated Fat: 1.1g; Sodium: 261mg

Lobster Tarragon Stew

Serves: 4 , Cooking time: 30 minutes

Ingredients:

- 1 tablespoon olive oil
- 2 onions, diced
- 2 cloves of garlic, minced
- 1 carrot, chopped
- 2 lobsters, shelled
- 1-pound ripe tomatoes, chopped
- 2 tablespoon tomato paste
- 1/3 clam juice
- 1 tablespoon tarragon

Directions for Cooking:

1. Place a heavy bottomed pot on medium high fire and heat pot for 3 minutes.
2. Once hot, add oil and stir around to coat pot with oil.
3. Sauté the onion, tomatoes and garlic for 10 minutes.
4. Stir in tomato paste, clam juice, and carrot. Cook for 5 minutes.
5. Add lobsters and mix well.
6. Cover and simmer for 5 minutes.
7. Serve and enjoy a sprinkle of tarragon.

Nutrition Information:

Calories per Serving: 149.9; Carbs: 13.3g; Protein: 14.5g; Fats: 4.3g; Saturated Fat: 1g; Sodium: 341mg

Easy Steamed Crab Legs

Serves: 4 , Cooking time: 10 minutes

Ingredients:
- 2 pounds frozen crab legs
- 4 tablespoons low fat butter
- 1 tablespoon lemon juice, freshly squeezed

Directions for Cooking:
1. Place a heavy bottomed pot on medium high fire, fill with 5 cups water and bring to a boil.
2. Add crab legs, cover and steam for 10 minutes. Once done, turn off fire and let it rest for 5 minutes.
3. Meanwhile, in a microwave safe bowl, melt butter. Once melted, add lemon juice and mix well.
4. Serve crab legs with lemon-butter dip on the side.

Nutrition Information:
Calories per Serving: 201.9; Carbs: 2.2g; Protein: 44g; Fats: 1.9g; Saturated Fat: .3g; Sodium: 297mg

Tasty Corn and Clam Stew

Serves: 4 , Cooking time: 25 minutes

Ingredients:
- 1-lb clam
- 1 cup frozen corn
- ½ cup water
- 4 cloves garlic
- 1 tsp oil
- 1 tsp celery seeds
- 1 tsp Cajun seasoning

Directions for Cooking:
1. Place a nonstick saucepan on medium high fire and heat pot for 3 minutes.
2. Once hot, add oil and stir around to coat pot with oil.
3. Sauté the garlic for a minute.
4. Add remaining ingredients, except for clams and mix well. Cook for 3 minutes.
5. Stir in clams.
6. Cover, bring to a boil, lower fire to a simmer, and simmer for 5 minutes.
7. Serve and enjoy. Discard any unopened clam.

Nutrition Information:
Calories per Serving: 120; Carbs: 23.2g; Protein: 2.3g; Fats: 2g; Saturated Fat: .2g; Sodium: 466mg

Seafood Curry Recipe from Japan

Serves: 4 , Cooking time: 30 minutes

Ingredients:
- 3 onions, chopped
- 2 cloves of garlic, minced
- 1-inch ginger, grated
- 1 tsp oil
- 3 cups water
- 1 2-inch long kombu or dried kelp
- 6 shiitake mushrooms, halved
- 12 manila clams, scrubbed
- 6 ounces medium-sized shrimps, peeled and deveined
- 6 ounces bay scallops
- 1 package Japanese curry roux
- ¼ apple, sliced

Directions for Cooking:
1. Place a heavy bottomed pot on medium high fire and heat pot for 3 minutes.
2. Once hot, add oil and stir around to coat pot with oil.
3. Sauté the onion, ginger and garlic for 5 minutes.
4. Add remaining ingredients and mix well.
5. Cover, bring to a boil, lower fire to a simmer, and simmer for 5 minutes. Let it rest for 5 minutes.
6. Serve and enjoy. Discard any unopened clams.

Nutrition Information:
Calories per Serving: 183.7; Carbs: 17.9g; Protein: 22.4g; Fats: 2.5g; Saturated Fat: .5g; Sodium: 294mg

Steamed Asparagus and Shrimps

Serves: 6 , Cooking time: 25 minutes
Ingredients:
- 1-pound shrimps, peeled and deveined
- 1 bunch asparagus, trimmed
- 1 teaspoon oil
- ½ tablespoon Cajun seasoning

Directions for Cooking:
1. In a heat-proof dish that fits inside saucepan, add all ingredients. Mix well.
2. Place a large saucepan on medium high fire. Place a trivet inside saucepan and fill pan halfway with water. Cover and bring to a boil.
3. Cover dish with foil and place on trivet.
4. Cover pan and steam for 10 minutes. Let it rest in pan for another 5 minutes.
5. Serve and enjoy.

Nutrition Information:
Calories per Serving: 79.8; Carbs: .4g; Protein: 15.5g; Fats: 1.8g; Saturated Fat: .3g; Sodium: 209mg

Coconut Milk Sauce over Crabs

Serves: 6 , Cooking time: 20 minutes
Ingredients:
- 2-pounds crab quartered
- 1 can coconut milk
- 1 lemongrass stalk
- 1 thumb-size ginger, sliced
- 1 onion, chopped
- 3 cloves of garlic, minced
- Pepper

Directions for Cooking:
1. Place a heavy bottomed pot on medium high fire and add all ingredients.
2. Cover, bring to a boil, lower fire to a simmer, and simmer for 10 minutes.
3. Serve and enjoy.

Nutrition Information:
Calories per Serving: 244.1; Carbs: 6.3g; Protein: 29.3g; Fats: 11.3g; Saturated Fat: 8.8g; Sodium: 356mg

Cajun Shrimp Boil

Serves: 4 , Cooking time: 40 minutes
Ingredients:
- 2 corn on the cobs, halved
- 1/2 kielbasa sausage, sliced into 2-inch pieces
- 1 cup chicken broth, low sodium
- 1 tablespoon old bay seasoning
- 1 tsp celery seeds
- 4 garlic cloves, smashed
- 1 teaspoon crushed red peppers
- 4 small potatoes, brushed and halved
- 1 onion, chopped
- 1-pound shrimps
- 1 tbsp olive oil
- Pepper

Directions for Cooking:
1. Place a heavy bottomed pot on medium high fire and heat pot for 3 minutes.
2. Once hot, add oil and stir around to coat pot with oil.
3. Sauté the garlic, onion, potatoes, and sausage for 5 minutes.
4. Stir in corn, broth, old bay, celery seeds, and red peppers. Cover and cook for 5 minutes.
5. Stir in shrimps and cook for another 5 minutes.
6. Serve and enjoy.

Nutrition Information:
Calories per Serving: 549.5; Carbs: 69.4g; Protein: 44.8g; Fats: 10.3g; Saturated Fat: 2.1g; Sodium: 289mg

Sautéed Savory Shrimps

Serves: 8 , Cooking time: 15 minutes

Ingredients:

- 2 pounds shrimp, peeled and deveined
- 1 tablespoon olive oil
- 4 cloves garlic, minced
- 2 cups frozen sweet corn kernels
- ½ cup chicken stock, low sodium
- 1 tablespoon lemon juice
- Pepper
- 1 tablespoon parsley for garnish

Directions for Cooking:

1. Place a heavy bottomed pot on medium high fire and heat pot for 3 minutes.
2. Once hot, add oil and stir around to coat pot with oil.
3. Sauté the garlic and corn for 5 minutes.
4. Add remaining ingredients and mix well.
5. Cover, bring to a boil, lower fire to a simmer, and simmer for 5 minutes.
6. Serve and enjoy.

Nutrition Information:

Calories per Serving: 180.6; Carbs: 11.4g; Protein: 25.2g; Fats: 3.8g; Saturated Fat: .6g; Sodium: 111mg

Sweet and Spicy Dolphinfish Filets

Serves: 2 , Cooking time: 25 minutes

Ingredients:

- 2 Dolphinfish filets
- Pepper to taste
- 2 cloves of garlic, minced
- 1 thumb-size ginger, grated
- ½ lime, juiced
- 2 tablespoons honey
- 2 tablespoons sriracha
- 1 tablespoon orange juice, freshly squeezed

Directions for Cooking:

1. In a heat-proof dish that fits inside saucepan, add all ingredients. Mix well.
2. Place a large saucepan on medium high fire. Place a trivet inside saucepan and fill pan halfway with water. Cover and bring to a boil.
3. Cover dish with foil and place on trivet.
4. Cover pan and steam for 10 minutes. Let it rest in pan for another 5 minutes.
5. Serve and enjoy.

Nutrition Information:

Calories per Serving: 348.4; Carbs: 22.3g; Protein: 38.6g; Fats: 2.2g; Saturated Fat: .5g; Sodium: 183mg

Steamed Ginger Scallion Fish

Serves: 2 , Cooking time: 30 minutes

Ingredients:

- 3 tablespoons soy sauce, low sodium
- 2 tablespoons rice wine
- 1 teaspoon minced ginger
- 1 teaspoon garlic
- 1-pound firm white fish

Directions for Cooking:

1. In a heat-proof dish that fits inside saucepan, add all ingredients. Mix well.
2. Place a large saucepan on medium high fire. Place a trivet inside saucepan and fill pan halfway with water. Cover and bring to a boil.
3. Cover dish with foil and place on trivet.
4. Cover pan and steam for 10 minutes. Let it rest in pan for another 5 minutes.
5. Serve and enjoy.

Nutrition Information:

Calories per Serving: 409.5; Carbs: 5.5g; Protein: 44.9g; Fats: 23.1g; Saturated Fat: 8.3g; Sodium: 115mg

Simply Steamed Alaskan Cod

Serves: 2 , Cooking time: 15 minutes

Ingredients:

- 1-lb fillet wild Alaskan Cod
- 1 cup cherry tomatoes, halved
- Salt and pepper to taste
- 1 tbsp balsamic vinegar
- 1 tbsp fresh basil chopped

Directions for Cooking:

1. In a heat-proof dish that fits inside saucepan, add all ingredients except for basil. Mix well.
2. Place a large saucepan on medium high fire. Place a trivet inside saucepan and fill pan halfway with water. Cover and bring to a boil.
3. Cover dish with foil and place on trivet.
4. Cover pan and steam for 10 minutes. Let it rest in pan for another 5 minutes.
5. Serve and enjoy topped with fresh basil.

Nutrition Information:

Calories per Serving: 195.2; Carbs: 4.2g; Protein: 41g; Fats: 1.6g; Saturated Fat: .3g; Sodium: 126mg

Enchilada Sauce on Mahi Mahi

Serves: 2 , Cooking time: 25 minutes

Ingredients:

- 2 Mahi Mahi fillets, fresh
- ¼ cup commercial enchilada sauce
- Pepper to taste

Directions for Cooking:

1. In a heat-proof dish that fits inside saucepan, place fish and top with enchilada sauce.
2. Place a large saucepan on medium high fire. Place a trivet inside saucepan and fill pan halfway with water. Cover and bring to a boil.
3. Cover dish with foil and place on trivet.
4. Cover pan and steam for 10 minutes. Let it rest in pan for another 5 minutes.
5. Serve and enjoy topped with pepper.

Nutrition Information:

Calories per Serving: 143.1; Carbs: 8.9g; Protein: 19.8g; Fats: 15.9g; Saturated Fat: 2.5g; Sodium: 225mg

Coconut Curry Fish Fillet

Serves: 4 , Cooking time: 25 minutes

Ingredients:

- 1 tablespoon olive oil
- ½ teaspoon mustard seeds
- 1-pound tilapia fillets, cut into thick strips
- 1 can coconut milk
- 1 tablespoon ginger, grated
- 15 curry leaves
- ½ onion, sliced
- ½ green bell pepper, sliced
- ½ yellow bell pepper, sliced
- 2 medium carrots, peeled and cut into ½-inch thick circles
- ½ teaspoon turmeric powder
- 2 teaspoons coriander powder
- 1 teaspoon cumin powder
- 1 teaspoon garam masala
- Pepper to taste

Directions for Cooking:

1. Place a heavy bottomed pot on medium high fire and heat pot for 3 minutes.
2. Once hot, add oil and stir around to coat pot with oil.
3. Sauté the mustard seeds, ginger, onion, curry leaves, turmeric, coriander, cumin, carrots, and garam masala for 7 minutes.
4. Add remaining ingredients and mix well.
5. Cover, bring to a boil, lower fire to a simmer, and simmer for 5 minutes.
6. Serve and enjoy.

Nutrition Information:

Calories per Serving: 164; Carbs: 4.9g; Protein: 23.5g; Fats: 5.6g; Saturated Fat: 1.2g; Sodium: 82 mg

Fish Filet in Sweet Orange Sauce

Serves: 4 , Cooking time: 15 minutes

Ingredients:

- 1 ½-lbs white fish fillets
- Juice and zest of 2 oranges
- 1 thumb-size ginger, grated
- Pepper to taste
- 1 tbsp honey
- 4 spring onions, chopped

Directions for Cooking:

1. In a heat-proof dish that fits inside saucepan, whisk well orange juice, orange zest, ginger, honey, and pepper. Place fish and marinate for 10 minutes. Top with green onions and cover dish with foil
2. Place a large saucepan on medium high fire. Place a trivet inside saucepan and fill pan halfway with water. Cover and bring to a boil.
3. Place dish on trivet.
4. Cover pan and steam for 10 minutes. Let it rest in pan for another 5 minutes.
5. Serve and enjoy topped with pepper.

Nutrition Information:

Calories per Serving: 141.9; Carbs: 6.5g; Protein: 26.5g; Fats: 1.1g; Saturated Fat: .2g; Sodium: 519mg

Salmon with Garlic-Oregano

Serves: 2 , Cooking time: 15 minutes

Ingredients:

- 1 tablespoon red wine vinegar
- 1 tablespoon lemon juice, freshly squeezed
- 1 clove of garlic, minced
- ¼ teaspoon dried oregano
- 1-pound salmon fillets, fresh
- 2 sprigs rosemary
- Pepper
- 1 tablespoon feta cheese, crumbled

Directions for Cooking:

1. In a heat-proof dish that fits inside saucepan, whisk well red wine vinegar, lemon juice, garlic and oregano. Place fish and marinate for 10 minutes. Top with rosemary and feta cheese. Cover dish with foil
2. Place a large saucepan on medium high fire. Place a trivet inside saucepan and fill pan halfway with water. Cover and bring to a boil.
3. Place dish on trivet.
4. Cover pan and steam for 10 minutes. Let it rest in pan for another 5 minutes.
5. Serve and enjoy topped with pepper.

Nutrition Information:

Calories per Serving: 361.8; Carbs: 6.3g; Protein: 45.9g; Fats: 17g; Saturated Fat: 11.4g; Sodium: 377mg

Chipotle Salmon Asparagus

Serves: 2 , Cooking time: 15 minutes

Ingredients:

- 1-lb salmon fillet, skin on
- 2 teaspoon chipotle paste
- A handful of asparagus spears, trimmed
- 1 lemon, sliced thinly

Directions for Cooking:

1. In a heat-proof dish that fits inside saucepan, whisk well red wine vinegar, lemon juice, garlic and oregano. Place fish and marinate for 10 minutes. Top with rosemary and feta cheese. Cover dish with foil
2. Place a large saucepan on medium high fire. Place a trivet inside saucepan and fill pan halfway with water. Cover and bring to a boil.
3. Place dish on trivet.
4. Cover pan and steam for 10 minutes. Let it rest in pan for another 5 minutes.
5. Serve and enjoy topped with pepper.

Nutrition Information:

Calories per Serving: 161.1; Carbs: 2.8g; Protein: 35g; Fats: 1.1g; Saturated Fat: .2g; Sodium: 325mg

Lemon Chili Halibut

Serves: 2 , Cooking time: 30 minutes

Ingredients:
- 1-lb halibut fillets
- 1 lemon, sliced
- 1 tablespoon chili pepper flakes
- Pepper

Directions for Cooking:
1. In a heat-proof dish that fits inside saucepan, place fish. Top fish with chili flakes, lemon slices and pepper. Cover dish with foil
2. Place a large saucepan on medium high fire. Place a trivet inside saucepan and fill pan halfway with water. Cover and bring to a boil.
3. Place dish on trivet.
4. Cover pan and steam for 10 minutes. Let it rest in pan for another 5 minutes.
5. Serve and enjoy topped with pepper.

Nutrition Information:
Calories per Serving: 216.4; Carbs: 4.2g; Protein: 42.7g; Fats: 3.2g; Saturated Fat: .7g; Sodium: 158mg

Sumptuously Tasty Poached Salmon

Serves: 4 , Cooking time: 10 minutes

Ingredients:
- 16-ounce salmon fillet with skin
- 4 scallions, chopped
- Zest of 1 lemon
- ½ teaspoon fennel seeds
- 1 teaspoon white wine vinegar
- 1 bay leaf
- ½ cup dry white wine
- 1 cup chicken broth, low sodium
- ¼ cup fresh dill
- Pepper
- 2 cups spinach

Directions for Cooking:
1. Place a heavy bottomed pot on medium high fire.
2. Add all ingredients, except for spinach and mix well.
3. Cover, bring to a boil, lower fire to a simmer, and simmer for 5 minutes.
4. Remove salmon with a slotted spoon and serve on a bed of spinach leaves.

Nutrition Information:
Calories per Serving: 225; Carbs: 4.4g; Protein: 34.3g; Fats: 7.8g; Saturated Fat: 3g; Sodium: 226mg

Salmon and Rice Pilaf

Serves: 4 , Cooking time: 25 minutes

Ingredients:
- ½ cup Jasmine rice
- ¼ cup dried vegetable soup mix
- 1 cup chicken broth
- 1 pinch saffron
- 1-lb wild salmon fillets

Directions for Cooking:
1. Place a heavy bottomed pot on medium high fire and add all ingredients and mix well.
2. Cover, bring to a boil, lower fire to a simmer, and simmer for 10 minutes.
3. Turn off fire, fluff rice and shred salmon. Let it rest for 5 minutes.
4. Serve and enjoy.

Nutrition Information:
Calories per Serving: 578.5; Carbs: 93.7g; Protein: 31.8g; Fats: 8.5g; Saturated Fat: 2g; Sodium: 286mg

Grilled Salmon Teriyaki Steaks

Serves: 2 , Cooking time: 10 minutes

Ingredients:

- 1-lb salmon fillet, skin on
- 1 tbsp teriyaki sauce
- 1 tbsp honey
- ½ tsp pepper
- 1 tsp sesame seeds

Directions for Cooking:

1. Preheat grill to 400ºF.
2. In a small bowl, whisk well pepper, honey, and teriyaki sauce.
3. Grease grate and place salmon filet. Brush tops with sauce.
4. Grill for 5 minutes and brush tops with sauce again. Sprinkle top with sesame seeds.
5. Continue grilling for 2 to 4 minutes or until desired doneness is reached.
6. Serve on a bed of spinach leaves and enjoy.

Nutrition Information:

Calories per Serving: 416.2; Carbs: 11.3g; Protein: 60.8g; Fats: 14.2g; Saturated Fat: 2.9g; Sodium: 237mg

Microwaved Golden Pompano

Serves: 2 , Cooking time: 25 minutes

Ingredients:

- ½-lb pompano
- 1 tbsp soy sauce, low sodium
- 1-inch thumb ginger, diced
- 1 clove garlic, minced
- 1 stalk green onions, chopped
- 1 tsp sesame oil
- ¼ cup water
- 1 lemon, halved
- 1 tsp pepper

Directions for Cooking:

1. In a microwavable casserole dish, mix well all ingredients except for pompano, green onions and lemon.
2. Squeeze a half of the lemon in dish and slice into thin circles the other half.
3. Place pompano in dish and add lemon circles on top of fish.
4. Cover top of casserole dish with a microwave safe plate.
5. Microwave for 5 minutes.
6. Remove from microwave, turn over fish, sprinkle green onions, top with microwavable plate.
7. Return to microwave and cook for another 3 minutes.
8. Let it rest for 3 minutes more.
9. Serve and enjoy.

Nutrition Information:

Calories per Serving: 244.5; Carbs: 6.3g; Protein: 22.2g; Fats: 14.5g; Saturated Fat: 4.6g; Sodium: 197mg

Chapter 12 Snack Recipes

Lemon Glazed Blueberry Scones

Serves: 8 , Cooking time: 20 minutes

Ingredients:

- 1/2 cup freshly squeezed lemon juice
- 2 cups confectioners' sugar, sifted
- 1 tablespoon unsalted butter
- 2 cups all-purpose flour
- 1 tablespoon baking powder
- 2 tablespoons sugar
- 5 tablespoons unsalted butter, cold, cut in chunks
- 1 cup fresh blueberries
- 1 cup heavy cream, plus more for brushing the scones

Directions for Cooking:

1. Make the lemon glaze by mixing lemon juice, confectioner's sugar, and butter. Microwave for 30 seconds and mix well until smooth and creamy. Set aside.
2. Preheat the oven to 400°F.
3. Sift together the flour, baking powder, and sugar. Using 2 forks or a pastry blender, cut in the butter to coat the pieces with the flour. The mixture should look like coarse crumbs. Fold the blueberries into the batter.
4. Make a well in the center and pour in the heavy cream. Fold everything together just to incorporate; do not overwork the dough.
5. Evenly divide dough into 8. Form each dough into triangles.
6. Place the scones on an ungreased cookie sheet and brush the tops with a little heavy cream. Bake for 15 to 20 minutes until beautifully browned.
7. Let the scones cool a bit before you apply the glaze.
8. Serve and enjoy

Nutrition Information:
Calories per Serving: 356; Carbs: 60.2g; Protein: 4.2g; Fats: 11.8g; Saturated Fat: 7.2g; Sodium: 13mg

Blueberry Coffee Cake Muffins

Serves: 16 , Cooking time: 25 minutes

Ingredients:

- 12 tablespoons (1 1/2 sticks) unsalted butter, at room temperature
- 1 1/2 cups sugar
- 3 extra-large eggs, at room temperature
- 1 1/2 teaspoons pure vanilla extract
- 8 ounces (about 1 cup) sour cream, light
- 1/4 cup skim milk
- 2 1/2 cups all-purpose flour
- 2 teaspoons baking powder
- 1/2 teaspoon baking soda
- 2 half-pints fresh blueberries

Directions for Cooking:

1. Preheat the oven to 350°F and line muffin tins with muffin liners.
2. Cream butter and sugar until light and fluffy in a large mixing bowl for 5 minutes with a mixer.
3. On low speed, add the eggs 1 at a time, then add the vanilla, sour cream, and milk.
4. Add baking soda and baking powder. Mix for a minute.
5. Add flour and beat until just mixed.
6. With a spatula, fold in blueberries.
7. Evenly add batter on to prepared muffin tins, filling each cup just over the top.
8. Bake for 25 minutes or until muffins are lightly browned on top.
9. Serve and enjoy. Muffins can be store in a tightly lidded container in the fridge for up to a week.

Nutrition Information:
Calories per Serving: ; Carbs: 26.2g; Protein: 3g; Fats: 7.6g; Saturated Fat: 4.6g; Sodium: 64mg

Healthy Blueberry & Banana Muffins

Serves: 12 , Cooking time: 25 minutes

Ingredients:

- 3/4 cup mashed ripe banana
- 3/4 cup + 2 tablespoons unsweetened almond milk
- 1 teaspoon apple cider vinegar
- 1/4 cup pure maple syrup
- 1 teaspoon pure vanilla extract
- 1/4 cup coconut oil, melted
- 1/2 teaspoon baking soda
- 2 teaspoons baking powder
- 4 tablespoons coconut sugar
- 1 1/2 teaspoons cinnamon
- 2 cups white spelt flour
- 1 1/4 cups frozen or fresh blueberries
- 1/2 cup walnut halves, chopped

Directions for Cooking:

1. Preheat oven to 350°F.
2. In a large mixing bowl, whisk well all wet ingredients.
3. Slowly add in dry ingredients, mixing well every after each addition.
4. Line 12 muffin tins with cupcake liners and evenly fill liners with batter.
5. Bake for 25 minutes.
6. Serve and enjoy.

Nutrition Information:

Calories per Serving: 226.5; Protein: 5g; Carbs: 33.4g; Fat: 8.1g; Saturated Fat: 4.3g; Sodium: 67mg

Tart Raspberry Crumble Bar

Serves: 9 , Cooking time: 45 minutes

Ingredients:

- 1/2 cup whole toasted almonds
- 1 3/4 cups whole wheat flour
- 1/4 teaspoon salt
- 3/4 cup cold, unsalted butter, cut into cubes
- 3 tablespoons cold water, or more if needed
- 1/2 cup granulated sugar
- 18-ounce fresh raspberries

Directions for Cooking:

1. In a food processor, pulse almonds until copped coarsely. Transfer to a bowl.
2. Add flour and salt into food processor and pulse until a bit combined. Add butter and pulse until you have a coarse batter. Evenly divide batter into two bowls.
3. In first bowl of batter, knead well until it forms a ball. Wrap in cling wrap, flatten a bit and chill for an hour for easy handling.
4. In second bowl of batter, add sugar. In a pinching motion, pinch batter to form clusters of streusel. Set aside.

5. When ready to bake, preheat oven to 375oF and lightly grease an 8x8-inch baking pan with cooking spray.
6. Discard cling wrap and evenly press dough on bottom of pan, up to 1-inch up the sides of the pan, making sure that everything is covered in dough.
7. Evenly spread raspberries. Top with streusel.
8. Pop in the oven and bake until golden brown and berries are bubbly, around 45 minutes.
9. Remove from oven and cool for 20 minutes before slicing into 9 equal bars.
10. Serve and enjoy or store in a lidded container for 10-days in the fridge.

Nutrition Information:

Calories per Serving: 235.7; Protein: 4.4g; Carbs: 29.1g; Fat: 11.3g; Saturated Fat: 6.5g; Sodium: 73mg

Choco-Chip Cookies with Walnuts and Oatmeal

Serves: 24 , Cooking time: 16 minutes

Ingredients:

- ½ tsp salt
- ½ tsp baking soda
- 1 tsp ground cinnamon
- ½ cup whole wheat pastry flour
- ½ cup all-purpose flour
- 2 cups rolled oats (not quick cooking)
- 4 tbsp cold unsalted butter, cut into pieces
- ½ cup tahini

- 2/3 cup packed light brown sugar
- 6 packets Stevia
- 1 tbsp vanilla extract
- 1 large egg white
- 1 large egg
- ½ cup chopped walnuts
- 1 cup semisweet Choco chips

Directions for Cooking:

1. Position two racks in the middle of the oven, leaving at least a 3-inch space in between them. Preheat oven to 350oF and grease baking sheets with cooking spray.
2. In medium bowl, whisk together salt, baking soda, cinnamon, whole wheat flour, all-purpose flour and oats.
3. In a large bowl, with a mixer beat butter and tahini until well combined.
4. Add brown sugar and Stevia, mixing continuously until creamy.
5. Mix in vanilla, egg white and egg and beat for a minute.
6. Cup by cup mix in the dry ingredients until well incorporated.
7. Fold in walnuts and Choco chips.
8. Get two tablespoonfuls of the batter and roll with your moistened hands into a ball.
9. Evenly place balls into prepped baking sheets at least an inch apart.
10. Pop in the oven and bake for 16 minutes. Ten minutes into baking time, switch pans from top to bottom and bottom to top. Continue baking for 6 more minutes.
11. Remove from oven, cool on a wire rack. Allow pans to cool completely before adding the next batch of cookies to be baked.
12. Cookies can be stored for up to 10 days in a tightly sealed container or longer in the fridge.

Nutrition Information:

Calories per Serving: 150.6; Protein: 3.8g; Carbs: 15.4g; Fat: 8.2g; Saturated Fat: 2.8g; Sodium: 87mg

Healthy Chocolate Mousse

Serves: 4 , Cooking time: 0 minutes

Ingredients:

- 1 large, ripe avocado
- 1/4 cup sweetened almond milk
- 1 tbsp coconut oil
- 1/4 cup cocoa or cacao powder
- 1 tsp vanilla extract

Directions for Cooking:

1. In food processor, process all ingredients until smooth and creamy.
2. Transfer to a lidded container and chill for at least 4 hours.
3. Serve and enjoy.

Nutrition Information:

Calories per Serving: 125; Protein: 1.2g; Carbs: 6.9g; Fat: 11.0g; Saturated Fat: 4.0g; Sodium: 22.0 mg

Healthy Banana-Choco Ice Cream

Serves: 4 , Cooking time: 0 minutes

Ingredients:

- 3 medium bananas, peeled and frozen
- 3 tbsp Unsweetened Cocoa Powder
- 1/2 tsp peppermint extract

Directions for Cooking:

1. Place all ingredients in a blender and puree until it resembles a soft serve ice cream.
2. Evenly divide into 4 bowls.
3. Serve and enjoy.

Nutrition Information:

Calories per Serving: 88; Protein: 1.7g; Carbs: 22.6g; Fat: 0.8g; Saturated Fat: 0.4g; Sodium: 2.0 mg

Pumpkin Walnut Cookie

Serves: 24 , Cooking time: 30 minutes

Ingredients:
- 1 tbsp baking powder
- ½ tsp salt
- 1½ tsp pumpkin pie spice mix
- 1¼ cups whole wheat flour
- 1½ cups flour
- ½ cup vegetable oil
- 2 eggs
- 1 cup brown sugar
- 3 packets Stevia
- 1 ¾ cups pumpkin, cooked and pureed (15 oz. can)
- 1 cup walnuts or hazelnuts, chopped
- 1 cup raisin

Directions for Cooking:
1. Grease a cookie sheet with cooking spray and preheat oven to 400oF.
2. In a medium bowl mix baking powder, salt, pumpkin pie spice mix, whole wheat flour, and flour.
3. In a large bowl beat eggs and oil thoroughly.
4. Add in brown sugar and stevia beat for at least 3 minutes.
5. Mix in pumpkin puree and beat well.
6. Slowly add the dry ingredients beating well after each addition.
7. Fold in nuts and raisins.
8. Using a 1 tbsp measuring spoon, get two saltspoonfuls of the dough and place on cookie sheet at least an inch apart. With the bottom of a spoon, flatten cookie.
9. Pop into the oven and bake until golden brown, around 10 minutes.
10. Once done, remove from oven, serve and enjoy or store in tightly lidded containers for up to a week.

Nutrition Information:
Calories per Serving: 230.4; Protein: 5.8g; Carbs: 22.1g; Fat: 13.2g; Saturated Fat: 5g; Sodium: 82mg

Healthy Buckwheat Groats and Seeds Granola

Serves: 18 , Cooking time: 30 minutes

Ingredients:
- 1 1/2 cups raw buckwheat groats
- 1 1/2 cups rolled oats
- 1/4 cup chopped pecans
- 1/4 cup chopped cashews
- 1/2 cup unsweetened coconut flakes
- 2 tbsp sunflower seeds
- 4 tbsp pepitas
- 3/4 tsp ground cinnamon
- 1/4 cup olive oil
- 1/2 cup maple syrup
- 3 tbsp almond butter
- 3 tbsp coconut sugar
- 1/3 cup dried blueberries

Directions for Cooking:
1. Preheat oven to 325ºF.
2. In a large mixing bowl, mix well groats, oats, pecans, cashews, coconut flakes, sunflower seeds, pepitas, and cinnamon.
3. Place a small nonstick pot on medium fire and heat oil for 2 minutes. Stir in maple syrup and mix well. Add almond butter and coconut sugar. Mix thoroughly until smooth and creamy.
4. Pour sauce into bowl of groats and toss well to coat and mix.
5. Lightly grease a baking sheet with cooking spray.
6. Evenly spread granola on to baking sheet. Pop in the oven and bake for 30 minutes or until a deep golden brown. Halfway through cooking time, toss around granola for even cooking.
7. Remove from oven and toss in dried fruit. Allow to cool completely.
8. Evenly divide into ¼ cups. Store in zip lock bags for up to 3 weeks.

Nutrition Information:
Calories per Serving: 184; Protein: 3.8g; Carbs: 19.7g; Fat: 10g; Saturated Fat: 2g; Sodium: 26mg

Easy Coconut-Carrot Cake Balls

Serves: 16 , Cooking time: 0 minutes

Ingredients:

- 3/4 cup peeled and finely shredded carrot
- 1 cup packed pitted medjool dates
- 1 ¾ cups raw walnuts
- 3/4 tsp ground cinnamon
- 1/2 tsp ground ginger
- 1 pinch ground nutmeg
- 2 tsp vanilla extract
- 5 tbsp almond flour
- 1/4 cup raisins
- ¼ cup desiccated coconut flakes

Directions for Cooking:

1. In food processor, process dates until it clumps. Transfer to a bowl.
2. In same food processor, process walnuts, cinnamon, ginger, and nutmeg. Process until it resembles a fine meal.
3. Add the processed dates, extract, almond flour, and shredded carrots. Pulse until you form a loose dough but not mushy. Do not over-pulse. Transfer to a bowl.
4. Pulse desiccated coconut into tinier flakes and transfer to a small plate.
5. Divide the carrot batter into 4 and then divide each part into 4 to make a total of 16 equal sized balls.
6. Roll the balls in the coconut flakes, place in a lidded contained, and refrigerate for 2 hours before enjoying.
7. Can be stored in the fridge for a week and up to a month in the freezer.

Nutrition Information:

Calories per Serving: 77.9; Protein: 1.5g; Carbs: 3.8g; Fat: 6.3g; Saturated Fat: 1g; Sodium: 8mg

Tart Raspberry Crumble Bar

Serves: 9 , Cooking time: 45 minutes

Ingredients:

- 1/2 cup whole toasted almonds
- 1 3/4 cups whole wheat flour
- 1/4 teaspoon salt
- 3/4 cup cold, unsalted butter, cut into cubes
- 3 tablespoons cold water, or more if needed
- 1/2 cup granulated sugar
- 18-ounce fresh raspberries

Directions for Cooking:

1. In a food processor, pulse almonds until copped coarsely. Transfer to a bowl.
2. Add flour and salt into food processor and pulse until a bit combined. Add butter and pulse until you have a coarse batter. Evenly divide batter into two bowls.
3. In first bowl of batter, knead well until it forms a ball. Wrap in cling wrap, flatten a bit and chill for an hour for easy handling.
4. In second bowl of batter, add sugar. In a pinching motion, pinch batter to form clusters of streusel. Set aside.
5. When ready to bake, preheat oven to 375oF and lightly grease an 8x8-inch baking pan with cooking spray.
6. Discard cling wrap and evenly press dough on bottom of pan, up to 1-inch up the sides of the pan, making sure that everything is covered in dough.
7. Evenly spread raspberries. Top with streusel.
8. Pop in the oven and bake until golden brown and berries are bubbly, around 45 minutes.
9. Remove from oven and cool for 20 minutes before slicing into 9 equal bars.
10. Serve and enjoy or store in a lidded container for 10-days in the fridge.

Nutrition Information:

Calories per Serving: 235.7; Protein: 4.4g; Carbs: 29.1g; Fat: 11.3g; Saturated Fat: 6.5g; Sodium: 73mg

Garlic-Parmesan Knots

Serves: 12 , Cooking time: 12 minutes

Ingredients:

- 2 tbsp Olive oil
- 3 tbsp Minced garlic
- 1 13.8-oz refrigerated pizza crust
- ¼ cup grated Parmesan cheese, low fat

Directions for Cooking:

1. Preheat oven to 400°F.

2. Roll dough out onto a cutting board. Cut dough into equal ¼-inch strips. Wrap each strip into knots
3. Mix olive oil & garlic in a bowl. Dip each knot into the mixture.
4. Lightly grease baking pan with cooking spray. Add knots to pan.

5. Bake until golden brown, around 12 minutes
6. Dust with Parmesan.
7. Serve and enjoy.

Nutrition Information:
Calories per Serving: 145.6; Carbs: 11g; Protein: 4.7g; Fats: 8.2g; Saturated Fat: 8.3; Sodium: 254mg

Chia Cinnamon Pudding

Serves: 2 , Cooking time: 0 minutes
Ingredients:
- 2 teaspoons unsweetened cacao powder
- 2 tablespoons chia seeds
- 1 packet Stevia
- 1/2 teaspoon cinnamon powder
- 1/3 cup almond milk
- 1/8 teaspoon vanilla extract

Directions for Cooking:

1. In a small bowl, mix well all ingredients.
2. Refrigerate for 4 hours.
3. Evenly divide into suggested servings and enjoy.

Nutrition Information:
Calories per Serving: 22.9; Carbs: 4.3g; Protein: .3g; Fats: .5g; Saturated Fat: .002g; Sodium: 28mg

Easy Baked Parmesan Chips

Serves: 10 , Cooking time: 10 minutes
Ingredients:
- 1 cup grated Parmesan cheese, low fat

Directions for Cooking:
1. Lightly grease a cookie sheet and preheat oven to 400°F.
2. Evenly sprinkle parmesan cheese on cookie sheet into 10 circles. Placing them about ½-inch apart.

3. Bake until lightly browned and crisped.
4. Let it cool, evenly divide into suggested servings and enjoy.

Nutrition Information:
Calories per Serving: 42; Carbs: 1.4g; Protein: 2.8g; Fats: 2.8g; Saturated Fat: 1.5g; Sodium: 180mg

Flaxseed, Maple & Pumpkin Muffin

Serves: 12 , Cooking time: 20 minutes
Ingredients:
- 1 tbsp cinnamon
- 1 cup pure pumpkin puree
- 1 tbsp pumpkin pie spice
- 1 tbsp olive oil
- 1 egg
- 1/2 tbsp baking powder
- 1/2 tsp apple cider vinegar
- 1/2 tsp vanilla extract
- 1/3 cup erythritol
- 1 3/4 cup all-purpose flour
- 1/4 cup Walden Farm's Maple Syrup

Directions for Cooking:

1. Line 12 muffin tins with muffin liners and preheat oven to 350°F.
2. In a blender, add all ingredients and blend until smooth and creamy, around 5 minutes.
3. Evenly divide batter into prepared muffin tins.
4. Pop in the oven and bake for 20 minutes or until tops are lightly browned.
5. Let it cool. Evenly divide into suggested servings and place in meal prep containers.

Nutrition Information:
Calories per Serving: 169.8; Carbs: 21.1g; Protein: 5.6g; Fats: 7g; Saturated Fat: 1.3g; Sodium: 36mg

Peanut Butter Cookies

Serves: 24 , Cooking time: 15 minutes

Ingredients:

- ¼ tsp salt
- 1 cup unsweetened peanut butter
- 1 tsp baking soda
- 1 tsp stevia powder
- 1/8 tsp xanthan gum
- 2 cups almond flour
- 2 large eggs
- 2 tbsp butter
- 2 tsp pure vanilla extract
- 4 ounces softened cream cheese
- 5 drops liquid Splenda

Directions for Cooking:

1. Line a cookie sheet with a non-stick liner. Set aside.
2. In a bowl, mix xanthan gum, flour, salt and baking soda. Set aside.
3. On a mixing bowl, combine the butter, cream cheese and peanut butter.
4. Mix on high speed until it forms a smooth consistency. Add the sweetener. Add the eggs and vanilla gradually while mixing until it forms a smooth consistency.
5. Add the almond flour mixture slowly and mix until well combined.
6. The dough is ready once it starts to stick together into a ball.
7. Scoop the dough using a 1 tablespoon measuring spoon and drop each cookie on the prepared cookie sheet. You will make around 24 cookies
8. Press the cookie with a fork and bake for 10 to 12 minutes at 350°F.
9. Let it cool and enjoy or store in an airtight container.

Nutrition Information:

Calories per Serving: 59.5; Carbs: 2.9g; Protein: 1.4g; Fats: 4.7g; Saturated Fat: 1.9g; Sodium: 266mg

No Cook Choco and Coconut Bars

Serves: 9 , Cooking time: 0 minutes

Ingredients:

- 1 tbsp Stevia
- ¾ cup shredded coconut, unsweetened
- ½ cup ground nuts (almonds, pecans, or walnuts)
- ¼ cup unsweetened cocoa powder
- 4 tbsp coconut oil

Directions for Cooking:

1. In a medium bowl, mix shredded coconut, nuts and cocoa powder.
2. Add Stevia and coconut oil.
3. Mix batter thoroughly.
4. In a 9x9 square inch pan or dish, press the batter and for 30-minutes place in the freezer.
5. Evenly divide into suggested servings and enjoy or store in airtight container.

Nutrition Information:

Calories per Serving: 99.7; Carbs: 2.7g; Protein: 1.3g; Fats: 9.3g; Saturated Fat: 5.7g; Sodium: 22mg

Carrot Cake Oatmeal Cookies

Serves: 12 , Cooking time: 20 minutes

Ingredients:

- 2 ripe bananas
- 2 cups old-fashioned rolled oats
- ½ cup carrots, shredded
- 3 tablespoons dried cranberries, chopped
- 3 tablespoons walnuts, chopped
- 2 tablespoons coconut flakes
- 1 ½ teaspoon ground cinnamon
- 1 ¼ teaspoon pure vanilla extract

Directions for Cooking:

1. Preheat the oven to 350^0F and line a baking sheet with parchment paper.
2. In a bowl, mash the banana and add the oats, carrots, cranberries, walnuts, coconut, cinnamon, and vanilla.
3. Mix to create a dough. Divide dough into half and divide it in thirds again. Now you have a total of 6 doughs.
4. Using your hands, divide each dough into two and form small balls and place on the baking sheet.
5. Flatten the balls with your hands.
6. Place in the oven and bake for 20 minutes or until golden brown.

Nutrition Information:

Calories per Serving: 109.1; Carbs: 16g; Protein: 3.4g; Fats: 3.5g; Saturated Fat: .7g; Sodium: 7mg

Lemon Ginger and Tapioca Pudding

Serves: 4 , Cooking time: 10 minutes

Ingredients:

- 1 can coconut milk, organic
- 1 cup plain and unsweetened almond milk
- 3 tablespoons raw honey
- 1 tablespoon lemon zest
- 1 teaspoon grated ginger
- 1/8 teaspoon salt
- ¼ cup small pearl tapioca, cooked according to package instruction

Directions for Cooking:

1. In a saucepan, place all ingredients.
2. Turn on the heat and allow simmering for 10 minutes.
3. Allow to cool before putting into containers.
4. Chill before serving.

Nutrition Information:

Calories per Serving: 265; Carbs: 30.7g; Protein: 1.8g; Fats: 15g; Saturated Fat: 12.7g; Sodium: 130mg

Crispy Apple Chips

Serves: 4 , Cooking time: 2 hours

Ingredients:

- 3 small apples, cored, peeled, and sliced thinly

Directions for Cooking:

1. Preheat the oven 275^0F.
2. Line a baking sheet with parchment paper.
3. Carefully arrange the apple slices on the baking sheet making sure that no apples are overlapping.
4. Bake for 2 hours or until crispy.

Nutrition Information:

Calories per Serving: 64.2; Carbs: 15.4g; Protein: .2g; Fats: .2g; Saturated Fat: .1g; Sodium: 1mg

Chapter 13 Dessert Recipes

Yogurt with Fresh Strawberries and Honey

Serves:4 , Cook Time: 5 minutes

Ingredients:
- 1-pint strawberries, fresh
- 4 teaspoons honey
- 3 cups plain low-fat yogurt
- 4 tablespoons toasted sliced almonds

Directions for Cooking:
1. Clean and slice the strawberries thinly. Set aside.
2. Place ¾ cup of the yogurt in each of the 4 glasses or dishes.
3. Distribute the strawberries evenly into the glasses.
4. Top with a teaspoon of honey and garnish with toasted almonds.
5. Chill in the fridge before serving.

Nutrition Information:
Calories per Serving: 169; Protein: 7g; Carbs: 21g; Fat: 3g; Saturated Fat: 1g; Sodium: 93mg

Boiled Honeyed Plantain Bananas

Serves:2 , Cook Time: 10 minutes

Ingredients:
- 4 small pieces of plantain bananas
- ½ cup water
- 2 tablespoons honey

Directions for Cooking:
1. Peel the plantain bananas and slice into halves.
2. Place in a saucepan the ingredients.
3. Heat over low medium flame until the water boils.
4. Allow to simmer for 10 minutes.
5. Serve hot or cold.

Nutrition Information:
Calories per Serving: 208; Protein: 1g; Carbs: 35g; Fat: 0.5g; Saturated Fat: 0g; Sodium: 4mg

Colorful Fruit Skewers

Serves:6 , Cook Time: 10 minutes

Ingredients:
- 84 strawberries, stems removed
- 1-pint blueberries
- 84 grapes
- 24 to 28 wooden skewers

Directions for Cooking:
1. Thread the strawberries, blueberries, and grapes into the skewers alternately.
2. Place on a plate and refrigerate the fruit skewers until ready to plate.

Nutrition Information:
Calories per Serving: 115; Protein: 2g; Carbs: 28g; Fat: 0.7g; Saturated Fat: 0g; Sodium: 3mg

Summer Berries with Yogurt

Serves:6 , Cook Time: 10 minutes

Ingredients:
- 1 cup sliced strawberries
- 1 cup fresh blueberries
- 1 cup fresh raspberries
- 1 teaspoon grated orange zest
- 3 tablespoon fresh orange juice
- 1-pint low fat plain yogurt

Directions for Cooking:
1. Combine all ingredients except for the yogurt in a bowl.
2. Place the fruit mixture in glass bowls.
3. Top with low-fat yogurt.
4. Place in the fridge and allow to chill before serving.

Nutrition Information:
Calories per Serving: 88; Protein: 4g; Carbs: 23g; Fat: 0.3g; Saturated Fat: 0g; Sodium: 13mg

Banana Berry Ice Cream

Serves:3 , Cook Time:5minutes

Ingredients:

- 3 large bananas, cut into 1-inch pieces and freeze
- 1 cup frozen berries
- ½ cup non-fat milk
- 1 ½ teaspoon vanilla extract

Directions for Cooking:

1. Place all ingredients in a food processor until the frozen fruit reaches the consistency of a soft ice cream.
2. Pour in a bowl and serve while still chilled.

Nutrition Information:

Calories per Serving: 232; Protein: 4g; Carbs: 48g; Fat: 3; Saturated Fat: 1g; Sodium: 58mg

Grilled Peaches with Honey and Yogurt

Serves:2 , Cook Time: 4 minutes

Ingredients:

- 2 large ripe peaches, cut in half
- ¼ cup fat-free Greek yogurt
- 1/8 teaspoon cinnamon
- 2 tablespoons honey

Directions for Cooking:

1. Heat the grill to low heat.
2. Grill the peaches for 2 to 4 minutes on each side until soft.
3. While the peaches are grilling, combine the yogurt and cinnamon in a small bowl.
4. Take the peaches out once cooked and drizzle with the honey sauce.
5. Top with a tablespoon of yogurt.
6. Serve chilled or warm.

Nutrition Information:

Calories per Serving:140; Protein: 3g; Carbs: 34g; Fat: 0.5g; Saturated Fat: 0g; Sodium: 0.4mg

Coconut Chocolate Parfait

Serves:1 , Cook Time: 5 minutes

Ingredients:

- ½ cup frozen fruit, unsweetened
- 2/3 cup plain low-fat kefir
- 1 tablespoon mini dark chocolate chips
- 1 tablespoon shredded coconut, unsweetened

Directions for Cooking:

1. Place frozen fruits into a bowl
2. Pour in the kefir
3. Sprinkle with dark chocolate and shredded coconut.
4. Serve chilled or immediately.

Nutrition Information:

Calories per Serving: 341; Protein: 9g; Carbs: 52g; Fat: 3g; Saturated Fat: 1.5g; Sodium: 170mg

Berry Yogurt Popsicles

Serves:6 , Cook Time: 60 minutes

Ingredients:

- 1 cup blueberries
- 1 cup blackberries
- 1 cup non-fat plain yogurt
- 1 ¼ cup non-fat milk

Directions for Cooking:

1. Place all ingredients in a blender and pulse until smooth.
2. Pour the mixture into molds or cups.
3. Insert popsicle sticks.
4. Freeze for an hour or until the popsicle hardens.

Nutrition Information:

Calories per Serving: 136; Protein: 5g; Carbs: 27g; Fat: 2g; Saturated Fat: 0.5g; Sodium: 38mg

Basmati Rice Pudding with Oranges

Serves:6 , Cook Time: 25 minutes

Ingredients:

- ¾ cup basmati rice, or any long-grain rice
- ½ vanilla bean, split lengthwise
- 4 cups fat-free evaporated milk
- 4 tablespoons honey
- 2 tablespoon chopped pistachios
- 3 large navel oranges, peeled and segmented

Directions for Cooking:

1. In a heavy saucepan, boil 2 cups of water. Once the water is boiling, add the rice and cover the pan. Reduce the heat to a simmer.
2. Cook the rice for 20 minutes until tender.
3. Add in the vanilla bean, evaporate milk, and honey.
4. Stir to combine all ingredients.
5. Cook for another 5 minutes.
6. Top with pistachios and oranges before serving.
7. Serve warm.

Nutrition Information:

Calories per Serving: 249; Protein: 8g; Carbs: 50g; Fat: 2g; Saturated Fat: 0.5g; Sodium: 89mg

Baked Stuffed Apples

Serves:4 , Cook Time: 25 minutes

Ingredients:

- 4 Golden Delicious apples, peeled and cored
- ¼ cup flaked coconut
- ¼ cup chopped dried apricots
- 2 teaspoons grated orange zest
- ½ cup orange juice
- 2 tablespoons honey

Directions for Cooking:

1. Arrange the apples in a baking dish. Set aside.
2. In a bowl, combine the coconut, apricots, and orange zest.
3. Fill the center of the apples with the coconut mixture.
4. In another bowl, combine the orange juice and honey.
5. Pour over the apples.
6. Place the apples in the oven and bake for 20 to 25 minutes until the apples are soft.
7. Cool before serving.

Nutrition Information:

Calories per Serving: 167; Protein:1 g; Carbs: 41g; Fat: 0.3g; Saturated Fat: 0g; Sodium: 21mg

Yummy Melon Slush

Serves:4 , Cook Time: 5 minutes

Ingredients:

- 5 ice cubes, crushed
- 4 cups ripe cantaloupe
- ¼ cup fresh orange juice

Directions for Cooking:

1. Place all ingredients in a blender and blend until smooth.
2. Pour in a glass and serve immediately.

Nutrition Information:

Calories per Serving: 68; Protein: 2g; Carbs: 16g; Fat: 0.3g; Saturated Fat: 0g; Sodium: 29mg

Almond Rice Pudding

Serves:6 , Cook Time: 30 minutes

Ingredients:

- 3 cups low-fat milk
- 1 cup brown rice
- ¼ cup honey
- 1 teaspoon vanilla
- ¼ teaspoon almond extract
- Cinnamon to taste
- ¼ cup toasted almonds

Directions for Cooking:

1. In a medium saucepan, place the milk and rice.
2. Bring to a boil and reduce the heat for 30 minutes or until the rice is soft.

3. Remove from heat and add in honey, vanilla extract, almond extract, and cinnamon.
4. Stir to combine.
5. Toss almonds for garnish.

Nutrition Information:
Calories per Serving: 201; Protein: 6g; Carbs: 41g; Fat: 1g; Saturated Fat:0 g; Sodium: 54mg

Watermelon Wedges with Lemon

Serves:1 , Cook Time: 5 minutes
Ingredients:
- ½ cup freshly squeezed lemon juice
- 3 tablespoons honey
- Three-inch-thick slices of chilled watermelon, quartered

Directions for Cooking:

1. In a mixing bowl, combine the lemon juice and honey.
2. Drizzle over the watermelon wedges.
3. Serve chilled.

Nutrition Information:
Calories per Serving: 222; Protein: 0.3g; Carbs: 61g; Fat: 0.7g; Saturated Fat: 0g; Sodium: 4

Icy Cold Watermelon Sorbet

Serves:8 , Cook Time: 4 hours
Ingredients:
- 8 cups cubed watermelon, seed and rind removed
- 2 tablespoon lemon juice

Directions for Cooking:
1. Place all ingredients in a blender and pulse until smooth.

2. Put in an ice cream maker and allow to freeze.
3. If you don't have any ice cream maker, you can put it in a lidded container and place in the fridge for 4 hours until it hardens.

Nutrition Information:
Calories per Serving: 47; Protein: 0.9g; Carbs: 11g; Fat: 0.2g; Saturated Fat: 0g; Sodium: 2mg

Skinny Pina Colada Popsicles

Serves:4 , Cook Time: 2 hours
Ingredients:
- 1 1/3 cups pineapple, diced
- ¼ cup pineapple juice, fresh
- ½ cup light coconut milk
- 1 teaspoon coconut water

Directions for Cooking:
1. Place all ingredients in a blender.

2. Blend until smooth.
3. Place in popsicle molds and free for at least 2 hours until the popsicles harden.

Nutrition Information:
Calories per Serving: 128; Protein: 1g; Carbs: 17g; Fat: 7g; Saturated Fat: 4g; Sodium: 7mg

Raspberry Jell-O Parfaits

Serves:3 , Cook Time: 10 minutes
Ingredients:
- 1 box organic gelatin
- 1 cup fresh raspberries, pureed
- ¾ cup fresh blueberries

Directions for Cooking:
1. Place gelatin in a bowl and add a cup of boiling water.
2. Transfer in a saucepan.
3. Stir until the gelatin dissolves.

4. Add in the pureed raspberries.
5. Place the blueberries in bowls.
6. Ladle the raspberry gelatin mixture into the blueberries.
7. Allow to chill and set in the fridge for at least 20 minutes.

Nutrition Information:
Calories per Serving: 134; Protein: 1g; Carbs: 34g; Fat: 0.3g; Saturated Fat: 0g; Sodium: 4mg

Mulled Pears and Apples

Serves:8 , Cook Time: 30 minutes

Ingredients:

- 4 quarts apple juice
- 2 cinnamon sticks
- 1 large crystallized ginger
- 6 whole cloves
- 1 lemon, halved
- 4 Fuji apples
- 4 Anjou pears

Directions for Cooking:

1. In a heavy pot, place the apple juice. In a cloth bag, place the cinnamon sticks, ginger, and cloves. Tie the cloth bag and place in the apple juice.
2. Bring to a boil and reduce the heat to medium. Once it reaches to a boil, reduce the heat and simmer for 15 minutes.
3. While the apple juice is boiling, squeeze the lemon in a bowl filled with water.
4. Core the apples and pears and drop into the bowl with lemon water until ready.
5. Add the fruits into the boiling liquid and simmer for 20 minutes until tender.
6. Turn off the heat and discard the cloth bag.
7. Allow to cool.
8. Serve the fruit with the apple juice.

Nutrition Information:

Calories per Serving: 317; Protein: 1g; Carbs: 54g; Fat: 0.8g; Saturated Fat: 0g; Sodium: 12mg

Frozen Fruit Tart

Serves:6 , Cook Time: 30 minutes

Ingredients:

- 1 cup shredded coconut, desiccated
- 3 tablespoons coconut oil
- 2 ¼ cups low-fat vanilla yogurt
- 12 ounces fresh blackberries
- 12 ounces fresh strawberries, cleaned and sliced

Directions for Cooking:

1. In a bowl, mix together the coconut shreds and coconut oil.
2. Press the mixture lightly into the bottom of a pie plate.
3. Place in the fridge and allow to harden.
4. Meanwhile, mix the vanilla yogurt, blackberries and strawberries.
5. Pour into prepared tart crust.
6. Chill for at least 30 minutes before serving.

Nutrition Information:

Calories per Serving: 215; Protein: 5g; Carbs: 31g; Fat: 8g; Saturated Fat: 4g; Sodium: 105mg

Blueberry Panna Cotta

Serves:6 , Cook Time: 3 hours

Ingredients:

- 2 tablespoons cold water
- 1 ½ teaspoon unflavored gelatin, organic
- ½ cup light cream
- 6 ounces fat-free yogurt, vanilla
- 1 tablespoon honey
- 1 cup fresh blueberries, for serving

Directions for Cooking:

1. In a small bowl, pour the water and add the gelatin. Place in a microwave and heat for 15 seconds. Whisk to dissolve the gelatin.
2. Stir in the cream, yogurt, and honey.
3. Divide the mixture into 6 small cups and chill for at least 3 hours.
4. Run a knife along the edges of the cup and unmold the panna cotta into a plate.
5. Top with blueberries on top.
6. Serve.

Nutrition Information:

Calories per Serving: 125; Protein: 2g; Carbs:21 g; Fat: 4g; Saturated Fat: 1g; Sodium: 42mg

TraditionalBaked Apples

Serves:4 , Cook Time: 35 minutes

Ingredients:
- 4 Fuji apples
- 2 teaspoons lemon juice
- 6 teaspoons golden raisins
- 2 teaspoons cinnamon
- 2 teaspoons honey
- A dash of vanilla extract
- ½ cup apple juice

Directions for Cooking:
1. Preheat the oven to 350^{0}F for 5 minutes.
2. Core the apple but do not cut through to make sure that the bottom remains intact.
3. Place the apples in a baking dish.
4. Drizzle with lemon juice.
5. Fill the center of the apple with raisins. Drizzle with honey, vanilla extract, and cinnamon.
6. Pour the apple juice at the bottom of the baking dish and bake for 30 to 35 minutes.
7. Baste the apples with the apple juice every 5 minutes.
8. Let it rest for 3 minutes before serving.

Nutrition Information:
Calories per Serving: 154; Protein: 0.5g; Carbs: 0.4g; Fat: 0.4g; Saturated Fat: 0g; Sodium: 4mg

Vanilla Poached Peaches

Serves:4 , Cook Time: 15 minutes

Ingredients:
- 1 cup water
- ¼ cup honey
- 1 vanilla bean, split and scraped
- 4 large peaches, halved and cored
- Mint leaves for garnish

Directions for Cooking:
1. In a saucepan, place the water, honey, and vanilla bean scrapings.
2. Heat the mixture over low heat for 10 minutes or until the sauce thickens.
3. Add the peaches and poach for 5 minutes.
4. Transfer the poaches in bowls and garnish with mint leaves.

Nutrition Information:
Calories per Serving: 133; Protein: 2g; Carbs: 34g; Fat: 0.4g; Saturated Fat: 0g; Sodium: 2mg

Summer Fruit Gratin

Serves:10 , Cook Time: 55 minutes

Ingredients:
- 1-pound fresh cherries, pitted and halved
- 4 cups different types of stone fruits (peaches and apricots), pitted and sliced
- 4 tablespoons whole wheat flour
- ½ cup rolled oats
- ¼ cup sliced almonds
- 2 tablespoons honey
- 1/8 teaspoon ground cinnamon
- 1/8 teaspoon ground nutmeg

Directions for Cooking:
1. Preheat the oven to 350^{0}F for 5 minutes.
2. In a bowl, mix together the cherries and stone fruits. Sprinkle with a tablespoon of whole wheat flour and toss to coat.
3. Place in a baking dish and set aside.
4. In another bowl, mix together the remaining flour with oats, almond, honey, cinnamon, and nutmeg.
5. Sprinkle the mixture on top of the fruit mixture.
6. Place inside the oven and bake for 45 to 55 minutes.
7. Serve warm or at room temperature.

Nutrition Information:
Calories per Serving: 141; Protein: 2g; Carbs: 36g; Fat: 0.6g; Saturated Fat: 0g; Sodium: 7mg

Strawberry Balsamic Sorbet

Serves:4 , Cook Time: 10 minutes

Ingredients:

- ¾ cup balsamic vinegar
- 4 cups strawberries, hulled and halved
- 1 tablespoon dark honey

Directions for Cooking:

1. In a saucepan, place the balsamic vinegar and bring to a boil over medium low heat. Allow to simmer for 5 minutes or until it has reduced. Turn off the flames and allow to cool.
2. In a blender, place the strawberries and pulse until smooth.
3. Add the balsamic reducing and honey and blend until well-incorporated.
4. Pour into ice cream maker or place in a lidded container and refrigerate overnight.
5. Scoop then serve cold.

Nutrition Information:

Calories per Serving:104; Protein: 1g; Carbs: 23g; Fat: 0.4g; Saturated Fat: 0g; Sodium: 13mg

Seasonal Fruit Palette

Serves:6 , Cook Time: 5 minutes

Ingredients:

- ¼ teaspoon ground cinnamon
- ¼ teaspoon honey
- 2 cups fresh strawberries, hulled and cleaned
- 1 kiwi, peeled and sliced
- 1 peach, pitted and sliced
- 1 pear, pitted and sliced
- 1 plum, pitted and sliced
- A handful of fresh mint leaves

Directions for Cooking:

1. In a bowl, combine all ingredients and toss to coat.
2. Place inside the fridge and allow to chill for at least 30 minutes.
3. Serve chilled.

Nutrition Information:

Calories per Serving: 46; Protein: 0.8g; Carbs: 11g; Fat: 0.3g; Saturated Fat: 0g; Sodium: 12mg

Simply Poached Pears

Serves:4 , Cook Time: 30 minutes

Ingredients:

- 1 cup orange juice
- ¼ cup apple juice, fresh
- 1 teaspoon ground cinnamon
- 1 teaspoon ground nutmeg
- 4 whole pears, peeled and cored but leave the stem
- ½ cup fresh raspberries
- 2 tablespoons orange zest

Directions for Cooking:

1. In a bowl, combine the orange juice, apple juice, cinnamon, and nutmeg. Stir to mix evenly.
2. Place the pears in a baking dish and pour the juice.
3. Turn the stove to medium and simmer for 30 minutes while turning the pears every 5 minutes. Do not let the liquid boil – only simmer – until the sauce reduces and thickens.
4. Transfer the pears into individual bowls and garnish with raspberries and orange zest.

Nutrition Information:

Calories per Serving: 126; Protein: 1g; Carbs: 31g; Fat:0.6g; Saturated Fat: 0g; Sodium: 3mg

Orange Slices with Citrus Syrup

Serves:4 , Cook Time: 10 minutes

Ingredients:

- 4 oranges, peeled and segmented
- Zest from one orange
- 1 ½ cups fresh orange juice
- 4 fresh mint sprigs

Directions for Cooking:

1. Slice the peeled and segmented oranges and place in a bowl. Set aside in the fridge.
2. In a small saucepan, mix together the orange zest and orange juice. Heat over medium flame until it simmers. Allow the sauce to thicken for 10 minutes while stirring constantly. Allow to cool.
3. Pour the sauce over oranges and garnish with mint.

Nutrition Information:
Calories per Serving: 266; Protein: 2g; Carbs: 53g; Fat: 5g; Saturated Fat: 1g; Sodium: 3mg

Twisted Grilled Pineapple

Serves:6 , Cook Time: 10 minutes
Ingredients:
- 1 large pineapple, peeled and cored
- 1 tablespoon olive oil
- 1 teaspoon ground cinnamon
- 1 tablespoon fresh lime juice
- 1 tablespoon grated lime zest

Directions for Cooking:
1. Place all ingredients in a large bowl and toss to coat the pineapples with the rest of the ingredients.
2. Heat the grill to low and grill the pineapples for 4 minutes on both sides.
3. Serve hot or warm.

Nutrition Information:
Calories per Serving: 98; Protein: 0.9g; Carbs:20 g; Fat: 2g; Saturated Fat: 0.5g; Sodium: 2mg

Grilled Fruit with Balsamic Vinegar Syrup

Serves:6 , Cook Time: 10 minutes
Ingredients:
- 1 small pineapple, peeled and cut into wedges
- 2 large mangoes, cored and sliced
- 2 large peaches, cored and sliced
- 2 tablespoons honey
- ½ cup balsamic vinegar
- A handful of fresh mint

Directions for Cooking:
1. Prepare the grill to low heat.
2. In a bowl, combine the pineapples, mangoes, and peaches. Drizzle with honey and toss to coat.
3. Grill the fruits for 3 minutes on each side. Set aside.
4. In a small saucepan, heat the balsamic vinegar over low heat for 10 minutes until it thickens.
5. Drizzle the grilled fruits with the balsamic vinegar reduction.

Nutrition Information:
Calories per Serving: 187; Protein: 2g; Carbs: 47g; Fat: 0.6g; Saturated Fat: 0g; Sodium: 27mg

Fresh Fruit Kebabs with Lemon Lime Sauce

Serves:4 , Cook Time: 5 minutes
Ingredients:
- 6 pineapple chunks
- 6 strawberries, cleaned
- 1 kiwi, peeled and cubed
- ½ banana, cut into chunks
- 6 red grapes
- 4 ounces low-fat and sugar-free yogurt
- 1 teaspoon fresh lime juice
- 1 teaspoon lime zest
- 4 wooden or bamboo skewers

Directions for Cooking:
1. In a bowl, mix the yogurt, lime juice, and lime zest until well-combined. Set aside.
2. Thread 1 of each fruit through the skewers.
3. Drizzle with the lemon dip.

Nutrition Information:
Calories per Serving: 66; Protein: 2g; Carbs: 14g; Fat: 0.5g; Saturated Fat: 0g; Sodium: 16mg

Serves:4 , Cook Time: 60 minutes

Ingredients:

- 1/3 cup dried cherries, chopped
- 3 tablespoons chopped almonds
- 1 tablespoon wheat germ
- ½ teaspoon ground cinnamon
- 1/8 teaspoon ground nutmeg
- 6 small Golden Delicious apples
- ½ cup apple juice
- ¼ cup water

Directions for Cooking:

1. Preheat the oven to 350⁰F.
2. In a small bowl, toss the cherries, almonds, wheat germ, cinnamon, and nutmeg until well-combined.

3. Core the apples. Use a knife to core the apple stopping at ¾ inch from the bottom.
4. Stuff the cavity of the apples with the cherry mixture.
5. Place the stuffed apples in a baking dish and pour the apple juice and water.
6. Cover the baking dish with foil.
7. Place inside the oven and bake for 60 minutes.
8. Baste the apples with the juice every 10 minutes.
9. Serve warm.

Nutrition Information:

Calories per Serving: 145; Protein:1 g; Carbs: 33g; Fat: 1g; Saturated Fat: 0g; Sodium: 37mg

Serves:6 , Cook Time: 10 minutes

Ingredients:

- ½ cup slivered almonds
- ½ cup unsweetened coconut flakes
- 1 small pineapple, cubed
- 5 oranges, peeled and segmented
- 2 red apples, cored and diced
- 1 banana, peeled and sliced
- ½ cup orange juice
- Fresh mint leaves for garnish

Directions for Cooking:

1. Preheat the oven to 325⁰F.
2. Spread the almonds on a baking dish and bake for 10 minutes. Once toasted, place on a plate and set aside.

3. Add the coconuts in the baking dish and toast for another 10 minutes while stirring constantly.
4. Assemble the Ambrosia by combining the pineapple, oranges, apples, and bananas. Pour over the orange juice and toss to coat.
5. Place in individual bowls and garnish with mint, toasted almonds, and coconut.

Nutrition Information:

Calories per Serving: 170; Protein: 1g; Carbs: 36g; Fat: 2g; Saturated Fat: 0.5g; Sodium:23mg

Serves:6 , Cook Time: 5 minutes

Ingredients:

- 3 cups ripe watermelons, cubed
- 2 fresh ripe peaches, pitted and sliced
- ½ seedless cucumber, diced
- 2 tablespoons mint leaves
- 3 tablespoons honey

Directions for Cooking:

1. Place all ingredients in a bowl.
2. Toss to coat the fruits with the honey.
3. Serve chilled or as is.

Nutrition Information:

Calories per Serving:62; Protein: 0.6g; Carbs: 16g; Fat: 0.2g; Saturated Fat:0 g; Sodium: 18mg

Serves:3 , Cook Time: 5 minutes

Ingredients:

- 1 large ripe avocado
- ¼ cup almond milk
- ¼ cup cacao powder

- 1 teaspoon vanilla extract

Directions for Cooking:

1. Put all ingredients in a blender or food processor.
2. Pulse until smooth.
3. Pour into individual containers.

4. Chill for at least 30 minutes before serving.

Nutrition Information:
Calories per Serving: 137; Protein: 2g; Carbs: 11g; Fat: 11g; Saturated Fat: 2g; Sodium: 20mg

Sautéed Tropical Bananas

Serves:6 , Cook Time: 10 minutes
Ingredients:
- 1 tablespoon coconut oil
- 4 firm bananas approximately 1 pound in total weight
- 1 tablespoon honey
- ¼ cup water
- 1 tablespoon dark raisins

Directions for Cooking:
1. In a non-stick pan, heat the coconut oil over medium low flame.

2. Stir in the bananas and allow to brown slightly on all sides.
3. Stir in honey, water, and raisins.
4. Allow to simmer for a few minutes or until the water has reduced.
5. Serve warm.

Nutrition Information:
Calories per Serving: 145; Protein: 1g; Carbs: 27g; Fat: 5g; Saturated Fat: 2g; Sodium: 21mg

Warm Chocolate Pudding

Serves:6 , Cook Time: 10 minutes
Ingredients:
- 1 tablespoon ground flaxseed
- ¼ cup warm water
- 2 ¼ cups skim milk
- ¼ cup honey
- 2/3 cup unsweetened cocoa powder
- 1 teaspoon vanilla extract, alcohol-free
- 1 tablespoon cornstarch

Directions for Cooking:
1. In a small bowl, mix the flaxseed with warm water. Set aside.
2. In a medium saucepan,mix together the milk and honey. Bring to a simmer and adjust the heat to medium.

3. Meanwhile, mix the cocoa powder, vanilla extract and cornstarch into the cooled flaxseed mixture.
4. Once well combined, pour into the simmering milk and mix until the mixture thickens.
5. Transfer into bowls and allow to chill before serving.

Nutrition Information:
Calories per Serving: 169; Protein: 5g; Carbs: 35g; Fat: 1g; Saturated Fat: 0g; Sodium: 10mg

Tasty Peach Float

Serves:4 , Cook Time: 0 minutes
Ingredients:
- 15 ounces fresh ripe peaches, pitted and sliced
- 4 cups sugar-free low-fat ice milk
- 32 ounces seltzer water

Directions for Cooking:
1. In a bowl, mash the peaches with a fork.

2. Divide the peaches into 4 glasses and add a cup of icemilk.
3. Pour a cup of seltzer water.
4. Put ice if desired.

Nutrition Information:
Calories per Serving: 128; Protein:7g; Carbs22; Fat: 0.7g; Saturated Fat: 0g; Sodium: 133mg

Sliced Apples with Creamy Dip

Serves:8 , Cook Time: 5minutes
Ingredients:
- 8 ounces fat-free cream cheese, softened
- 2 tablespoons honey
- 1 ½ teaspoons vanilla

- 2 tablespoons peanuts, chopped and unsalted
- 4 medium-sized apples, cored and sliced
- ½ cup orange juice

Directions for Cooking:
1. In a bowl, combine the cream cheese, honey, and vanilla. Mix until the mixture becomes smooth and homogenous. Add in the peanuts
2. In another bowl, drizzle the apples with orange juice.
3. Serve the sliced apples with the cream cheese dip.

Nutrition Information:
Calories per Serving: 118; Protein: 6g; Carbs: 19g; Fat: 2g; Saturated Fat: 0.5g; Sodium: 102mg

Rainbow Ice Pops

Serves:6 , Cook Time: 10 minutes
Ingredients:
- 1 ½ cups diced fruits of your choice (cantaloupe, strawberries, or watermelon)
- ½ cup blueberries
- 2 cups apple juice, organic
- Popsicle molds and craft sticks

Directions for Cooking:
1. In a bowl, mix the fruit together and distribute into popsicle molds.
2. Pour in apple juice and insert craft sticks in the middle.
3. Place in the fridge to set and harden overnight.
4. Remove from the popsicle molds before serving.

Nutrition Information:
Calories per Serving: 60; Protein: 0.5g; Carbs: 14g; Fat: 0g; Saturated Fat: 0g; Sodium: 6mg

Watermelon Cranberry Agua Fresca

Serves:6 , Cook Time: 5 minutes
Ingredients:
- 2 ½ pounds watermelon, rind removed and diced
- 5 ice cubes
- 1 cup cranberry juice, naturally sweetened
- ¼ cup lime juice, freshly squeezed
- 1 lime, cut into 6 slices

Directions for Cooking:
1. Place all ingredients except for the lime slices in a blender.
2. Blend until smooth
3. Pour into a large pitcher and stir in the lime slices.
4. Serve immediately or refrigerate until later use.

Nutrition Information:
Calories per Serving: 84; Protein: 1g; Carbs: 20g; Fat: 0g; Saturated Fat: 0g; Sodium: 9mg

Wholegrain Banana Bread

Serves:6 , Cook Time: 60 minutes
Ingredients:
- ½ cup brown rice flour
- ½ cup amaranth flour
- ½ cup tapioca flour
- ½ cup millet flour
- ½ cup quinoa flour
- 1 teaspoon baking soda
- ½ teaspoon baking powder
- ¾ cup egg whites
- 2 tablespoons grapeseed oil
- ½ cup coconut sugar
- 2 cups mashed ripe bananas

Directions for Cooking:
1. Preheat the oven to 350⁰F.
2. Prepare a loaf pan by spraying it lightly with cooking spray. Set aside.
3. In a bowl, mix the first seven ingredients (dry ingredients).
4. In another bowl, combine the egg whites, oil, sugar, and mashed bananas. Pour into the dry ingredients and mix until well-combined.
5. Once all ingredients have been mixed, pour into the loaf pan.
6. Bake for 60 minutes or until a toothpick inserted in the middle comes out clean.

Nutrition Information:
Calories per Serving: 163; Protein: 4g; Carbs: 30g; Fat: 3g; Saturated Fat: 0.5g; Sodium: 67mg

Chapter 14 Smoothie Recipes

Fruity Tofu Smoothie

Serves: 2 , Cooking time: 0 minutes

Ingredients:

- 1 container silken tofu
- 1 cup packed spinach
- ½ cup frozen pineapple chunks
- 1 medium banana, frozen
- ¼ cup mango chunks, frozen
- 1 cup ice cold water
- 1 tbsp chia seeds

Directions for Cooking:

1. In a powerful blender, add all ingredients and puree until smooth and creamy.
2. Evenly divide into two glasses, serve and enjoy.

Nutrition Information:

Calories per Serving: 175; Protein: 6.0g; Carbs: 33.3g; Fat: 3.7g; Saturated Fat: 0.6g; Sodium: 22 mg

Almond Butter-Banana Smoothie

Serves: 1 , Cooking time: 0 minutes

Ingredients:

- 1 medium banana, peeled and frozen
- ½ cup spinach, packed
- 1 cup fat-free milk
- 1 tbsp almond butter
- ½ cup ice cubes

Directions for Cooking:

1. In a powerful blender, blend all ingredients until smooth and creamy.
2. Serve and enjoy.

Nutrition Information:

Calories per Serving: 293; Protein: 13.5g; Carbs: 42.5g; Fat: 9.8g; Saturated Fat: 1.1g; Sodium: 143mg

Creamy Oats, Greens & Blueberry Smoothie

Serves: 1 , Cooking time: 0 minutes

Ingredients:

- ½ cup cooked oatmeal, frozen
- 1 cup salad greens
- ½ cup fresh frozen blueberries
- 1 tbsp sunflower seeds
- 1 cup fat-free milk, cold

Directions for Cooking:

1. In a powerful blender, blend all ingredients until smooth and creamy.
2. Serve and enjoy.

Nutrition Information:

Calories per Serving: 280; Protein: 14.0g; Carbs: 44.0g; Fat: 6.8g; Saturated Fat: 0.9g; Sodium: 283 mg

Banana-Peanut Butter 'n Greens Smoothie

Serves: 1 , Cooking time: 0 minutes

Ingredients:

- 1 medium banana, frozen
- 1 tbsp all-natural peanut butter
- 1 cup almond milk, cold
- 1 cup Romaine lettuce, chopped and packed

Directions for Cooking:

1. In a heavy-duty blender, add all ingredients.
2. Puree until smooth and creamy.
3. Serve and enjoy.

Nutrition Information:

Calories per Serving: 349.3; Protein: 8.1g; Carbs: 57.4g; Fat: 9.7g; Saturated Fat: 1.2g; Sodium: 273mg

Mango-Banana 'n Orange Smoothie

Serves: 2 , Cooking time: 0 minutes

Ingredients:

- ½ cup orange juice, freshly squeezed
- ½ cup mango chunks
- ½ banana, cut into chunks
- 1/3 cup plain yogurt
- ¼ cup oats
- 8 ice cubes

Directions for Cooking:

1. Place all ingredients in a blender.
2. Pulse until smooth.
3. Pour in a glass and enjoy.

Nutrition Information:

Calories per Serving: 145; Carbs: 30.0g; Protein: 4.4g; Fats: 1.6g; Saturated Fat: 0.3g; Sodium: 31mg

Raspberry 'n Kale Smoothie

Serves: 2 , Cooking time: 0 minutes

Ingredients:

- 1 cup fresh kale, destemmed and chopped
- 1 cup almond milk, unsweetened
- 1 cup spinach, fresh
- 1 medium banana, peeled and frozen
- ¼ cup fresh raspberries
- ¼ cup fresh pineapple chunks
- 1 tbsp chia seeds
- ½ cup cold water

Directions for Cooking:

1. Place all ingredients in a blender.
2. Pulse until smooth.
3. Serve and enjoy.

Nutrition Information:

Calories per Serving: 188.7; Carbs: 40.3g; Protein: 2.6g; Fats: 1.9g; Saturated Fat: .1g; Sodium: 103mg

Berry-Banana Yogurt Smoothie

Serves: 2 , Cooking time: 0 minutes

Ingredients:

- 5-6 ice cubes
- ½ cup blueberries, frozen
- ½ banana, frozen
- 1 container 5.3oz non-fat Greek yogurt
- ¼ cup quick cooking oats
- 1 cup almond milk
- ¼ cup of chopped Collard Greens, middle stem removed and discarded

Directions for Cooking:

1. In a microwave safe cup, microwave on high for 2.5 minutes the 1 cup almond milk and ¼ cup oats.
2. Once oats are cooked, add 2 ice cubes to cool it down quick and mix.
3. Then pour the rest of the ingredients, along with the slightly cool oat mixture, in a blender and puree until mixture is smooth and creamy.
4. Serve and enjoy.

Nutrition Information:

Calories per Serving: 183.5; Carbs: 37g; Protein: 3.7g; Fats: 2.3g; Saturated Fat: .2g; Sodium: 94mg

Nutty Pina Colada Smoothie

Serves: 2 , Cooking time: 2.5 minutes

Ingredients:

- 6 ice cubes
- ¼ tsp coconut extract
- ½ cup diced fresh pineapple
- 1 medium banana, peeled and frozen
- 1 container 6oz Greek yogurt
- ¼ cup quick cooking oats
- 1 cup Almond Milk
- 1 cup Swiss Chard, destemmed and torn
- ¼ cup Dandelion Greens

Directions for Cooking:

1. In a microwave safe mug, mix almond milk and oats. Microwave for 2.5 minutes. Once

done, remove from microwave and mix. Add 3 ice cubes and mix again.
2. Place all ingredients in a blender, including cooked oats and begin blending until you have a smooth and creamy mixture.

3. Serve and enjoy.
Nutrition Information:
Calories per Serving: 197.9; Carbs: 39.9g; Protein: 4.4g; Fats: 2.3g; Saturated Fat: .2g; Sodium: 137mg

Pomegranate and Cactus Pear Smoothie

Serves: 2 , Cooking time: 0 minutes
Ingredients:
- ½ cup cold water
- 2 ½ tbsp goji berries
- ¼ cup raw almonds
- 1 medium banana, peeled and frozen
- 1 cup frozen blueberries
- 2 cactus pears, juiced and fleshed, strain out seeds and peel
- ½ cup fresh pomegranate juice

Directions for Cooking:
1. In a blender, mix all ingredients and blend until the mixture becomes smooth and creamy.
2. Serve and enjoy.
Nutrition Information:
Calories per Serving: 137.8; Carbs: 31.1g; Protein: 1.1g; Fats: 1g; Saturated Fat: .2g; Sodium: 8mg

Cran-Banana Spinach Smoothie

Serves: 2 , Cooking time: 0 minutes
Ingredients:
- 1 cup cold water
- 3 dates
- 1 stalk celery
- 2 cups baby spinach
- 1 medium banana, peeled and frozen
- ½ cup cranberries

Directions for Cooking:
3. Add all ingredients in a blender and puree until you have a smooth and creamy mixture.
4. Serve and enjoy.
Nutrition Information:
Calories per Serving: 136.4; Carbs: 31.4g; Protein: 1.8g; Fats: .4g; Saturated Fat: .1g; Sodium: 35mg

Berry Green and Leafy Smoothie

Serves: 2 , Cooking time: 0 minutes
Ingredients:
- 8 oz filtered water
- 1 tbsp ground flax seeds
- 1 cup green leaf lettuce, chopped
- 2 cups chopped dandelion greens
- 8 large strawberries, frozen
- 1 large mango, peeled and pitted
- 1 medium banana, peeled and frozen

Directions for Cooking:
1. Blend all ingredients in blender until smooth and creamy.
2. Serve and enjoy.
Nutrition Information:
Calories per Serving: 262.5; Carbs: 49.5g; Protein: 5.1g; Fats: 4.9g; Saturated Fat: .8g; Sodium: 53mg

Green and Leafy Ginger-Apple Smoothie

Serves: 2 , Cooking time: 0 minutes
Ingredients:
- 8 ice cubes
- 1 tsp freshly grated ginger root
- 2 large handfuls baby spinach
- 1 medium apple, cored
- 1 medium carrots, chopped
Directions for Cooking:

1. Blend all ingredients in blender until smooth and creamy.
2. Serve and enjoy.
Nutrition Information:
Calories per Serving: 76.4; Carbs: 16.8g; Protein: 1.4g; Fats: .4g; Saturated Fat: .1g; Sodium: 46mg

Escarole, Pineapple and Apple Smoothie

Serves: 2 , Cooking time: 0 minutes

Ingredients:

- 1 head escarole lettuce
- 1 stalk celery
- 2 cups pineapple, cubed
- 2 apples, cored
- 1 cup almond milk

Directions for Cooking:

1. Blend all ingredients in blender until smooth and creamy.
2. Serve and enjoy.

Nutrition Information:

Calories per Serving: 397.8; Carbs: 87g; Protein: 5.7g; Fats: 3g; Saturated Fat: .2g; Sodium: 134mg

High Protein, Green and Fruity Smoothie

Serves: 2 , Cooking time: 0 minutes

Ingredients:

- 1 cup spinach, packed
- 1 cup ice cold water
- ½ medium banana, peeled and frozen
- ½ avocado, peeled, pitted, and frozen
- 1 tbsp almond butter
- ¼ cup packed Kale, stem discarded, and leaves chopped
- 1 cup frozen broccoli florets

Directions for Cooking:

1. Puree almond butter, kale and water until smooth and creamy.
2. Add remaining ingredients in blender and blend until smooth and creamy.
3. Serve and enjoy.

Nutrition Information:

Calories per Serving: 180.9; Carbs: 13.8g; Protein: 4.2g; Fats: 12.1g; Saturated Fat: 1.6g; Sodium: 44mg

Dandelion and Beet Greens Detox Smoothie

Serves: 2 , Cooking time: 0 minutes

Ingredients:

- 6 ice cubes
- 1 cup almond milk
- 2 tbsp almond butter
- 1 medium banana, peeled and frozen
- 1 cup dandelion greens
- 1 cup beet greens

Directions for Cooking:

1. Blend all ingredients in blender until smooth and creamy.
2. Serve and enjoy.

Nutrition Information:

Calories per Serving: 97.2; Carbs: 31.1g; Protein: 5.9g; Fats: 10.8g; Saturated Fat: 1.2g; Sodium: 186mg

Beans, Peaches and Greens Smoothie

Serves: 2 , Cooking time: 0 minutes

Ingredients:

- Pinch of nutmeg
- 1/8 tsp cinnamon
- ¼ canned white beans, rinsed and drained well
- 1 cup frozen peaches
- 1 cup almond milk
- ¼ cup quick cooking oats
- 1 cup packed lettuce (any kind)
- ¼ cup Italian parsley
- 6 cubes of ice

Directions for Cooking:

1. Blend all ingredients in blender until smooth and creamy.
2. Serve and enjoy.

Nutrition Information:

Calories per Serving: 231.8; Carbs: 50g; Protein: 3g; Fats: 2.2g; Saturated Fat: .1g; Sodium: 99mg

Berry Nutty Smoothie

Serves: 2 , Cooking time: 0 minutes

Ingredients:

- 1 cup frozen mix berries
- ½ cup almond milk
- ¼ cup raw cashews
- 1 cup packed Romaine lettuce
- ¼ cup packed Swiss chard, packed, chopped and stems discarded
- 1 cup ice cubes or cold water - optional

Directions for Cooking:

1. Blend all ingredients in blender until smooth and creamy.
2. Serve and enjoy.

Nutrition Information:

Calories per Serving: 80.8; Carbs: 8g; Protein: 1.4g; Fats: 2.4g; Saturated Fat: .3g; Sodium: 57mg

Fat Burning Pumpkin Smoothie

Serves: 2 , Cooking time: 0 minutes

Ingredients:

- 6 Ice cubes
- Pinch of nutmeg
- ½ tsp ginger
- 1 tsp cinnamon
- 1 small frozen banana
- ½ cup pureed pumpkin
- 1 tbsp chia seeds
- ¼ cup rolled oats
- 1 cup almond milk

Directions for Cooking:

1. Overnight or for an hour, soak chia seeds and oats in almond milk. This will give your smoothie a finer consistency.
2. When ready, blend all ingredients in blender until smooth and creamy.
3. Serve and enjoy.

Nutrition Information:

Calories per Serving: 171.7; Carbs: 33.6g; Protein: 3.7g; Fats: 2.5g; Saturated Fat: .2g; Sodium: 87mg

Grape-Avocado Smoothie

Serves: 2 , Cooking time: 0 minutes

Ingredients:

- 1 tbsp lime juice, fresh
- 2 tbsp avocado
- 6-oz Greek yogurt, plain
- 15 pcs red or green grapes
- 1 pear, peeled, cored and chopped
- 2 cups packed spinach leaves
- 6 ice cubes

Directions for Cooking:

1. Blend all ingredients in blender until smooth and creamy.
2. Serve and enjoy.

Nutrition Information:

Calories per Serving: 188.8; Carbs: 20g; Protein: 15.5g; Fats: 5.2g; Saturated Fat: .8g; Sodium: 69mg

Mango, Cucumber and Spinach Smoothie

Serves: 2 , Cooking time: 0 minutes

Ingredients:

- 6 ice cubes
- 1 cup orange juice, fresh
- 3 cups baby spinach
- 1 cup frozen mango, cubed and deseeded
- 2 apples, cored and chopped roughly
- 1 cucumber, ends removed and chopped roughly

Directions for Cooking:

1. Blend all ingredients in blender until smooth and creamy.
2. Serve and enjoy.

Nutrition Information:

Calories per Serving: 249.1; Carbs: 55.7g; Protein: 3.9g; Fats: 1.1g; Saturated Fat: .2g; Sodium: 43mg

Chapter 15 Canning Recipes

Preserved Chopped Tomatoes

Serves: 4 pieces of pint jars , Cooking time: 1 hour and 25 minutes

Ingredients:

- 5-lbs tomatoes, chopped
- 4 tbsp bottled lemon juice, divided

Directions for Cooking:

1. Place a heavy bottomed pot, fill with 5-inches of water, place a trivet on bottom, and place pot on medium high fire and bring water to a simmer. Place four pieces of pint jars on trivet.
2. Chop tomatoes to desired size.
3. Spread a hand towel on countertop and place one hot pint jar on top.
4. Add a tbsp of lemon juice to each hot pint jar.
5. Pack the tomatoes in each jar and leave ½-inch of headspace, this is important.
6. Remove air bubbles from jar, by pressing down on tomatoes. Wipe the rim of the jar clean. Center the lid on jar. Apply band until fingertip tight. Return to pot.
7. Repeat process for remaining jars and tomatoes.
8. Cover the pot, increase fire to high and boil jars for an hour and 25 minutes.
9. Allow jars to cool for 30 minutes inside pot. Remove from pot and place on top of hand towel and cool completely. Lid should not flex up and down when pressed after 24-hours of canning.
10. Store until ready for use.

Nutrition Information:
Calories per Serving: 94; Carbs: 19.1g; Protein: 6.6g; Fats: 1.1g; Saturated Fat: 0.1g; Sodium: 238mg

Canned and Herbed Tomatoes

Serves: 4 pieces of pint jars , Cooking time: 1 hour and 25 minutes

Ingredients:

- 5-lbs tomatoes, chopped
- 4 tbsp bottled lemon juice, divided
- 4 cloves garlic, smashed
- 4 tbsp dried rosemary
- 4 tsp pepper

Directions for Cooking:

1. Place a heavy bottomed pot, fill with 5-inches of water, place a trivet on bottom, and place pot on medium high fire and bring water to a simmer. Place four pieces of pint jars on trivet.
2. Chop tomatoes to desired size.
3. Spread a hand towel on countertop and place one hot pint jar on top.
4. Add a tbsp of lemon juice, 1 smashed clove of garlic, and 1 tbsp rosemary to each hot pint jar.
5. Pack the tomatoes in each jar and leave ½-inch of headspace, this is important.
6. Remove air bubbles from jar, by pressing down on tomatoes. Wipe the rim of the jar clean. Center the lid on jar. Apply band until fingertip tight. Return to pot.
7. Repeat process for remaining jars and tomatoes.
8. Cover the pot, increase fire to high and boil jars for an hour and 25 minutes.
9. Allow jars to cool for 30 minutes inside pot. Remove from pot and place on top of hand towel and cool completely. Lid should not flex up and down when pressed after 24-hours of canning.
10. Store until ready for use.

Nutrition Information:
Calories per Serving: 107; Carbs: 21.9g; Protein: 7.1g; Fats: 1.3g; Saturated Fat: 0.2g; Sodium: 240mg

Serves: 4 pieces of pint jars , Cooking time: 1 hour and 15 minutes

Ingredients:
- 10-lb tomatoes, chopped
- 1 large onion, chopped
- 8 cloves garlic, smashed and peeled
- 1 tbsp olive oil
- 4 tbsp bottled lemon juice
- 1 cup fresh basil

Directions for Cooking:
1. Place a heavy bottomed pot, fill with 5-inches of water, place a trivet on bottom, and place pot on medium high fire and bring water to a simmer. Place four pieces of pint jars on trivet.
2. Place another pot on medium high fire and heat for 3 minutes. Add oil and heat for 2 minutes. Stir in garlic and onions and sauté for 3 minutes. Stir in tomatoes and simmer for 20 minutes. Transfer to a blender, add ½ of basil and blend in two batches. Strain the pureed tomato mixture and discard seeds and peel. Return to pot and mix well.
3. Spread a hand towel on countertop and place one hot pint jar on top.
4. Add a tbsp of lemon juice to each hot pint jar.
5. Pack the tomato sauce in each jar and leave ½-inch of headspace, this is important.
6. Remove air bubbles from jar. Wipe the rim of the jar clean. Center the lid on jar. Apply band until fingertip tight. Return to pot.
7. Repeat process for remaining jars and tomatoes.
8. Cover the pot, increase fire to high and boil jars for 40 minutes.
9. Allow jars to cool for 30 minutes inside pot. Remove from pot and place on top of hand towel and cool completely. Lid should not flex up and down when pressed after 24-hours of canning.
10. Store until ready for use.

Nutrition Information:
Calories per Serving: 240; Carbs: 42.8g; Protein: 14.2g; Fats: 5.7g; Saturated Fat: 0.8g; Sodium: 479mg

Serves: 4 pieces of pint jars , Cooking time: 65 minutes

Ingredients:
- 10-lb tomatoes, chopped
- 1 tbsp olive oil
- 4 tbsp bottled lemon juice

Directions for Cooking:
1. Place a heavy bottomed pot, fill with 5-inches of water, place a trivet on bottom, and place pot on medium high fire and bring water to a simmer. Place four pieces of pint jars on trivet.
2. Place another pot on medium high fire and heat for 3 minutes. Add oil and heat for 2 minutes. Sauté tomatoes and simmer for 20 minutes. Transfer to a blender and blend in two batches. Strain the pureed tomato mixture and discard seeds and peel. Return to pot and mix well.
3. Spread a hand towel on countertop and place one hot pint jar on top.
4. Add a tbsp of lemon juice to each hot pint jar.
5. Pack the tomatoes in each jar and leave ½-inch of headspace, this is important.
6. Remove air bubbles from jar. Wipe the rim of the jar clean. Center the lid on jar. Apply band until fingertip tight. Return to pot.
7. Repeat process for remaining jars and tomatoes.
8. Cover the pot, increase fire to high and boil jars for 40 minutes.
9. Allow jars to cool for 30 minutes inside pot. Remove from pot and place on top of hand towel and cool completely. Lid should not flex up and down when pressed after 24-hours of canning.
10. Store until ready for use.

Nutrition Information:
Calories per Serving: 215; Carbs: 37.1g; Protein: 13.2g; Fats: 5.6g; Saturated Fat: 0.8g; Sodium: 477mg

Low-Sodium Tomato Ketchup

Serves: 4 pieces of pint jars , Cooking time: 2 hours

Ingredients:
- 2 tbsp celery seeds
- 4 tsp whole cloves
- 1 cinnamon stick
- 1 tsp whole spice
- 2 cups cider vinegar
- 12 pounds tomatoes, cored and quartered
- 2 cups chopped onions
- 1 tsp cayenne
- 1 cup granulated sugar
- ¼ cup coconut aminos

Directions for Cooking:
1. In a spice bag, add celery seeds, cloves, cinnamon stick, and all spice.
2. Place a small pot on medium high fire and add vinegar and spice bag. Once boiling, turn off fire and let spice infuse for 25 minutes.
3. Meanwhile, in a large pot, placed on medium high fire bring to a boil the tomatoes, onion, and cayenne pepper. Lower fire to a simmer and coo for 20 minutes while stirring every now and then. Pour in infused vinegar and continue simmering for 30 minutes until tomatoes are soft and mixture has thickened.
4. Slowly transfer tomato mixture into a sieve and press down to get the juices. Discard the solids. Return juice to pot, add sugar and coconut aminos. Continue simmering until you reach a thickened consistency to your liking, around 45 minutes.
5. Place a heavy bottomed pot, fill with 5-inches of water, place a trivet on bottom, and place pot on medium high fire and bring water to a simmer. Place four pieces of pint jars on trivet.
6. Spread a hand towel on countertop and place one hot pint jar on top.
7. Ladle ketchup in each jar and leave ½-inch of headspace, this is important.
8. Remove air bubbles from jar. Wipe the rim of the jar clean. Center the lid on jar. Apply band until fingertip tight. Return to pot.
9. Repeat process for remaining jars and ketchup.
10. Cover the pot, increase fire to high and boil jars for 15 minutes.
11. Allow jars to cool for 10 minutes inside pot. Remove from pot and place on top of hand towel and cool completely. Lid should not flex up and down when pressed after 24-hours of canning.
12. Store until ready for use.

Nutrition Information:
Calories per Serving: 482; Carbs: 103.2g; Protein: 17.3g; Fats: 3.8g; Saturated Fat: 0.6g; Sodium: 1170mg

Low-Sodium BBQ Sauce

Serves: 3 pieces of pint jars , Cooking time: 1 hour and 25 minutes

Ingredients:
- 20 cups chopped cored peeled tomatoes (about 21 medium)
- 2 cups finely chopped onions
- 5 cloves garlic, finely chopped
- 1 tbsp hot pepper flakes
- 1 tbsp celery seeds
- 1 1/2 cups lightly packed brown sugar
- 1 cup white vinegar
- 1/3 cup lemon juice
- 2 Tbsp coconut aminos
- 1-1/2 Tbsp ground mace
- 1 Tbsp dry mustard
- 1 tsp ground ginger
- 1 tsp ground cinnamon

Directions for Cooking:
1. In a large pot, add celery seeds, hot pepper flakes, onion, and tomatoes. Bring to a boil, lower fire to a simmer, and cook for 30 minutes while stirring every now and then. Cover pot.
2. In a sieve, add tomatoes in batches and press to get the juice. Discard the solids. Return juice in pot. Mix in cinnamon, ginger, mustard, mace, coconut aminos, lemon juice, vinegar, and sugar. Simmer for 30 minutes, stirring occasionally. Cook until desired thickness is achieved.
3. Place a heavy bottomed pot, fill with 5-inches of water, place a trivet on bottom, and place pot on medium high fire and bring

water to a simmer. Place four pieces of pint jars on trivet.
4. Spread a hand towel on countertop and place one hot pint jar on top.
5. Add a tbsp of lemon juice to each hot pint jar.
6. Pack the BBQ sauce in each jar and leave ½-inch of headspace, this is important.
7. Remove air bubbles from jar. Wipe the rim of the jar clean. Center the lid on jar. Apply band until fingertip tight. Return to pot.
8. Repeat process for remaining jars and BBQ sauce.

9. Cover the pot, increase fire to high and boil jars for 20 minutes.
10. Allow jars to cool for 10 minutes inside pot. Remove from pot and place on top of hand towel and cool completely. Lid should not flex up and down when pressed after 24-hours of canning.
11. Store until ready for use.

Nutrition Information:
Calories per Serving: 543; Carbs: 125.6g; Protein: 11.1g; Fats: 3.4g; Saturated Fat: 0.53g; Sodium: 141mg

Low-Sodium Beef Stock

Serves: 4 pieces of pint jars , Cooking time: 2 hours and 20 minutes
Ingredients:
- 4-lbs meaty beef bones
- 12 cups water
- 1 large onion, peeled and chopped
- 1 stalk celery, sliced
- 1 bay leaf
- 5 cloves garlic smashed
- 2 tbsp coconut aminos
- 1 tbsp peppercorns

Directions for Cooking:
1. Place a large heavy bottomed pot on high fire and add all ingredients. Mix well. Bring to a boil, lower fire, cover and simmer for 2 hours.
2. Turn off fire, skim off fat, strain broth and discard any solids.
3. In a pressure cooker, fill with 5-inches of water, add trivet on bottom, and place pot on medium high fire and bring water to a simmer. Place four pieces of pint jars on trivet.
4. Spread a hand towel on countertop and place one hot pint jar on top.

5. Ladle beef stock in each jar and leave ½-inch of headspace, this is important.
6. Remove air bubbles from jar. Wipe the rim of the jar clean. Center the lid on jar. Apply band until fingertip tight. Return to pot.
7. Repeat process for remaining jars and beef stock.
8. Close pressure cooker and pressure cook jars for 20 minutes. Allow for a natural release before opening pot.
9. Allow jars to cool for 30 minutes inside pot. Remove from pot and place on top of hand towel and cool completely. Lid should not flex up and down when pressed after 24-hours of canning.
10. Store until ready for use.

Nutrition Information:
Calories per Serving: 103; Carbs: 6.7g; Protein: 13.1g; Fats: 3.1g; Saturated Fat: 1.1g; Sodium: 75mg

Low-Sodium Chicken Stock

Serves: 4 pieces of pint jars , Cooking time: 1 hour and 25 minutes
Ingredients:
- 1 whole rotisserie chicken, chopped into pieces no skin
- 12 cups water
- 1 large onion, chopped
- 5 garlic cloves
- 1 tbsp peppercorns
- 2 tbsp coconut aminos

Directions for Cooking:

1. Place a large heavy bottomed pot on high fire and add all ingredients. Mix well. Bring to a boil, lower fire, cover and simmer for 2 hours.
2. Turn off fire, skim off fat, strain broth and discard any solids.
3. In a pressure cooker, fill with 5-inches of water, add trivet on bottom, and place pot on medium high fire and bring water to a

simmer. Place four pieces of pint jars on trivet.

4. Spread a hand towel on countertop and place one hot pint jar on top.
5. Ladle chicken stock in each jar and leave ½-inch of headspace, this is important.
6. Remove air bubbles from jar. Wipe the rim of the jar clean. Center the lid on jar. Apply band until fingertip tight. Return to pot.
7. Repeat process for remaining jars and chicken stock.
8. Close pressure cooker and pressure cook jars for 20 minutes. Allow for a natural release before opening pot.
9. Allow jars to cool for 30 minutes inside pot. Remove from pot and place on top of hand towel and cool completely. Lid should not flex up and down when pressed after 24-hours of canning.
10. Store until ready for use.

Nutrition Information:
Calories per Serving: 41; Carbs: 6.4g; Protein: 3.7g; Fats: 0.3g; Saturated Fat: 0.1g; Sodium: 31mg

Low-Sodium Vegetable Soup

Serves: 4 pieces of pint jars , Cooking time: 1 hour and 25 minutes

Ingredients:
- 10 cups water
- 5 stalks celery, chopped
- 5 large carrots, peeled and chopped
- 2 large onions, peeled and chopped
- 2 garlic cloves, smashed
- 1 head broccoli chopped
- 1 head cabbage, chopped
- 1 tbsp peppercorns
- 2 tbsp coconut aminos

Directions for Cooking:
1. Place a large heavy bottomed pot on high fire and add all ingredients. Mix well. Bring to a boil, lower fire, cover and simmer for an hour.
2. Turn off fire, strain broth and discard any solids.
3. In a pressure cooker, fill with 5-inches of water, add trivet on bottom, and place pot on medium high fire and bring water to a simmer. Place four pieces of pint jars on trivet.
4. Spread a hand towel on countertop and place one hot pint jar on top.
5. Ladle vegetable stock in each jar and leave ½-inch of headspace, this is important.
6. Remove air bubbles from jar. Wipe the rim of the jar clean. Center the lid on jar. Apply band until fingertip tight. Return to pot.
7. Repeat process for remaining jars and vegetable stock.
8. Close pressure cooker and pressure cook jars for 20 minutes. Allow for a natural release before opening pot.
9. Allow jars to cool for 30 minutes inside pot. Remove from pot and place on top of hand towel and cool completely. Lid should not flex up and down when pressed after 24-hours of canning.
10. Store until ready for use.

Nutrition Information:
Calories per Serving: 126; Carbs: 29.2g; Protein: 4.5g; Fats: 0.7g; Saturated Fat: 0.1g; Sodium: 144mg

No Salt Added Cannellini Beans

Serves: 4 pieces of pint jars , Cooking time: 1 hour and 25 minutes

Ingredients:
- 1 ½-pounds dried cannellini beans

Directions for Cooking:
1. Place beans in a pot and cover with water. Soak overnight.
2. When ready to can, rinse beans and return to pot. Cover with water and bring to a boil.

Once boiling, lower fire to a simmer while canning.

3. In a pressure cooker, fill with 5-inches of water, add trivet on bottom, and place pot on medium high fire and bring water to a simmer. Place four pieces of pint jars on trivet.

4. Spread a hand towel on countertop and place one hot pint jar on top.
5. Ladle beans and boiling water in each jar and leave 1-inch of headspace, this is important.
6. Remove air bubbles from jar. Wipe the rim of the jar clean. Center the lid on jar. Apply band until fingertip tight. Return to pot.
7. Repeat process for remaining jars and chicken stock.
8. Close pressure cooker and pressure cook jars for 1 hour and 15 minutes. Allow for a natural release before opening pot.
9. Allow jars to cool for 30 minutes inside pot. Remove from pot and place on top of hand towel and cool completely. Lid should not flex up and down when pressed after 24-hours of canning.
10. Store until ready for use.

Nutrition Information:
Calories per Serving: 566; Carbs: 102.1g; Protein: 40.1g; Fats: 1.4g; Saturated Fat: 0.2g; Sodium: 41mg

No Salt Added Red Kidney Beans

Serves: 4 pieces of pint jars , Cooking time: 1 hour and 25 minutes
Ingredients:
- 1 ½-pounds dried red kidney beans

Directions for Cooking:
1. Place beans in a pot and cover with water. Soak overnight.
2. When ready to can, rinse beans and return to pot. Cover with water and bring to a boil. Once boiling, lower fire to a simmer while canning.
3. In a pressure cooker, fill with 5-inches of water, add trivet on bottom, and place pot on medium high fire and bring water to a simmer. Place four pieces of pint jars on trivet.
4. Spread a hand towel on countertop and place one hot pint jar on top.
5. Ladle beans and boiling water in each jar and leave 1-inch of headspace, this is important.
6. Remove air bubbles from jar. Wipe the rim of the jar clean. Center the lid on jar. Apply band until fingertip tight. Return to pot.
7. Repeat process for remaining jars and chicken stock.
8. Close pressure cooker and pressure cook jars for 1 hour and 15 minutes. Allow for a natural release before opening pot.
9. Allow jars to cool for 30 minutes inside pot. Remove from pot and place on top of hand towel and cool completely. Lid should not flex up and down when pressed after 24-hours of canning.
10. Store until ready for use.

Nutrition Information:
Calories per Serving: 561; Carbs: 101.7g; Protein: 41.4g; Fats:0.4 g; Saturated Fat: 0.1g; Sodium: 19mg

No Salt Added Black Beans

Serves: 4 pieces of pint jars , Cooking time: 1 hour and 25 minutes
Ingredients:
- 1 ½-pounds dried black beans

Directions for Cooking:
1. Place beans in a pot and cover with water. Soak overnight.
2. When ready to can, rinse beans and return to pot. Cover with water and bring to a boil. Once boiling, lower fire to a simmer while canning.
3. In a pressure cooker, fill with 5-inches of water, add trivet on bottom, and place pot on medium high fire and bring water to a simmer. Place four pieces of pint jars on trivet.
4. Spread a hand towel on countertop and place one hot pint jar on top.
5. Ladle beans and boiling water in each jar and leave 1-inch of headspace, this is important.
6. Remove air bubbles from jar. Wipe the rim of the jar clean. Center the lid on jar. Apply band until fingertip tight. Return to pot.
7. Repeat process for remaining jars and chicken stock.

8. Close pressure cooker and pressure cook jars for 1 hour and 15 minutes. Allow for a natural release before opening pot.
9. Allow jars to cool for 30 minutes inside pot. Remove from pot and place on top of hand towel and cool completely. Lid should not flex up and down when pressed after 24-hours of canning.
10. Store until ready for use.

Nutrition Information:
Calories per Serving: 577; Carbs: 107.6g; Protein: 36.1g; Fats: 1.5g; Saturated Fat: 0.4g; Sodium: 15mg

No Salt Added Chickpeas

Serves: 4 pieces of pint jars , Cooking time: 1 hour and 25 minutes
Ingredients:
- 1 ½-pounds dried chickpeas

Directions for Cooking:
1. Place beans in a pot and cover with water. Soak overnight.
2. When ready to can, rinse beans and return to pot. Cover with water and bring to a boil. Once boiling, lower fire to a simmer while canning.
3. In a pressure cooker, fill with 5-inches of water, add trivet on bottom, and place pot on medium high fire and bring water to a simmer. Place four pieces of pint jars on trivet.
4. Spread a hand towel on countertop and place one hot pint jar on top.
5. Ladle beans and boiling water in each jar and leave 1-inch of headspace, this is important.
6. Remove air bubbles from jar. Wipe the rim of the jar clean. Center the lid on jar. Apply band until fingertip tight. Return to pot.
7. Repeat process for remaining jars and chicken stock.
8. Close pressure cooker and pressure cook jars for 1 hour and 15 minutes. Allow for a natural release before opening pot.
9. Allow jars to cool for 30 minutes inside pot. Remove from pot and place on top of hand towel and cool completely. Lid should not flex up and down when pressed after 24-hours of canning.
10. Store until ready for use.

Nutrition Information:
Calories per Serving: 643; Carbs: 107.1g; Protein: 34.8g; Fats: 10.3g; Saturated Fat: 1.0g; Sodium: 41mg

No Salt Added Tuna in Water

Serves: 6 pieces of half-pint jars , Cooking time: 1 hour and 40 minutes
Ingredients:
- 2.5-lbs boneless skinless tuna loin

Directions for Cooking:
1. In a pressure cooker, fill with 4-inches of water, add trivet on bottom, and place pot on medium high fire and bring water to a simmer. Place 6 pieces of half-pint jars on trivet.
2. Spread a hand towel on countertop and place one hot pint jar on top.
3. Bring a kettle of hot water to boil.
4. Wash tuna, discard blood line and connective tissue. Slice in 3-inch chunks.
5. Pack tuna in each jar, add boiling water, and leave 1-inch of headspace, this is important.
6. Remove air bubbles from jar. Wipe the rim of the jar clean. Center the lid on jar. Apply band until fingertip tight. Return to pot.
7. Repeat process for remaining jars and tuna.
8. Close pressure cooker and pressure cook jars for 1 hour and 40 minutes at 11-lbs psi. Allow for a natural release before opening pot.
9. Allow jars to cool for 30 minutes inside pot. Remove from pot and place on top of hand towel and cool completely. Lid should not flex up and down when pressed after 24-hours of canning.
10. Store until ready for use.

Nutrition Information:
Calories per Serving: 272; Carbs: 0g; Protein: 44.1g; Fats: 9.3g; Saturated Fat: 2.4g; Sodium: 74mg

Serves: 4 pieces of pint jars , Cooking time: 1 hour and 25 minutes

Ingredients:

- 8-lbs chicken breast, cut into 1-inch chunks

Directions for Cooking:

1. In a pressure cooker, fill with 5-inches of water, add trivet on bottom, and place pot on medium high fire and bring water to a simmer. Place 4 pieces of pint jars on trivet.
2. Spread a hand towel on countertop and place one hot pint jar on top.
3. Bring a kettle of hot water to boil.
4. Pack chicken chunks in each jar, add boiling water, and leave 1-inch of headspace, this is important.
5. Remove air bubbles from jar. Wipe the rim of the jar clean. Center the lid on jar. Apply band until fingertip tight. Return to pot.
6. Repeat process for remaining jars and tuna.
7. Close pressure cooker and pressure cook jars for 1 hour and 40 minutes at 11-lbs psi. Allow for a natural release before opening pot.
8. Allow jars to cool for 30 minutes inside pot. Remove from pot and place on top of hand towel and cool completely. Lid should not flex up and down when pressed after 24-hours of canning.
9. Store until ready for use.

Nutrition Information:

Calories per Serving: 1089; Carbs: 0g; Protein: 204.1g; Fats: 23.8g; Saturated Fat: 5.1g; Sodium: 408mg

Serves: 4 pieces of pint jars , Cooking time: 1 hour and 25 minutes

Ingredients:

- 7-lbs apples, cut into chunks seeds discarded
- 4 tbsp cinnamon
- 1 cup water

Directions for Cooking:

1. Place a large heavy bottomed pot on high fire and add all ingredients. Mix well. Bring to a boil, lower fire, cover and simmer for an hour. Puree with a handheld blender.
2. Turn off fire, strain broth and discard any solids.
3. In a pressure cooker, fill with 5-inches of water, add trivet on bottom, and place pot on medium high fire and bring water to a simmer. Place four pieces of pint jars on trivet.
4. Spread a hand towel on countertop and place one hot pint jar on top.
5. Ladle applesauce in each jar and leave ½-inch of headspace, this is important.
6. Remove air bubbles from jar. Wipe the rim of the jar clean. Center the lid on jar. Apply band until fingertip tight. Return to pot.
7. Repeat process for remaining jars and applesauce.
8. Close pressure cooker and pressure cook jars for 20 minutes. Allow for a natural release before opening pot.
9. Allow jars to cool for 30 minutes inside pot. Remove from pot and place on top of hand towel and cool completely. Lid should not flex up and down when pressed after 24-hours of canning.
10. Store until ready for use.

Nutrition Information:

Calories per Serving: 432; Carbs: 115.9g; Protein: 2.4g; Fats: 1.4g; Saturated Fat: 0.3g; Sodium: 10mg

Low-Sodium Pickle Relish

Serves: 4 pieces of pint jars , Cooking time: 45 minutes

Ingredients:

- 1 large onion, diced
- 1 tbsp salt
- 2 cups sugar
- 3 cups white vinegar
- 4 cloves garlic- minced
- 2 tsp Celery Seed
- 2 tsp Mustard Seed
- Dash turmeric
- 4-lbs cucumber, seeds discarded and flesh diced

Directions for Cooking:

1. In a large pot, mix well onion, cucumber, and salt. Leave for 2 hours. With a cheesecloth, press excess water from cucumber mixture. Return to pot.
2. In same pot add remaining ingredients and mix well. Bring to a boil and simmer for 10 minutes.
3. In a pressure cooker, fill with 5-inches of water, add trivet on bottom, and place pot on medium high fire and bring water to a simmer. Place four pieces of pint jars on trivet.
4. Spread a hand towel on countertop and place one hot pint jar on top.
5. Ladle pickle relish in each jar and leave 1/4-inch of headspace, this is important.
6. Remove air bubbles from jar. Wipe the rim of the jar clean. Center the lid on jar. Apply band until fingertip tight. Return to pot.
7. Repeat process for remaining jars and pickle relish.
8. Close pressure cooker and pressure cook jars for 30 minutes. Allow for a natural release before opening pot.
9. Allow jars to cool for 30 minutes inside pot. Remove from pot and place on top of hand towel and cool completely. Lid should not flex up and down when pressed after 24-hours of canning.
10. Store until ready for use.

Nutrition Information:

Calories per Serving: 521; Carbs: 12.3g; Protein: 4.0g; Fats: 1.2g; Saturated Fat: 0.2g; Sodium: 1767mg

Low-Sodium Jalapeno Rings

Serves: 8 pieces of 4-oz jars , Cooking time: 30 minutes

Ingredients:

- 1-lb jalapeno peppers sliced into rings
- 2 cups water
- 3 tbsp white sugar
- 2 clove garlic, minced
- ½ tsp oregano
- 1 tsp pickling salt

Directions for Cooking:

1. In a large pot, mix well all ingredients and bring to a boil. Allow to for 10 minutes.
2. In a pressure cooker, fill with 3-inches of water, add trivet on bottom, and place pot on medium high fire and bring water to a simmer. Place 8 pieces of 4-oz jars on trivet.
3. Spread a hand towel on countertop and place one hot pint jar on top.
4. Ladle jalapeno rings and water in each jar and leave 1/4-inch of headspace, this is important.
5. Remove air bubbles from jar. Wipe the rim of the jar clean. Center the lid on jar. Apply band until fingertip tight. Return to pot.
6. Repeat process for remaining jars and jalapeno rings.
7. Close pressure cooker and pressure cook jars for 20 minutes. Allow for a natural release before opening pot.
8. Allow jars to cool for 30 minutes inside pot. Remove from pot and place on top of hand towel and cool completely. Lid should not flex up and down when pressed after 24-hours of canning.
9. Store until ready for use.

Nutrition Information:

Calories per Serving: 36; Carbs: 8.7g; Protein: 0.6g; Fats: 0.2g; Saturated Fat: 0g; Sodium: 294mg

Serves: 4 pieces of pint jars , Cooking time: 1 hour and 30 minutes

Ingredients:

- 2.5-lbs mushrooms, chopped roughly
- 6 cloves garlic, smashed, peeled and minced
- 1 large onion, chopped
- 1 tbsp pepper
- 8 cups beef broth

Directions for Cooking:

1. In a large pot, add all ingredients and simmer for an hour.
2. In a pressure cooker, fill with 5-inches of water, add trivet on bottom, and place pot on medium high fire and bring water to a simmer. Place four pieces of pint jars on trivet.
3. Spread a hand towel on countertop and place one hot pint jar on top.
4. Ladle mushroom soup in each jar and leave 1/4-inch of headspace, this is important.
5. Remove air bubbles from jar. Wipe the rim of the jar clean. Center the lid on jar. Apply band until fingertip tight. Return to pot.
6. Repeat process for remaining jars and mushroom soup.
7. Close pressure cooker and pressure cook jars for 30 minutes. Allow for a natural release before opening pot.
8. Allow jars to cool for 30 minutes inside pot. Remove from pot and place on top of hand towel and cool completely. Lid should not flex up and down when pressed after 24-hours of canning.
9. Store until ready for use. To make it creamy when using, just add heavy cream or 2 tbsp flour to thicken.

Nutrition Information:

Calories per Serving: 120; Carbs: 22.2g; Protein: 8.1g; Fats: 1.8g; Saturated Fat: 0.4g; Sodium: 15mg

Serves: 4 pieces of pint jars , Cooking time: 55 minutes

Ingredients:

- 4.5-lbs pie pumpkin, peeled, deseeded, and chopped

Directions for Cooking:

1. Bring a pot of water and pumpkin cubes to a boil and let it simmer.
2. In a pressure cooker, fill with 5-inches of water, add trivet on bottom, and place pot on medium high fire and bring water to a simmer. Place four pieces of pint jars on trivet.
3. Spread a hand towel on countertop and place one hot pint jar on top.
4. Ladle pumpkin and water in each jar and leave 1-inch of headspace, this is important.
5. Remove air bubbles from jar. Wipe the rim of the jar clean. Center the lid on jar. Apply band until fingertip tight. Return to pot.
6. Repeat process for remaining jars and pumpkin and water.
7. Close pressure cooker and pressure cook jars for 55 minutes at 10-lbs psi. Allow for a natural release before opening pot.
8. Allow jars to cool for 30 minutes inside pot. Remove from pot and place on top of hand towel and cool completely. Lid should not flex up and down when pressed after 24-hours of canning.
9. Store until ready for use.

Nutrition Information:

Calories per Serving: 133; Carbs: 33.2g; Protein: 5.1g; Fats: 0.5g; Saturated Fat: 0.3g; Sodium: 5mg

Chapter 16 Dips, Gravies, And Sauces Recipes

Creamy Artichoke Dip

Serves:8 , Cook Time: 30 minutes

Ingredients:

- 1 can artichoke hearts in water, drained and rinsed thoroughly
- 4 cups raw spinach, chopped
- 2 cloves of garlic, minced
- 1 teaspoon ground black pepper
- 1 teaspoon fresh thyme, minced
- 1 tablespoon fresh parsley, minced
- 1 cup white beans, boiled for 4 hours until soft then drained
- 2 tablespoons Parmesan cheese, grated
- ½ cup low-fat sour cream

Directions for Cooking:

1. Preheat the oven to 350^{0}F.
2. In a mixing bowl, mix all ingredients until well-combined.
3. Pour into a heat-proof baking dish.
4. Bake for 30 minutes.
5. Serve warm.

Nutrition Information:

Calories per Serving: 78; Protein: 5g; Carbs: 10g; Fat: 2g; Saturated Fat: 1g; Sodium: 130mg

Amazing Avocado Dip

Serves:4 , Cook Time: 5 minutes

Ingredients:

- 1 ripe avocado, pitted and peeled
- ½ cup fat-free sour cream
- 2 teaspoons chopped onion
- 1/8 teaspoon hot sauce

Directions for Cooking:

1. In a small bowl,mash the avocado with a fork.
2. Stir in the rest of the ingredients.
3. Serve with baked tortilla or sliced vegetables.

Nutrition Information:

Calories per Serving: 85; Protein: 2g; Carbs: 8g; Fat: 5g; Saturated Fat: 1g; Sodium: 57mg

Basil and Sun-Dried Tomato Sauce

Serves:4 , Cook Time: 10 minutes

Ingredients:

- ½ cup sun-dried tomato, soaked in water then rinsed
- 1 tablespoon grass-fed butter
- 1 tablespoon whole wheat flour
- 1 cup unsalted chicken broth
- 1 tablespoon finely chopped fresh basil

Directions for Cooking:

1. In a food processor, pulse the sun-dried tomatoes until it becomes a smooth paste.
2. Heat grass-fed butter in a saucepan over low to medium heat.
3. Stir in the wheat flour and stir constantly until you form a roux.
4. Stir in the chicken broth and the tomato paste.
5. Mix until well combined and until the sauce thickens.
6. Add the basil last.

Nutrition Information:

Calories per Serving: 43; Protein:1g; Carbs:3g; Fat: 3g; Saturated Fat: 2g; Sodium: 101mg

Refreshing Citrus Vinaigrette

Serves:8 , Cook Time: 5 minutes

Ingredients:

- 1 cup water
- ½ cup orange juice, fresh
- ½ cup olive oil
- ¼ cup rice wine vinegar
- 2 tablespoons honey
- 1 tablespoon fresh thyme
- A pinch of ground black pepper

Directions for Cooking:

1. Mix all ingredients in a blender until smooth.
2. Place in a container until ready to use.
3. Store in the fridge to last for 2 weeks.
4. Shake well before using.
5. Use to flavor steaks and salads.

Nutrition Information:

Calories per Serving: 143; Protein: 0g; Carbs: 7g; Fat: 14g; Saturated Fat: 1g; Sodium: 89mg

Cranberry Orange Glaze for Meats

Serves:4 , Cook Time:20 minutes

Ingredients:

- 1 cup fresh cranberries, chopped
- 2/3 cup orange juice, freshly squeezed

Directions for Cooking:

1. Place all ingredients in a saucepan.
2. Bring to a boil over low heat while stirring constantly until the sauce thickens.
3. Remove from heat and transfer into a container.

Nutrition Information:

Calories per Serving: 36; Protein: 0g; Carbs: 9g; Fat: 0g; Saturated Fat: 0g; Sodium: 1mg

Dash House Ranch Dressing

Serves:20 , Cook Time: 5 minutes

Ingredients:

- 2 cups plain fat-free Greek yogurt
- ½ cup low-fat mayonnaise
- 2 tablespoons lemon juice, freshly squeezed
- 1 tablespoon dried dill weed, chopped
- ½ tablespoon onion powder
- ½ tablespoon garlic powder
- ¼ teaspoon black pepper

Directions for Cooking:

1. Combine all ingredients in a bowl until well-combine.
2. Using a spatula, transfer the sauce into clean bowls.
3. Drizzle over salad.
4. Keep inside the fridge for up to two weeks.

Nutrition Information:

Calories per Serving: 30; Protein: 2g; Carbs:2 g; Fat: 1g; Saturated Fat: 0g; Sodium: 88mg

Tzatziki Sauce for Wraps and Pita Bread

Serves:13 , Cook Time: 5 minutes

Ingredients:

- 2 large cucumbers, cut in half and seeds removed
- 16 ounces fat-free Greek yogurt, plain
- 1 ½ teaspoons fresh dill, chopped finely
- ½ teaspoon chopped garlic
- Ground black pepper to taste

Directions for Cooking:

1. Grate the cucumber.
2. Place the grated cucumber in a cheesecloth and press to drain the extra liquid.
3. Place the grated cucumber in a bowl and add in the rest of the ingredients.
4. Mix until well combined.
5. Place in a lidded container and keep in the fridge.
6. Serve cold.

Nutrition Information:

Calories per Serving: 28; Protein: 4g; Carbs: 3g; Fat: 0g; Saturated Fat: 0g; Sodium: 41mg

Creamy Mushroom Sauce for Pasta and Meats

Serves:12 , Cook Time: 20 minutes

Ingredients:

- 2 teaspoons olive oil
- 1 small onion
- 1 ½ cup fresh mushrooms,
- 2 tablespoons whole wheat flour, sifted
- 2 cups fat-free milk
- 1 tablespoon chopped chives
- A small pinch of salt
- Black pepper to taste

Directions for Cooking:

1. In a saucepan, heat oil over medium heat and sauté the onion until fragrant.
2. Stir in the mushrooms and sauté until wilted. Set aside.
3. Do not rinse the saucepan.
4. Using the same saucepan, stir in whole wheat flour while stirring constantly over low flame to form a roux.
5. Pour in the milk and stir in the sautéed mushrooms.
6. Allow the sauce to thicken.
7. Stir in the chive and add in salt and pepper to taste.

Nutrition Information:

Calories per Serving: 33; Protein: 2g; Carbs: 4g; Fat: 1g; Saturated Fat: 0g; Sodium:19 mg

Pepper Sauce Vinaigrette

Serves:10 , Cook Time: 15 minutes

Ingredients:

- 1 dried ancho chili pepper
- 1 dried chipotle chili pepper
- 1 dried New Mexico chili pepper
- ½ cup water
- 1 cup white vinegar
- 1/8 cup olive oil

Directions for Cooking:

1. In a food processor, mix all the chili peppers, water and white vinegar.
2. Pulse until smooth.
3. In a saucepan, pour the chili mixture and the olive oil.
4. Allow to simmer for 5 minutes or until the chili is cooked.
5. Place in a lidded container.
6. Keep inside the fridge to last for a month.

Nutrition Information:

Calories per Serving: 64; Protein: 0.5g; Carbs: 2g; Fat: 6g; Saturated Fat: 0g; Sodium: 3mg

Peanut Butter Hummus

Serves:16 , Cook Time: 5 minutes

Ingredients:

- 2 cups garbanzo or chickpea beans
- 1 cup water
- ½ cup organic and sugar-free peanut butter
- 1 teaspoon vanilla extract

Directions for Cooking:

1. Place all ingredients in a food processor.
2. Pulse until smooth.
3. Place in a container and refrigerate up to 1 month.

Nutrition Information:

Calories per Serving: 135; Protein: 7g; Carbs: 19g; Fat: 4g; Saturated Fat: 0g; Sodium: 47mg

Red Pepper Pesto for Pasta and Bread

Serves:12 , Cook Time: 10 minutes

Ingredients:

- 4 red bell peppers
- 3 cups fresh basil leaves
- 3 tablespoons pumpkin seeds
- 3 tablespoons grated Parmesan cheese
- 1 tablespoon olive oil
- 1 teaspoon minced garlic
- A dash of salt

Directions for Cooking:

1. Heat the grill to medium flame and grill the pepper on direct heat until the outer skin chars or blackens.
2. Remove the peppers from the heat and place in a bowl to cool.
3. Once cooled, peel the peppers and remove the seeds.

4. In a food processor, combine the rest of the ingredients including the pepper.
5. Process until the mixture is smooth.

Nutrition Information:
Calories per Serving: 45; Protein: 2g; Carbs: 4g; Fat: 3g; Saturated Fat: 1g; Sodium: 104mg

Savory Vegetable Dip

Serves:8 , Cook Time: 10 minutes
Ingredients:
- 3 cloves garlic peeled and cut in half
- ¾ cup chopped sun-dried tomatoes, soaked in water and drained
- 1 cup low fat cottage cheese
- 1/3 cup plain fat-free yogurt
- 1/3 cup low-fat mayonnaise

Directions for Cooking:

1. Place all ingredients in a food processor.
2. Blend until smooth.
3. Place in a container and refrigerate for 3 hours.
4. Serve with your favorite vegetables.

Nutrition Information:
Calories per Serving: 54; Protein: 4g; Carbs: 5g; Fat: 2g; Saturated Fat: 0g; Sodium: 49mg

Turkey, Poultry 'n Potato Gravy

Serves:8 , Cook Time: 15 minutes
Ingredients:
- 4 cups unsalted turkey stock
- 2 tablespoons fresh sage, chopped
- 2 tablespoons fresh thyme, chopped
- 1 cup skim milk
- ¼ cornstarch slurry

Directions for Cooking:
1. Place the turkey stock in a pot and add the sage, thyme, and milk.

2. Heat over medium flame and bring to a boil.
3. Once boiled, reduce the heat to low and stir in the cornstarch slurry.
4. Allow the sauce to thicken.
5. Serve with roasted turkey or gravy.

Nutrition Information:
Calories per Serving: 25; Protein: 1g; Carbs: 5g; Fat: 1g; Saturated Fat: 0g; Sodium: 14mg

Caramelized Balsamic Vinaigrette

Serves:8 , Cook Time: 20 minutes
Ingredients:
- ½ cup water
- 3 tablespoons honey
- ½ cup dark balsamic vinegar
- 2 tablespoons olive oil
- 4 garlic cloves, minced
- ¼ teaspoon ground black pepper

Directions for Cooking:

1. Heat a small saucepan over medium heat and add water, honey, balsamic vinegar, oil, garlic, and black pepper.
2. Bring to a boil until the liquid reduces.
3. Serve dressing for later use.

Nutrition Information:
Calories per Serving: 89; Protein: 0g; Carbs: 14g; Fat: 3g; Saturated Fat: 0g; Sodium: 62mg

Cilantro Lime Sauce

Serves:16 , Cook Time: 5 minutes

Ingredients:
- ¼ cup olive oil
- 2 cups low fat cottage cheese
- 1 clove of garlic, minced
- 2 whole limes, juiced freshly squeezed
- ½ cup cilantro, roughly chopped
- ½ teaspoon honey
- ¼ teaspoon ground black pepper

Directions for Cooking:

1. Place all ingredients in a food processor or blender.
2. Blend until smooth.
3. Place in a container and keep in the fridge for at least 2 weeks.
4. Serve on salad.

Nutrition Information:
Calories per Serving: 54; Protein: 4g; Carbs: 2g; Fat: 4g; Saturated Fat: 1g; Sodium: 109mg

Vegetable Salsa Dip

Serves:16 , Cook Time: 10 minutes

Ingredients:
- 1 cup finely chopped zucchini
- 1 cup finely chopped red onion
- 2 red bell peppers, seeded and finely chopped
- 2 green bell peppers, seeded and finely chopped
- 4 tomatoes, finely chopped
- 2 garlic cloves, minced
- ½ cup finely chopped fresh cilantro
- 1 teaspoon ground black pepper
- 2 teaspoons honey
- ¼ cup lime juice, freshly squeezed
- A dash of salt

Directions for Cooking:
1. Place all ingredients in a bowl.
2. Toss to mix all ingredients.
3. Serve with tortilla chips or crackers.

Nutrition Information:
Calories per Serving: 24; Protein: 1g; Carbs: 5g; Fat: 0g; Saturated Fat: 0g; Sodium: 79mg

Mango Salsa Dip

Serves:4 , Cook Time: 5 minutes

Ingredients:
- 2 mangoes, finely chopped
- ½ small red onion, minced
- 3 red Fresno peppers, minced
- 2 tablespoons minced cilantro
- Zest and juice from 1 lime
- 1 tablespoon olive oil

Directions for Cooking:
1. Place all ingredients in a bowl.
2. Mix until well-combined.
3. Serve with chips and crackers if desired.

Nutrition Information:
Calories per Serving: 100; Protein: 1g; Carbs: 15g; Fat: 4g; Saturated Fat: 0.5g; Sodium: 3mg

Gluten-Free Chicken Gravy

Serves:6 , Cook Time: 20 minutes

Ingredients:
- ½ cup finely chopped onion
- ½ cup finely chopped Cremini mushrooms
- 2 tablespoons chopped fresh parsley
- ½ cup low sodium or natural chicken broth

Directions for Cooking:
1. In a saucepan, sauté the onion and Cremini mushrooms for 5 minutes or until the mushrooms wilt.
2. Stir in the rest of the ingredients and allow the liquid to reduce by simmering for at least 10 minutes or as needed.
3. Serve with chicken.

Nutrition Information:
Calories per Serving: 3; Protein: 0.5g; Carbs: 0.5g; Fat: 3g; Saturated Fat: 0g; Sodium: 70mg

Light Peanut Dipping Sauce

Serves:6 , Cook Time: 5 minutes

Ingredients:

- ¼ cup natural peanut butter, reduced fat
- ¼ cup non-fat plain Greek yogurt
- 1 clove garlic, minced
- 1 teaspoon fresh ginger, minced
- 1 teaspoon sesame oil
- 1 tablespoon apple cider vinegar
- 1 tablespoon lime juice, freshly squeezed
- 1 teaspoon honey
- ¼ teaspoon red pepper flakes

Directions for Cooking:

1. Place all ingredients in a bowl.
2. Mix until well-combined.
3. Use it as dipping sauce for chicken, barbecued meats, or as topping for noodles.

Nutrition Information:

Calories per Serving: 87; Protein: 4g; Carbs: 6g; Fat: 8g; Saturated Fat: 0.8g; Sodium: 2mg

Creamy Herbed Dip

Serves:6 , Cook Time: 5 minutes

Ingredients:

- ½ cup tofu mayonnaise
- 2 tablespoons water
- 3 tablespoons chopped fresh chives
- 3 tablespoons chopped fresh basil
- 1 tablespoon chopped fresh thyme
- 2 tablespoons olive oil
- 1 tablespoon lemon juice
- ¼ teaspoon black pepper
- 2/3 cup non-fat Greek yogurt

Directions for Cooking:

1. Combine all ingredients in a bowl.
2. Mix until well-combined.
3. Serve with raw vegetables or chips.

Nutrition Information:

Calories per Serving: 179; Protein: 0.1g; Carbs: 0.5g; Fat: 10g; Saturated Fat: 1.2g; Sodium: 156mg

Skinny Ranch Dip

Serves:2 , Cook Time: 5 minutes

Ingredients:

- 2 tablespoons light mayonnaise
- 2 tablespoons fat-free plain Greek yogurt
- 2 tablespoons fresh chopped scallion
- A pinch of salt to taste

Directions for Cooking:

1. Combine all ingredients in a mixing bowl.
2. Stir to combine everything.
3. Keep in the fridge for a week.

Nutrition Information:

Calories per Serving: 61; Protein: 1g; Carbs: 3g; Fat: 4g; Saturated Fat: 0.9g; Sodium: 121mg

DASH Marinara Sauce

Serves:5 , Cook Time: 30 minutes

Ingredients:

- 2 tablespoons extra virgin olive oil
- 10 large fresh tomatoes, peeled and diced
- ½ teaspoon minced garlic
- 2 tablespoons chopped onion
- 1 tablespoon chopped fresh basil
- 1 teaspoon honey
- ½ teaspoon dried oregano
- 1/8 teaspoon ground black pepper

Directions for Cooking:

1. Heat the olive oil in a heavy skillet over medium flame.
2. Stir in the tomatoes, garlic, and onions until wilted and fragrant.
3. Stir in the rest of the ingredients.
4. Close the lid and allow the tomatoes to sweat for 30 minutes.

Nutrition Information:

Calories per Serving: 94; Protein: 3g; Carbs: 15g; Fat: 3g; Saturated Fat: 0.4g; Sodium: 57mg

Crockpot Spicy Beefy Tomato Sauce

Serves:8 , Cook Time: 8 hours

Ingredients:

- 3 ounces of lean ground beef
- 15 Roma tomatoes, chopped
- 2 small onions, chopped
- A dash of organic herb seasoning blend
- 5 teaspoons cayenne pepper

Directions for Cooking:

1. Place all ingredients in the crockpot and give a good stir.
2. Cover the lid and cook on low for 6 to 8 hours.

Nutrition Information:

Calories per Serving: 120; Protein: 8.6g; Carbs: 7g; Fat: 4g; Saturated Fat: 2g; Sodium: 62mg

Vegan Spicy Cilantro Cream Sauce

Serves:5 , Cook Time: 5 minutes

Ingredients:

- 1 cup raw cashews, soaked in water overnight then drained
- 1 cup water
- ¾ cup lemon juice
- 3 cloves garlic
- 1 teaspoon cayenne powder
- 1 teaspoon smoked paprika
- ¼ cup cilantro
- A tiny dash of salt

Directions for Cooking:

1. Place all ingredients except for the cilantro in a blender.
2. Pulse until smooth.
3. Once smooth, place the cilantro last and pulse again until the cilantro is roughly chopped.
4. Serve on salad or pasta.

Nutrition Information:

Calories per Serving: 93; Protein: 3g; Carbs: 5g; Fat: 7g; Saturated Fat: 1g; Sodium: 102mg

Creamy Cheesy Vegan Sauce

Serves:6 , Cook Time: 20 minutes

Ingredients:

- ½ cup chickpea flour
- ½ cup nutritional yeast flakes
- 1 teaspoon onion powder
- ½ teaspoon paprika
- ½ teaspoon dry mustard powder
- ½ teaspoon garlic powder
- ¼ teaspoon cayenne pepper
- 2 cups non-dairy milk
- 1/8 cup olive oil
- 1 teaspoon miso

Directions for Cooking:

1. Place all ingredients in a blender.
2. Pulse until smooth.
3. Transfer the mixture into a non-stick saucepan.
4. Turn on the stove to medium-low heat.
5. Bring the mixture to a simmer until the sauce thickens.
6. Make sure to stir constantly.
7. Serve with vegetables or use as a replacement of cheese when making mac and cheese.

Nutrition Information:

Calories per Serving: 126; Protein: 8g; Carbs: 10g; Fat: 5g; Saturated Fat: 0.8g; Sodium: 231mg

Appendix 1:21 Days Heart Healthy Diet Meal Plan

WEEK-1

Meal Plan	Breakfast	Lunch	Dinner	Side Dish Or Snack
DAY-1	Cucumber 'n Tomato Breakfast Wrap	Chicken Penne Pesto	Summertime Crab with Napa Cabbage	Crispy Apple Chips
DAY-2	Spinach 'n Tomato Egg Scramble	Herby Pasta and Lentils	Dill Relish on White Sea Bass	Peanut Butter Cookies
DAY-3	Stuffed Breakfast Zucchini	Simple Pasta Limon	Steamed Fish Mediterranean Style	Chia Cinnamon Pudding
DAY-4	Cheddar & Kale Frittata	Pasta Creole Style	Creamy Haddock with Kale	Garlic-Parmesan Knots
DAY-5	Avocado Cup with Egg	Veggie Stir Fry	Turkey Legs in Thai Sauce	Tart Raspberry Crumble Bar
DAY-6	No Cook Overnight Oats	Vegan Buddha Bowl	Honey Sesame Chicken	Lemon Glazed Blueberry Scones
DAY-7	Cereal with Cranberry-Orange Twist	Healthy Curried Tofu	Broccoli-Chicken Rice	Colorful Fruit Skewers

Meal Plan	Breakfast	Lunch	Dinner	Side Dish Or Snack
DAY-8	Nectarine & Shrimp Salad	Quesadillas with a Pear-Twist	Lip Smacking Good Hoisin Chicken	Banana Berry Ice Cream
DAY-9	Medley of Lentil Salad	Marinated Tofu Salad	3-Bean Cilantro Salad	Baked Stuffed Apples
DAY-10	Chicken Teriyaki Lettuce Wraps	Baked Chicken Pesto	Hearty Italian Bean Stew	Frozen Fruit Tart
DAY-11	Cobb Salad with a Thai Twist	Chicken Ala Cubana	Black Bean and Couscous Salad	Rainbow Ice Pops
DAY-12	Warm Salad of Pinto 'n Rice	Tasty Curried Chicken	Red Lentil and Cauliflower Curry	Tasty Peach Float
DAY-13	Steak-Blue Cheese 'n Fruits Salad	Chicken-Rice Pilaf	Marinated Pork Tenderloin	Summer Fruit Salad
DAY-14	Sweet Potato, Rice, & Black Bean Salad	Honey-Garlic Chicken	Beef with Cucumber Raita	Sautéed Tropical Bananas

Meal Plan	Breakfast	Lunch	Dinner	Side Dish Or Snack
DAY-15	Artichoke, Red Pepper and Feta Frittata	Beef Stroganoff	Pork Tenderloin with Apples And Balsamic Vinegar	Flaxseed, Maple & Pumpkin Muffin
DAY-16	Scrambled Eggs with Spinach	Spicy Beef Curry	Coconut Curry Sea Bass	No Cook Choco and Coconut Bars
DAY-17	Kale and Mushroom Frittata	Exotic Thai Steak	Easy Steamed Crab Legs	Twisted Grilled Pineapple
DAY-18	Cauliflower and Egg Casserole	Savory Lobster Roll	Mouth-Watering Seafood Curry	Almond Rice Pudding
DAY-19	Corned Beef Hash	Cajun Shrimp Boil	Roast Rack of Lamb	Berry Yogurt Popsicles
DAY-20	Danish Puff Pastry	Tasty Corn and Clam Stew	Fish Filet in Sweet Orange Sauce	Yummy Melon Slush
DAY-21	Easy Brekky Bread Pudding	Lobster Tarragon Stew	Grilled Prawn Kebab	Crispy Apple Chips

Appendix 2: Recipes Index

196

Made in the USA
Monee, IL
07 June 2021